Writers of Wales

Ruth Bidgood

Writers of Wales

Ruth Bidgood

Matthew Jarvis

University of Wales Press

Cardiff 2012

www.uwp.co.uk

British Library Cataloguing-in-Publication Data
A catalogue record for this book is available from the British Library.

ISBN 978-0-7083-2522-3
e-ISBN 978-0-7083-2523-0

Printed and typeset in Wales by Dinefwr Press, Llandybïe

To Kate, Danny and Ethan

And with grateful thanks to William Marx

Contents

Preface   ix

List of Illustrations   xiii

Abbreviations   xv

1   Finding Mid-Wales   1

2   Towards a Poetics of Abergwesyn   22

3   Myth and the Sacred   45

4   The Necessity of Darkness   68

5   Other Histories   95

6   A Mid-Wales Epic   121

Appendix A   Publication in magazines during the 1960s   131

Appendix B   Two unpublished early poems   133

Appendix C   Unpublished letter to *Poetry Wales*   135

Notes   139

Select Bibliography   159

Index   175

Preface

This book is intended to be a study of Ruth Bidgood's poetry. Whilst she is primarily known as a poet, Ruth is also a noted local historian, having published over seventy items in this field, including a full-length book, various pamphlets and numerous articles (listed in the Select Bibliography to this volume). However, my focus here is unambiguously on her poetic work and development. Her local history publications are thus attended to only insofar as they are directly useful for the analysis of her poetry. Moreover, whilst wishing to sketch out and acknowledge the story of her life, this study is certainly not intended to be primarily a work of biographically based literary criticism. Thus, I open the book with biographical material and I draw on relevant biographical detail as necessary throughout. But I do not generally seek to prioritize the life as a way of understanding the poetry, apart from in the obvious sense that, for Ruth, poetry as a whole was seemingly kick-started by one very important personal decision: her move to mid-Wales in the mid-1960s. Moreover, I only very occasionally approach the poetry as a way into understanding its author's life. Rather, my primary commitment in this volume is overwhelmingly to the poetic text itself – often, here, within the context of the land and culture of the mid-Wales region to which this particular poet has manifestly had such a deep, strong and long reaction.

*   *   *

This book has been longer in the making than I had hoped. Or, to put it somewhat more accurately, it took me longer to get around to than I had initially expected, not least because I found that being the primary child-carer for two young boys distracted me far too pleasurably from preceding writerly tasks. So I am grateful both to Ruth and to the University of Wales Press for bearing with me. In particular, I am grateful to them for understanding that caring for my two boys, Danny and Ethan, always took precedence. And to both of my boys: thank you so much for keeping me company in the midst of all my writing.

The book itself could not have been produced without the support of many people. Most obvious amongst these, of course, is Ruth Bidgood herself with whom I have enjoyed a pleasurable correspondence for some years. Ruth has generously offered always-constructive comments on the text itself, as well as absolutely invaluable background information about her poetry. Without her kind input, this book would be poverty-stricken by comparison with what I hope it finally offers. I have also been kindly assisted by the staff of the University of Wales Press (particularly commissioning editor, Sarah Lewis), who have fielded my numerous queries with considerable patience. I am, moreover, much indebted to the Anthony Dyson fund at the university in Lampeter. This fund is a result of Dyson's bequest to the university. It not only provides for my ongoing post (as Anthony Dyson Fellow in Poetry, in the School of Cultural Studies, at what is now the University of Wales Trinity Saint David), but has also covered the publication costs of this volume. Without the money provided by the Dyson fund it is possible that this book would never have appeared, and I am profoundly grateful for the support given to me in this respect.

I am also grateful to a wide variety of people who have helped me during my research for this volume, either professionally or through the diverse kindnesses of friendship: the staff at the National Library of Wales, particularly Iwan ap Dafydd, Jayne Day and Will Troughton; Jane Aaron; David Arnold of the University of Worcester; Stephen Barnes, current vicar of St Mary's, Seven Sisters; John Barnie; Peter Barry; Martin Bidgood; Charles Boase, former publisher of Gwasg Boase; Kirsti Bohata; Norman Burns, archivist of the Cwm Dulais Historical Society;

Claire Connolly; James and Stephanie Coutts; Martin Crampin; Stuart Douglas, general manager of the Dulais Valley Partnership; Gerald England, editor of *New Hope International Review*; Alice Entwistle; Paula Fahey of the *Country Life* Picture Library; Mick Felton of Seren Books; Peter Finch, former chief executive of Literature Wales; Glyn Jenkins; Ian Jones, Rhydlewis; Sally Roberts Jones; Lionel Madden; William Marx; Glyn Mathias; John Parham; Bronwen Price of Literature Wales; Dafydd Prys of *Planet*; Fran Rhydderch; Lleucu Siencyn, chief executive of Literature Wales; Wynn Thomas; Luke Thurston; Miriam Valencia of The Poetry Library; Amy Wack of Seren Books; Damian Walford Davies; Nina Wedell of the Ewyas Lacy Study Group; Dilys Wood, founder of the Second Light Network; Albert and Margaret Wright; Andrew Wright; Paul Wright; and Steven Wright of UCL Special Collections. Any errors in the text are, of course, my own. But ultimate thanks must, as always, go to my wife, Kate: the writing is really all for you.

*   *   *

For permission to reproduce the poetry of Ruth Bidgood, I am grateful to Ruth Bidgood, the Arts Council of Wales/Cyngor Celfyddydau Cymru, BBC Cymru Wales, Canterbury Press, Cinnamon Press and Seren Books. For permission to reproduce Ruth Bidgood's unpublished work and material from personal correspondence with her, I am grateful to Ruth Bidgood. For permission to reproduce the photographs within the volume, I am grateful to Ruth Bidgood (figures 1–4, 6–7 and 9–14), Martin Bidgood (figure 5), the Roland Mathias Prize (figure 8), the National Library of Wales/Llyfrgell Genedlaethol Cymru (figure 9) and the Radnorshire Society (figure 10). For permission to reproduce the cover image, I am grateful to Bernard Mitchell.

Aberystwyth
January 2012

List of Illustrations

The picture section is placed between pages 80 and 81.

Cover image: Ruth Bidgood, Abergwesyn, 1997.
   (Photograph: Bernard Mitchell, reproduced by kind
   permission of the photographer.)

1 Ruth Jones with her parents, Revd William Herbert Jones
   (1874–1945) and Hilda Jones née Garrett (1887–1971), in
   Seven Sisters (Blaendulais), Glamorgan, c.1924. (Photograph:
   family photograph, Ruth Bidgood's private papers.)

2 Ruth Jones aged eleven (1933/4), in Aberafan, Port Talbot.
   (Photograph: family photograph, Ruth Bidgood's private
   papers.)

3 Ruth Jones, Women's Royal Naval Service, 1943.
   (Photograph: unknown professional photographer.)

4 Ruth Bidgood, with her children (left to right) Anthony,
   Janet and Martin; August 1960, near Rhayader.
   (Photograph: David Edgar Bidgood.)

5 David Edgar Bidgood, 1966. (Photograph: Martin Bidgood.)

6 Tŷhaearn, Abergwesyn, March 1967. (Photograph: Ruth
   Bidgood.)

7 Abergwesyn, April 1999. Tŷhaearn is the house towards the
   right-hand side of the picture. (Photograph: Ruth Bidgood.)

8 Ruth Bidgood receiving applause on her award of the 2011
   Roland Mathias Prize; The Guildhall, Brecon, 8 April 2011.
   (Photograph: Roland Mathias Prize.)

9 Clearance of Coed Trallwm, Cnyffiad Valley, December 1966. This was the scene that inspired the early poem 'Tree-felling'. (Photograph: Ruth Bidgood, by permission of Llyfrgell Genedlaethol Cymru/The National Library of Wales.)

10 Llanddewi Hall, Radnorshire, April 1972. (Photograph: Ruth Bidgood, reprinted by kind permission of the Radnorshire Society.)

11 Cluniau-fawr, Camarch Valley, August 1967. (Photograph: Ruth Bidgood.)

12 Ruins of Digiff, Irfon Valley, June 1984. (Photograph: Ruth Bidgood.)

13 On Rhiw Garreg-lwyd, above Tŷhaearn, February 1986. (Photograph: Ruth Bidgood.)

14 View up the Camarch Valley, March 2004. (Photograph: Ruth Bidgood.)

Abbreviations

FM	*The Fluent Moment* (Bridgend: Seren, 1996)
GT	*The Given Time* (Swansea: Christopher Davies, 1972)
'H'	'Heartland', *Poetry Wales*, 26/3 (1991)
HV	*Hearing Voices* (Blaenau Ffestiniog: Cinnamon, 2008)
'HW'	'History is now and Wales: Ruth Bidgood interviewed by Jason Walford Davies', *Planet*, 137 (1999)
K	*Kindred* (Bridgend: Poetry Wales Press, 1986)
LC	*Lighting Candles: New and Selected Poems* (Bridgend: Poetry Wales Press, 1982)
N&S	*New & Selected Poems* (Bridgend: Seren, 2004)
NWH	*Not Without Homage* (Swansea: Christopher Davies, 1975)
PB	*Parishes of the Buzzard* (Port Talbot: Gold Leaf, 2000)
PM	*The Print of Miracle* (Llandysul: Gomer, 1978)
RB	Personal communication from Ruth Bidgood to the author of this volume
SoP	*Symbols of Plenty: Selected Longer Poems* (Norwich: Canterbury Press, 2006)
SP	*Selected Poems* (Bridgend: Seren, 1992)
SW	*Singing to Wolves* (Bridgend: Seren, 2000)
TB	*Time Being* (Bridgend: Seren, 2009)

1

Finding Mid-Wales

The poet and local historian Ruth Bidgood is primarily associated
with the remote mid-Wales village of Abergwesyn (some eleven-
and-a-half miles to the west of Builth Wells) and more generally
with the surrounding areas of north Breconshire and Radnorshire. However, her connection with Abergwesyn did not begin
until she was in her early forties, in the mid-1960s, and she did
not live there full-time until a decade later. Nonetheless, it was
the association with Abergwesyn that, in Bidgood's early middle
age, seemed abruptly to instigate her life as both poet and local
historian. Her first collection of poetry, *The Given Time*, was
published in 1972 – the year she turned fifty. As the dust jacket
notes to this volume indicate, 'It was not until . . . she came to
live for part of each year in Abergwesyn, North Breconshire, that
she started to write', with the same remarks even going so far as
to suggest that, without her involvement with mid-Wales, none
of the poems in the book 'would have been written'. As Bidgood
has stated, bar poetry written at school, 'There were no pre-
Abergwesyn poems.'[1] However, since her arrival in the mid-
Wales area in the mid-1960s, she has published twelve volumes
of poetry as well as an array of work on local history (a full-
length book, various pamphlets and nearly seventy articles). In
the words of Jason Walford Davies, Bidgood's arrival in Abergwesyn, now more than four-and-a-half decades ago, occasioned
a 'striking conversion' to writing ('HW', 49).

*   *   *

Ruth Bidgood's life before Abergwesyn is essentially a story of physical, though not emotional, movement out of Wales. Born on 20 July 1922 in the mining village of Seven Sisters (Blaendulais), Glamorgan, Ruth Jones was the only child of Revd William Herbert Jones (1874–1945) – known as Herbert, and then vicar of St Mary's Anglican church in the village[2] – and his wife Hilda (née Garrett, 1887–1971), 'a former teacher in Aberdare' (RB) and a native of the West Country (figure 1).[3] Herbert Jones, who came from Conwy, had grown up in what is now the National Trust property of Aberconwy House, which his parents had run as a temperance hotel.[4] He was a Welsh speaker ('HW', 47) and whilst his daughter never learnt more than 'a little' of the language ('H', 7) – a situation she has described as 'a deep regret' ('HW', 47) – she did learn from him what she has called a 'love of Wales and a conviction of Welshness' ('H', 7). Bidgood notes that she was always keen to 'know more about the Welsh side' of her family, and 'didn't want to be half English at all'. Indeed, this 'mixture' of heritage was something that she suggests caused her 'sorrow' when she was young ('HW', 47). Bidgood recalls a relatively bookish home environment in her childhood years. Her father's study contained 'a great many' theological works, and there were 'a lot' of nineteenth-century novels around the house as well as some poetry volumes (RB). Shelley was the first of the latter that she remembers reading. Describing herself as 'a very early reader', Bidgood recollects a fondness for Christmas annuals, whilst one of the novels to which she found herself 'addicted' was Sabine Baring-Gould's *Eve* (RB). Her particular memory of a 'gory accident with a scythe' (RB) in this book is perhaps significant, given the interest identifiable in her own writing with violent or gruesome events.[5]

In 1929, the Jones family moved twelve miles south when Herbert became vicar of St Mary's church in Aberafan, Port Talbot.[6] This meant that, in 1933, the young Ruth joined the grammar school that was then called Port Talbot Secondary School,[7] and so came into contact with the English master Philip Burton (best known for his formative role in the life of

Bidgood's fellow pupil at the school, Richard Jenkins – later, Richard Burton). Philip Burton's influence was to be a strong one on Bidgood's future direction, even if she was not particularly conscious of such influence at the time,[8] and it is telling that she dedicated her first volume of poetry to him. Perhaps most importantly, she has credited him specifically with 'mak[ing] me believe that some day I could be a writer, though I doubt if he thought it would take so long, or that the form of writing would be poetry' ('H', 7).[9] Clearly having caught something of Burton's 'enormous enthusiasm for life and letters' ('H', 7), Bidgood set her sights on admission to Oxford to read English. Thus, she entered St Hugh's College in 1940 (RB), albeit only after her headmaster had talked her out of a 'somewhat melodramatic attempt to give education a miss and join up' at the start of World War II ('H', 7).

University was an experience much treasured by Bidgood, and she 'flung' herself into it 'with zest'. Moreover, she actively sustained her Welsh engagements whilst away from Wales itself as she 'helped to run the Celtic Society', which she has described as 'a meeting-place for Welsh undergraduates' ('H', 7). However, Oxford seems to have done nothing for Bidgood's creative life, even if (as she has put it) the 'academic habit of meticulous analysis . . . was a useful corrective to woolly romanticism' ('H', 7). University thus saw the production of no poetry at all, although Bidgood discovered through her studies a particular enthusiasm for Thomas Wyatt and John Donne ('H', 8). Called up to the Women's Royal Naval Service (figure 3) after finishing her degree in 1943, Bidgood spent most of her service life in Alexandria working as a coder, following initial stationing in the south-west of England (Devon and Cornwall) and then Scotland. Ironically, perhaps, whilst an English degree at Oxford had brought her nowhere near the actual writing of poetry, military service led her closer. In response to Jason Walford Davies's shrewd question as to whether it could be said 'that the kind of intense involvement with language' which being a coder required 'is related in some way to the poetic process', Bidgood replied:

Yes, I think it probably is akin to writing poetry . . . My particular line was dealing with signals that didn't make any sense, deciding how the script had got into the state it was in, what minute changes of letters and figures would cause it to start making sense again. ('HW', 49)

Alongside the formative belief that she could be a writer, inspired in her by Philip Burton, the wartime business of coding thus helped foster an acute sensitivity to linguistic minutiae – as well as a capacity to deal with puzzling detail, which Bidgood has connected with the particular challenges of local history ('HW', 49).

In some ways, the stage was now set for the creative and scholarly life for which Bidgood has subsequently become known. However, the last piece of the jigsaw, her arrival in mid-Wales, was not to fall into place for nearly another two decades. In that long period, Bidgood worked for 'about a year' (RB) for *Chambers's Encyclopædia* in London; got married in 1946 (to David Edgar Bidgood; figure 5); moved to the town of Coulsdon in 1949 – 'not far from London, in Surrey suburbia', in Bidgood's description ('H', 8); and had three children (the first in London, the latter two after the move to Coulsdon). During these years, which were overwhelmingly dedicated to being a full-time mother, there seems to have been a rather forced attempt on Bidgood's part to engage emotionally with England:

At the time there seemed little hope of getting back to Wales – I made a conscious effort to identify with the England I seemed likely to live in, even deciding on English names [Anthony, Janet and Martin; figure 4] for the children. (RB)

Pulling against this, however, Wales formed a constant undertow. As Bidgood has explained, 'Increasingly I wanted to come back, not to my native Glamorganshire, but to mid-Wales' ('H', 8). Mid-Wales had held a particular attraction for Bidgood since a visit there in her teens when she had holidayed with her parents and a school-friend in Llandrindod. 'We had no car,' she recalls, 'so hired a car and driver to take us to the Elan Valley', and she found that 'this wilder side of Radnorshire appealed to me very much' (RB). But it was not until the mid-1960s that a small legacy enabled her and her husband to buy 'a corrugated Victorian bungalow' in the region. This became the family holiday house for the next ten years (their regular presence meaning that they were 'accepted as something more than "summer residents"') and Bidgood's permanent, full-time home after divorce in 1974 (RB).[10] As Bidgood has explained:

> Houses in the Welsh countryside were then very cheap. We didn't manage to find a suitable one in Radnorshire, but were told of a bungalow in a beautiful North Breconshire valley, and found it was in Abergwesyn, which I had spotted on the map and been fascinated by – it looked so remote . . . We bought it in spring 1964. (RB)

The bungalow was called Tŷhaearn ('iron house'; figure 6), and Bidgood's arrival there was the key moment in the generation of her writing career. She recounts that, whilst living in Surrey, neither the history nor the natural world of the surrounding area 'touch[ed] me at all'. However, as soon as she came to mid-Wales, 'immediately there was the call of the land and the ruins – drawing me up the side-valleys into the remains of communities' ('HW', 49). The upshot, 'within about a year' of buying Tŷhaearn, was a surge of poetry production and local history work ('HW', 49). Bidgood's return to Wales, in other words, coupled with a rediscovery of Edward Thomas's poetry around 1966 ('H', 8), 'was powerful enough to start me off quite compulsively writing'. It was, she has explained, 'as if I was making up for lost time'.[11]

* * *

Ruth Bidgood's poetically productive life thus began in 1965, whilst her 1966 reacquaintance with Edward Thomas's work was inspirational in the sense that she saw in his poetry 'a sort of uncertainty' that she found both appealing and 'formative' ('HW', 50). 'The influence of place and the influence of this writer came together', she has suggested, and she was quickly spurred on not only to write but also to read 'more of what was being written in Wales in the English language' ('H', 8). Publication of her poetry soon followed, from mid-1967 onwards, in countryside magazines (the long-standing English magazines *Country Life* and *The Countryman*, as well as Wales's relatively new *Country Quest*[12]), in explicitly literary periodicals (*The Anglo-Welsh Review*, *Poetry Wales* and Vera Rich's London-based *Manifold*) and also in Tudor David's increasingly important social/cultural periodical *London Welshman*.[13] Indeed, whilst Bidgood's first volume of poetry did not appear until 1972, she had an extremely lively publication record in magazines during the final three years of the 1960s, publishing more than forty poems over a period of about thirty months.[14]

This early material is an interesting mixture. For example, the very first of her poems to appear, 'Tree-felling', is rooted in the country life with which Bidgood has been much associated over the course of her career. Published in the June 1967 edition of the Wrexham-edited *Country Quest*,[15] this poem portrays a group of men 'felling the oaks' on a 'rainy hill'. The event has a notable violence about it:

> A great black horse drags the logs in chains,
> Wrenching strong hoofs from the mud.
>
> Mist, and blue smoke from burning brushwood,
> And steam from the sweating, struggling horse,
> Soften the yellow of cut wood,
> And mask raw mutilation.

Although the scene is somewhat 'Soften[ed]' by mist, smoke and steam, the horse finds itself 'Wrenching' and 'struggling', with the description of the logs making them sound like prisoners (they are 'in chains'), whilst either the 'cut wood' or the landscape itself has been nothing short of mutilated. Notwithstanding the poem's appearance in a magazine of rural life, it is manifestly not some easy celebration of the then-contemporary countryside.

Rather, there is brutality here, made even more incomprehensible by the fact that, as the poem's third stanza makes clear, such brutality is not the act of strangers, nor is it vindictive. Instead, the men are 'acquiescent in the end of a landscape / Of which they had been a part.' Destruction here is effectively self-destruction, and seemingly complacent self-destruction at that. As such, in the fourth and final stanza, the horse becomes an 'archaic beast', part of the now-disappearing world that he is forced to tear to pieces. Indeed, at the poem's end, it is quite clear that Bidgood sees this destruction in terms of a manifest cultural downgrading, as the great horse 'heav[es] behind him / The ruins of a kindlier world.' For Bidgood, in other words, the destruction of the oaks is, in an act of grimly muddy violence, suggestive of a rather brutal sort of regression.

'Tree-felling' is not explicitly a mid-Wales poem; indeed, it does not even identify itself as a poem about Wales. Significantly, however, it dates from a point just after the years 1947–65, during which time official UK forestry policy had pursued a programme of especially intense, and equally contentious, coniferization of Welsh land. According to William Linnard, part of this process involved the 'wholesale coniferization of low-grade broadleaved semi-natural woodlands, *mainly oak*'. More-over, as Linnard also notes, 'In Wales especially', such actions, coupled with the 'large-scale planting of pure blocks of conifers, with insensitive boundary lines', were 'giving forestry a bad name'.[16] Within this context, 'Tree-felling' starts to look very much like a response to precisely this post-war grubbing up of indigenous Welsh woodland. That Bidgood herself confirms 'Tree-felling' to be 'an Abergwesyn poem' should thus come as no surprise. As she has indicated, it specifically dramatizes events in the nearby Cnyffiad Valley (RB), where the land which the poem describes being cleared – the land of Coed Trallwm on the slopes of Bryn Mawr – was indeed subsequently turned over, wholesale, to coniferous plantation.[17] Coed Trallwm was predominantly a broadleaved wood; however, it had also con-tained conifers in one stand of mixed trees.[18] Bidgood's December

1966 photograph of what she has identified as the scene which inspired 'Tree-felling' (RB; figure 9) suggests that the poem draws specifically on the clearing of this latter area of mixed woodland: whilst the trees across the back of the photograph are broadleaved, the logs in the foreground, which form a primary focus for the poem itself, are apparently not. Given Linnard's remarks about the particular impact of coniferization on Welsh broadleaved woods, it is thus especially striking that 'Tree-felling' renders this scene so that the only trees mentioned by the poem are oaks. 'Tree-felling', in effect, partially reimagines its origins in a way that precisely emphasizes the destruction of established, oak-based woodlands in Wales during this period. Indeed, although the poem's final lines rely on a rather naively romantic vision of a 'kindlier world' from which the present is a lamentable fall, they also mark the piece as an unequivocally critical response to the landscape changes it figures. From this sort of perspective, then, 'Tree-felling' is very much part of that hostile Welsh reaction to Westminster-driven forestry policy in mid-twentieth-century Wales to which Kirsti Bohata points when she observes that the Forestry Commission has had a persistent reputation in Wales as 'one arm of a centralized, often arrogant and alien, London government'.[19]

Whilst the relationship of 'Tree-felling' with Bidgood's mid-Wales only becomes apparent through the provision of socio-historical context or authorial gloss, other early pieces are entirely overt responses to that area which had proved so generative for Bidgood's poetic life. For example, the second of her poems to be published in the major weekly magazine *Country Life* was 'Llanddewi Hall, Radnorshire'.[20] Llanddewi Hall (figure 10), 'built on a level site to the N. of the village of Llanddewi Ystrad-enny, on the E. side of the river Ithon' and dating from around 1550,[21] was to be the subject of one of Bidgood's most extended pieces of local history research, which ran to seven substantial articles published between 1974 and 1980 in the journal *Transactions of the Radnorshire Society*.[22] These articles focused specifically on the history of the families who lived in the hall, starting with the Phillips family in the mid-sixteenth century.[23] Whilst the families are present in the poem, too, its ultimate focus is arguably elsewhere – on the house itself. At its opening, the difference between this piece and 'Tree-felling' is striking, with house and hills offered up as manifestations of a sort of gentleness and seemingly part of that earlier, 'kindlier world' to which 'Tree-felling' referred:

> Century after century, under these quiet hills
> The quiet house has kept its counsel,
> Sheltered grief and happiness, been home
> To Phillips, Hanmer, Burton and the rest

Emphasizing both temporal continuity ('Century after century') and the physical pleasures of the house itself, the poem goes on to celebrate 'cool thick walls' and 'polished stair', and suggests that this was a place about which 'many men found goodbye hard to say'. Such goodbyes were hard, Bidgood contends, 'Even in death', not only because the house was loved but also because its owners 'thought imagined heavens less beautiful than this'. The mid-Wales past as embodied in this particular building is, in this sense, not only 'kindlier' but more-than-heavenly. Indeed, in the third stanza, imagining 'one of the squires' of the house 'deep in his cups' and staggering on the stairs, Bidgood proposes, precisely, that 'the strength of the house [was] / A reassurance and somehow a redemption.' In other words, Llanddewi Hall is nothing less than a spiritually benevolent force, working against the more negative tendencies of its various inhabitants. Bidgood has conceded that some of her early poetry was 'tinged with the nostalgia I imbibed from the older people of Abergwesyn, who felt it acutely' ('H', 8), and this particular piece might be considered to have just this sort of nostalgic aspect to it – presenting the past in terms of a fundamentally uncomplicated and perpetually positive relationship between residents and always-sheltering house. However, any such nostalgia is ultimately less important than the poem's overriding invocation of the sacred. For not only is Bidgood's Llanddewi Hall more-than-heavenly and redemptive, it is also (in the final stanza) 'the place of comfort' to which spirits beyond death may return. Indeed, in closing words which are suggestive of a sort of Eucharistic exchange, it is a place where 'Century after century, love was sought and given.' Llanddewi Hall is thus, in Bidgood's poetic rendition of it, what the religious historian Mircea Eliade calls 'a strong, significant space'; it is 'qualitatively different' from what lies around it (most obviously, as the particular place of consolation for the dead) and is thus a 'sacred space'.[24] Or, to put it in different terms, in this poem, Bidgood seemingly offers up Llanddewi Hall as a kind of spiritual haven, sanctifying the diverse lives that have gone on within it.

Not all of Bidgood's earliest published poems are about mid-Wales. 'In the Suburbs', for example, seems to respond directly to life in Coulsdon.[25] Over its four stanzas, however, it constitutes as sharp a rejection of suburban England as 'Llanddewi Hall, Radnorshire' constitutes an embrace of rural Wales. In the opening three stanzas, then, the poem observes various intrusions onto the neatness of suburban physical order and cultural sensibilities. Thus, stanza one describes how:

> Two gardens away down a suburban road
> Eight puppies crying make a country sound,
> Half-quack, half-howl, and wholly primitive,
> In overweening lust for milk and warmth.

Bidgood here proposes a disjunction between the 'suburban road' and the 'country sound' of the puppies, the implication being that their 'wholly primitive' noise is fundamentally at odds with their immediate surroundings. Similarly, stanza two observes how 'Tame golden-rod has seeded in the nettles.' The plant has 'exceeded' what Bidgood calls the 'neat limits' which the 'commuters' have set for it and the unruly actions of the non-human world thus seem to be offered up as a mockery of orderly suburban intentions. Finally, in stanza three, a squirrel startles 'A muster of housewives' at a bus stop. Bidgood compares the animal to the people, to the manifest detriment of the latter: the squirrel, the poem's speaker says pointedly, is 'gazing with more self-possession / Than theirs'. Having become more overtly critical of suburban scenes and characters as it has progressed, the poem concludes with a full-blooded attack:

> Build, build the walls, fence in, defend the garden,
> Observe protective laws of taste and measure.
> Talk sensibly of manageable feelings,
> And if you hear a cry out there, don't listen.

For Bidgood, it seems, suburbia is all about a desperate attempt to defend oneself against that which is outside immediate 'taste' and 'measure'. It is about ignoring that which is excessive, and that which is 'out there' in the non-human world. It appears, in short, to be about fear and limits. As a part of Bidgood's discovery of mid-Wales, then, 'In the Suburbs' would seem to represent a counterbalancing, emphatic rejection of non-rural life. The ecocritic Terry Gifford has suggested that 'the desire to retreat to a static rural idyll away from the disordered stresses of modernity' is effectively what defines pastoral literature in its conservative, quietist mode.[26] There are clearly elements of this sort of pastoral tendency within Bidgood's earliest poetry of rural Wales, such as the rendition of Llanddewi Hall as, precisely, a sort of spiritually elevated idyll. However, it is clear from 'In the Suburbs' that modern suburbia is not rejected by Bidgood because it is stressful and difficult, but because it is too ordered. In other words, whatever the relationship of Bidgood's poetry with the pastoral – an issue to which I shall return – 'In the Suburbs' would seem to suggest that her engagement with the rural does not emerge out of a flight from some sort of perceived complexity.

Whilst 'In the Suburbs' might not itself be concerned with Wales, it clearly relates to issues that are fundamental to Bidgood's 1960s poetic embedding into Breconshire and Radnorshire.

However, other poems from this earliest period of magazine publication do seem to exist completely beyond the matrix of Bidgood's Welsh concerns, appropriately suggesting that it is inappropriate to reduce her to one strand of poetic engagement. 'Trespass', for example, which was published in the *London Welshman* in November 1967, is a brief meditation on the poet-speaker's growing age.[27] The poem explores the way in which the speaker feels herself to be the eponymous trespasser in summer – in which country, she says, 'It is the young who own the land.' The speaker, by contrast, recognizes that she has passed out of youth, and so 'Must tread the dead-leaf paths of autumn/ That to the barren winter go.' Formally somewhat four-square, employing even rhythms and full rhyme, this piece seems to represent a very early stylistic moment within Bidgood's work. It is, in this sense, significant that she did not include it in her first collection.[28] Nonetheless, and whilst not wishing to reduce the poem merely to the life of its author,[29] it is hard not to suggest that it is strikingly indicative of Bidgood's relatively late arrival to poetry that a piece on her 'lost title' to the youthful realm of summer should be amongst her earliest work.

'Shoes' is another of Bidgood's earliest magazine publications that exists entirely beyond the bounds of her mid-Wales concerns. This piece, which was published in the *London Welshman* in June 1968, is about a mother, her daughter and the passage out of childhood.[30] The opening stanza thus tells of the daughter 'Hurrying out to a dance', leaving the house empty of sound except for the 'far-off hum of traffic' and the 'dim boom' of the wind. The second stanza then focuses sharply on the daughter's eponymous shoes:

> A pair of her shoes lay on the hearthrug
> At a strange angle, like something broken.
> Her mother stooped to pick them up,
> But changed her mind and left them there
> Through the long evening – pieces of childhood
> Not yet quite tidied away.

The shoes, symbolic of the last remaining fragments of a childhood, are kept in view by a mother who seemingly does not wish to see that part of her daughter's life tidied away just yet. However, the poem suggests that this wistful act is effectively futile: the daughter has already gone, with the mother left alone to the consequently stretched-out time of a solitary 'long evening'.

If 'Shoes' is centrally to do with the mother-daughter relationship, Bidgood's first poem to be published in *Poetry Wales*, 'Warning', has a similar focus on matters to do with female life. Within this context, it is important to note that Bidgood refuses to appear in women-only anthologies, and has made it unequivocally plain that she has no desire to be thought of as a woman poet ('HW', 54). Indeed, her response to Deryn Rees-Jones's 1991 gender-oriented reading of her work was fundamentally dismissive, albeit kindly so ('HW', 54).[31] Similarly, in an unpublished letter to *Poetry Wales* about her long radio poem 'Hymn to Sant Ffraid', she rejects gender-based aspects of Kenneth R. Smith's reading of the poem and notes that, whilst she enjoyed meeting Smith, their conversation had 'what might have seemed an unpropitious start, when I had to tell him I don't much like being called a "woman poet"'.[32] However, Bidgood is equally clear that she is 'much in sympathy with all efforts to remove assorted unfairnesses to women' (RB), and that 'I'm not the least anti-feminist. Most of what they want, I want' ('HW', 54). Indeed, her refusal to be included in women-only anthologies grows, for her, from a sense that 'being put into a little box labelled "Women Poets" without the slightest idea of how I stand in relation to "Poets"' is 'a limiting thing' and 'doesn't do any real service to the cause of women' ('HW', 54).

'Warning', then, is a poem that seems to key in very directly to this notion of doing 'service to the cause of women', as it delivers a sharp attack on the propagation of patriarchal structures through the passing on of fear and ignorance in father–son relationships.[33] Thus, the speaker of the poem, who is effectively the voice of patriarchy itself, uses the first stanza to declare:

> Father, warn your son against women,
> for are they not the enemy
> whom you were bred to fear,
> the draining mouth of succubus,
> the devil in the thighs?
> O father, warn your son against women.

Over the course of the poem, the speaker urges the father to 'Teach' his son variously to 'defeat these curious creatures' every day; to treat falling in love with a woman as the opportunity for him to 'take a captive'; to consider the highest social good to be 'the handclasp / of a brother' and thus to 'treasure' beery evenings amongst men when women are kept elsewhere; and to know no more accurate sense of women than 'a stereotype of lust or chastity / fit for the Christian Fathers'. The upshot, says the speaker, will be the son's protection against 'ever knowing / a complete love, ever progressing / past casual venery or tentative friendship / that ends in retreat, defeat'. The poem's point is thus abundantly clear: that the modes of suspicion, subjugation and (self-)deception on which patriarchy depends are utterly destructive, not only for the women whose imprisonment is their primary target but also for the men whom they reduce to bullies and emotional failures.

*   *   *

The acceptance of 'Warning' by *Poetry Wales* seems to have been a particular source of pride for Bidgood. As she recalls, 'I got [a poem] into Poetry Wales, which was a great day – I certainly thought so at the time.'[34] Her excitement about placing work with this particular periodical was understandable. *Poetry Wales*, formed in 1965 under the pioneering editorship of Meic Stephens, was a crucial publication in a Welsh context because it was this magazine that was the focal point for a new explosion in English-language poetry in Wales (following on from the slightly earlier work of Tudor David's London-based monthly *London Welshman*).[35] Anglophone poetry in Wales had fallen into the doldrums in the

1950s after the deaths of Dylan Thomas and Idris Davies (both in 1953).[36] However, by the latter part of the 1960s – substantially because of *Poetry Wales* itself – Stephens was able to observe that 'Anglo-Welsh poets' suddenly seemed to be 'as numerous as blackberries in the woods', and he was able to talk of this revitalized poetic life as 'the second flowering of Anglo-Welsh verse'.[37] Admittedly, it does not seem that Bidgood was especially prominent within this 1960s Welsh literary context. Most obviously, she only began publishing in the final three years of the decade, whilst it is also the case that much of her poetry from 1967 to 1969 appeared in countryside and broad cultural magazines rather than in explicitly literary periodicals. Indeed, in this context it is telling that a total of only seven of her poems appeared in *Poetry Wales* and *The Anglo-Welsh Review* during the 1960s, and these only over the final year-and-a-half of the decade. Moreover, whilst she had a strong record of 1960s publication in the *London Welshman* (eight poems in the two-and-a-half years from the summer of 1967), this magazine had an extremely broad Welsh cultural agenda and perhaps did not create literary impact in the same way as appearing in *Poetry Wales* or *The Anglo-Welsh Review*. Nonetheless, Bidgood was emphatically conscious of being part of the new and particular literary energy within anglophone Wales, observing that 'I was very aware of it. Roland Mathias and Raymond Garlick were very encouraging – I can remember that. *I felt I was doing something Welsh*' ('HW', 49–50; emphasis added).

It was, then, within this recently revivified poetic milieu that Bidgood's first volume, *The Given Time*, appeared in 1972 from Swansea publisher Christopher Davies. Writing in the *London Welshman* in December 1966, John Tripp – poet, journalist and key figure within Wales's English-language poetic revival in the 1960s – observed 'the new "verbal toughness", as it has been called, the new literary honesty shared by the latest generation of [anglophone] Welsh poets. There is a control and a cutting back of rhetoric, and real point to the subject-matter, with little obscurity.'[38] Bidgood's work in *The Given Time* suggests that her own poetry took a not dissimilar stylistic line. For example, the fourth poem of the collection, 'Chimneys' (*GT*, p. 15), is typified by precisely the sort of linguistic openness to which Tripp appeared, at least in part, to have been referring. The point of 'Chimneys', then, is to recount a 'trick of sun and shade' which deceives the speaker into thinking that she has seen a house where one does not exist. As the first two stanzas explain:

> Far away, we saw three chimneys in the trees
> Across the valley, on a little hill
> Beyond the first hill's shoulder
>
> Shading our eyes from the sidelong evening sun,
> We gazed and guessed till we could almost see
> The roofs of beast-house, stable and barn.

In their use of easy, speech-like phrases such as 'we saw three chimneys in the trees' and 'we could almost see / The roofs', these lines achieve the sort of unfussy clarity towards which Tripp's remarks seemingly gestured. Indeed, in a similar fashion, the closest Bidgood comes here to what Tripp called 'rhetoric' would seem to be the alliteration of 'gazed and guessed', whilst the poem as a whole certainly avoids obscurity. Thus, for example, although 'Chimneys' does not actually identify the location with which it is concerned, the poem's opening two stanzas provide entirely sufficient context for a reader to understand its subsequent action. The whole, in short, suggests an approachable and distinctly conversational poetic manner. Admittedly, this gently contemplative piece, with its similarly low-key register – its most striking choice of words being the description of a 'plunging valley' – can hardly be said to reflect Tripp's notion of 'verbal toughness'. 'Local Character' (*GT*, p. 44), however, certainly can. Here, then, in a poem of a considerable drama, Bidgood tells of a man who was notable for his emotional wildness, whose 'rough laughter / towered up to the rough crags' and whose 'rages / swelled and boomed through the trembling valley'. Thrown from his pony one day, the eponymous 'Character' gashes his head and is subsequently shown 'horrifically cursing', staggering home, 'lurch[ing] over the yard' and 'bellowing' at his wife. He is, the poem indicates, 'magnificent in meanness'. Such descriptions emphasizing the near-feral qualities of her chosen subject (laughter towering upwards; rages swelling and booming; horrific cursing; lurching; bellowing), Bidgood's verbal character here is almost aggressive. Significantly, however, such increased linguistic forcefulness does not move this poem away from the approachably conversational mode that was identifiable in 'Chimneys', and which seems to characterize her more mature work over *The Given Time* as a whole. Thus, in 'Local Character', the poem's narrative unwinds over sentences which spill easily from line to line:

> When he died, the earth he had bullied
> and the weather he had matched with his extremes
> let him down – there were no landslides,
> no thunderspouts for his passing,
> and in the gentle anti-climax of the grave
> he lies now quiet as any. (*GT*, p. 44)

In such lines, with their comfortably flowing syntax and relaxed rhythms, the suggestion of something related to speech is again strong – this, perhaps, being what Tripp meant by his notion of stylistic 'honesty'. Moreover, whilst the poem is structured around a clear rhetorical pattern (the four stanzas start, respectively, 'When he was young', 'When he was grown', 'When he was old' and 'When he died'), this hardly constitutes formal intricacy, with repetition simply being used to stage the passing of time. In other words, whilst the dominant stylistic note of such work is not exactly one of plainness, and whilst its diction may sometimes be colourful, it is manifestly rooted in a general avoidance of complexity and obscurity in both manner and reference. Bidgood's work was, it seems, substantially in tune with the poetic approach that Tripp's 1966 analysis had proposed as fundamental to the new energy of the Second Flowering.

None of this is to say, of course, that Bidgood's first collection is of one stylistic stamp throughout. From rather different approaches identifiable in poems such as 'The Malcontent', 'Walls', 'Old Film', 'Pattern' and 'Island', it is clear that Bidgood was still exploring a variety of forms. Bidgood has written of her early attempts at using 'a tighter structure than the conversational one that became more typical of me' and her sense that this sort of 'more formal shape' proved in some way 'unsatisfying or restrictive' – though she stresses that 'I've always admired it when well done by others' (RB). 'The Malcontent' (*GT*, p. 47) certainly takes a 'more formal shape' than either 'Chimneys' or 'Local Character', albeit a very simple one, being constructed of two rhyming quatrains and using full rhymes throughout. The consequence, at least in the first stanza, is perhaps most obviously seen in the poem's syntactic patterns, which appear to be some-what disjointed:

> You, never satisfied with the rose you see,
> Never accepting the dry denial of stone,
> Or limitation in love – so, inevitably, alone –
> Spoilt child who cannot compromise or agree;
>
> Only, perhaps, at the feared and destined close
> Of all neat possibilities will you, blind,
> See through the rock spring-water, find
> The kiss that was never given and the impossible rose.

The syntax of the opening stanza here is essentially a clutter of short phrases, possibly embedded in what might be the awkwardly broken apostrophe of 'You, . . . / Spoilt child.' 'Walls' (*GT*, p. 52) is a similar case. Again, the use of a simple scheme of full rhyme (each four-line stanza rhyming the second and fourth lines) seems to drive the poem away from speech-like patterns and towards a far more mannered syntactic approach ('Walls stand in space, in time, / Are here, are then'). 'Old Film' (*GT*, p. 57), 'Pattern' (*GT*, p. 63) and 'Island' (*GT*, p. 64), by con-trast, all adopt a very short-lined format, of no more than four words to a line. 'Old Film' and 'Island' additionally abandon punctuation. The first stanza of 'Island' might appropriately suggest the impression of such work:

> island is image
> venture nostalgia
> aspiration
> symbol dream
> opportunity

The intensely reduced form that Bidgood adopts here is a world away from the more discursive approach of 'Chimneys', 'Local Character' or 'Llanddewi Hall, Radnorshire' (which is also collected in *The Given Time*). And whilst it is the case that neither the rhymed and syntactically more mannered approach nor the miniaturist mode went on to form a significant part of Bidgood's subsequent output, their presence in *The Given Time* certainly seems to suggest a poet who was self-consciously working through various formal possibilities at the beginning of her career.

If aspects of Bidgood's approach to style in *The Given Time* indicate a certain kinship with the new generation of anglophone Welsh poets that John Tripp had discussed in the *London Welshman* in 1966, then the collection's primary poetic rootedness in mid-Wales suggests another important connection with this particular generation – especially within the context of her important sense that she was 'doing something Welsh' ('HW', 50). In 1967, in his keynote *Poetry Wales* article 'The Second Flowering', Meic Stephens emphasized what he saw as the Wales-identifying quality of the 'new' anglophone poets (by which he meant those writers who had appeared since 1960):

Only this much is clear: the new poets, with one or two lone wolves to remind us that labels in poetry are so often phoney, all recognise that they have a great deal in common, including a social background, roots if you like in a particular community. They are also willing to associate as Welshmen and have their work discussed with reference to the culture of Wales.[39]

Bidgood's specific choice of a Welsh publishing house for *The Given Time* is thus important. 'I don't think', she has observed, that 'I considered sending my first collection to an English house at all' (RB). Moreover, whilst her arrangement of material in the collection itself was done somewhat naively (by her own admission), there was a clear sense of the need to begin her choices with Wales-oriented material. As she has explained, 'I was totally ignorant of the processes of [book] publication':

> I had no idea that I would have any say in choice or arrangement of the poems if the book was accepted . . . I got together a batch of poems with a Welsh connection (as I had chosen a Welsh publisher and felt from the start identified with Wales), then thought they didn't seem enough, added a batch of rather different poems, and finally some more Welsh-flavoured ones . . . I was very pleased to have an immediate acceptance, and waited to see what was chosen and how it would be arranged, being rather surprised to find everything accepted, and the order I had bundled them up in not changed at all. (RB)

In this sense, the arrangement of material in *The Given Time* thus retains, in fascinatingly unedited form, Bidgood's simple initial impulse to begin with Wales. And this impulse was strikingly in tune with Meic Stephens's sense of how the generation of the Second Flowering was pursuing – and indeed *should* pursue – its poetics. Lauding most highly the work of Raymond Garlick, Harri Webb and John Tripp, whom he saw as making 'their vision of a free Wales the theme for poems that I consider to be among the finest written about this country', Stephens used his 1967 article to set out his sense of what anglophone Welsh verse should be:

> I am not suggesting that all Anglo-Welsh poets should feel obliged to write about Welsh nationhood, but I am convinced that before a poet writing in English can fully justify his position as Anglo-Welsh, he needs either to write about Welsh scenes, Welsh people, the Welsh past, life in contemporary Wales, or his own analysis of all these, or else attempt to demonstrate in his verse those more elusive

characteristics of style and feeling which are generally regarded as belonging to Welsh poetry.[40]

For Stephens, then, the poetry of anglophone Welsh writers had to be committed to Wales, if not actively as a cause to be supported then at least as an object of primary scrutiny. Of course, Stephens's editorship of *Poetry Wales* made him a significant shaping force in terms of what sort of material was actually published by anglophone Welsh writers in the period. But his sentiments in this article also reflected strong tendencies in 1960s anglophone Welsh poetry in general.[41] In any case, the Wales-weighted approach of *The Given Time* manifestly made it a clear inheritor of such a sensibility and milieu, with its second poem, appropriately titled 'Mid-Wales' (*GT*, p. 12), thus acting as an important early credo. Whilst acknowledging the sadness that the ruins of the area so often seem to create ('Some in her ruins / See only dereliction'), the speaker of 'Mid-Wales' urges the reader to understand that 'a life is not invalidated / By having ended':

> These tumbled stones are language
> In which a life is written –
> Read, and rejoice that it was lived.
> Drink with joy the silence offered
> In this cup of hills, this Grail.

Taking the sense of sacred space that was suggested in 'Llanddewi Hall, Radnorshire' and radically extending it to the whole of mid-Wales's rural landscape, 'Mid-Wales' positions itself as a fundamental celebration of the area – whether or not the life of the place has essentially ceased – and argues for a joyous immersion in it. In Bidgood's own manner, this effectively serves notice of that poetic commitment to Welsh place and life for which Meic Stephens had argued in 1967. It is, then, the precise nature of that early commitment, in terms of its construction of a poetics of the Abergwesyn area and of the mid-Wales region more broadly, that is my primary concern in the next chapter.

2
Towards a Poetics of Abergwesyn

The immediate reception of *The Given Time* was broadly positive. Jeremy Hooker's response in *The Anglo-Welsh Review* began with carefully qualified praise. This was, he said, 'potentially, the best first book of poems to appear in Wales for some time'. Its problem, he suggested, was that it was a 'very uneven' long collection which contained 'a fine shorter one'[1] – remarks that are entirely consistent with Bidgood's own surprise at having every one of the poems that she had submitted selected for the volume (RB). Hooker quickly identified Bidgood's stylistic character ('naturalness'; 'a colloquial poetry using speech rhythms'), and saw her primary concern with the 'life of the past as it is renewed or changed by memory' as evidence of a poet who had crucially discovered a theme. This was, moreover, a theme that should, he suggested, remain 'inexhaustible'.[2] David Shayer, writing in *Poetry Wales*, responded in very similar terms. *The Given Time* was, he urged, 'one of the best of the Christopher Davies poetry volumes to appear to date', although he observed a 'number of thinner pieces towards the end which could well have been left out'.[3] Indeed, his analysis of Bidgood's concerns in this volume still provides an excellent starting-point for understanding her poetic:

> The setting for many of the poems is the Welsh countryside, and I think that perhaps this is where the appeal of the writing lies, with the feel of wild mid-Wales and its empty valleys and forests conveyed so convincingly that one can almost smell the country. There are a number of principal themes or preoccupations; the relationship between man's pattern-making efforts (farming, buildings) and nature's

constant encroaching tide of weed and forest; the importance of the past and what its survival should teach us; and – despite the valuable secrets which the past holds – the overwhelming importance of the here-and-now and of the patterns we create in it for the future.[4]

It was left to John Tripp, writing in *Planet*, to sound a more sceptical note. Bidgood, he suggested, 'tends to be a victim of dusty cliché, and the indolent phrase'. Whilst some years earlier he had (as I noted in chapter 1) praised the poets of the Second Flowering for their pursuit of an unfussy style, the stylistic stamp of *The Given Time* was, he seemed to suggest, relaxed to the point of carelessness. Tripp's assessment of the book's concerns similarly emphasized its 'tranquil' vision of 'the Welsh countryside and its history', and argued that this 'exceptionally gentle' poet had produced poems which 'make a pleasant picture of a region she is obviously wedded to'.[5] Whilst Tripp may have had a point in terms of a certain tendency towards the use of well-worn language at this early stage (something that Jeremy Hooker also observed),[6] I would suggest that his criticism of her 'indolent phrase' is simply a misunderstanding of the 'speech rhythms' that Hooker more accurately identified. Similarly, and as I hope to show, Tripp's suggestion of a kind of uniform gentleness to her work does seem to constitute a significant misreading – and one which becomes especially clear in the light of her subsequent development. The balance of this early criticism, however, was manifestly on the positive side. Indeed, Peter Elfed Lewis even went so far as to take Sam Adams bluntly to task for failing to include Bidgood in his Carcanet anthology *Ten Anglo-Welsh Poets* (1974). Since Adams's volume 'concentrates on the period from 1967', Lewis argued, 'the omission of Ruth Bidgood, the most gifted Anglo-Welsh poet to have come to light during these years, is particularly regrettable'.[7]

*   *   *

Bidgood's first three collections came out swiftly over a period of just six years: after *The Given Time* in 1972, *Not Without Homage* appeared in 1975, winning a Welsh Arts Council prize in 1976 in the process, whilst 1978 saw the publication of *The Print of Miracle*.[8] In all of these books, the mid-Wales area was the single most substantial impetus behind and focus for her poetry, radiating out from her personal locus of Abergwesyn to include Breconshire more broadly, Radnorshire, Cardiganshire and (occasionally) north Carmarthenshire.[9] Of the sixty-five poems in *The Given Time*, for example, nearly the entire first half of the book emerges out of mid-Wales places or experiences, as do many of the final dozen poems in the volume.[10]

The opening and title poem of *The Given Time* thus announces a number of important themes within Bidgood's early poetics of mid-Wales. Moreover, it immediately suggests that John Tripp's reading of such material as offering merely a 'pleasant picture' of the region was too thin. Essentially, 'The Given Time' (*GT*, p. 11) begins with destruction, as the poet peers into the future and sees the house on which the poem focuses as nothing more than 'a darkness, / Irregularity, among the ordered trees' of the forest which has swamped it. Crucially, it is not just the physical presence of the house that has been driven into darkness by the advancing trees: its cultural significance has also been lost as there is, Bidgood observes, 'Not a memory left, not a line of its story.' The particularities of local history, the poem suggests, will be lost here to the growing trees. Of course, and to redirect David Shayer's early response to Bidgood's poetry, this is not just a matter of what Shayer called 'nature's constant encroaching tide' impacting upon human constructions.[11] Rather, those '*ordered* trees' (emphasis added) should recall William Linnard's observation of the contemporaneous 'large-scale planting of pure blocks of conifers, with insensitive boundary lines'.[12] In other words, the trees which have swallowed the house in the opening stanza of 'The Given Time' are human-planted. Indeed, in the second stanza, during the present ('this time decreed as mine') the forest is merely 'tiny trees' and it is thus clear that the plantation in question is part of that unpopular mid-twentieth-century policy of Welsh afforestation which I noted in chapter 1.

In this context, it is pertinent that Bidgood's subsequent book of local history, *Parishes of the Buzzard* (which appeared in 2000), notes the 'conversion of huge tracts of North Breconshire into forest' since 'about the time of the Second World War' (*PB*, p. 184), whilst the house to which the poem substantially responds – identified by Bidgood as Cluniau-fawr in the Camarch Valley (RB; figure 11) – was indeed swallowed up by Forestry Commission coniferous woodland.[13] 'The Given Time' is thus not a generalized response to mid-Wales rural life. Rather, it emerges out of and is manifestly a response to very particular – and distinctly politicized – Welsh landscape conditions in the mid-twentieth century.

However, the poem is also a deliberate attempt to counteract the impact of such conditions and their future effects. The second stanza's focus on the present moment recognizes that, with the house only yet 'lapped / By the first waves of forest-land', its identity still survives, even though its life has gone:

> The house has lost its life, not yet identity –
> It is known hereabouts, stories are still told
> Of men who lived there. Silent, it poses questions,
> Troubles me with half-answers, glimpses, echoes. (*GT*, p. 11)

Crucially, in the present, the cultural significance of the house remains, in the sense that at least some of its stories survive, even if it now only offers up troubling 'half-answers' in its abandoned state. Indeed, it is this sense of the present as troubled which dominates the poem's third and final stanza. Accepting her existence in the present ('this given time') means, the speaker suggests, that she both lives in 'the haunted present' and 'know[s] the forest's shadow'. In other words, living in the present means that she is troubled not only by the past (that which is haunting) but also by the future (the shadow cast by the grown trees that are to come). It is, then, this troubled present that seems to springboard the poem's speaker into an act of imagination which, by the end of the poem, restores to her a time 'where in the winds of the past the house rose whole, / A shape of life in a living valley.' Thus, at the very start of her first collection, the cultural act of Bidgood's poetry is fundamentally restorative. In other words, it constitutes an attempt to re-find, through an act of imagination, the lost life of a particular mid-Wales valley and consequently to escape the 'snatching branches' of destructive afforestation. Admittedly, what the poem thus imagines might seem to fit into Tony Curtis's slightly later criticism that Bidgood's early work was prone to 'rather mistily Romantic' tendencies:[14]

> Winter brightening the low rooms
> With snow-light and spark-spattering logs,
> Or spring's shadows playing like lambs,
> Racing with the sun like children over the fields.

The imagery here, in other words, concentrates on the picturesque flicker of fire in the hearth and of fleeting shadows over the land; there is no imagining of work in the house, for example, as there is in 'Llanddewi Hall, Radnorshire', which considers 'a farmer, coming in tired from lambing' (GT, p. 13). But whilst the particular imagery at the end of 'The Given Time' is arguably somewhat out of step with the rest of the piece, to concentrate on this would be a mistake: this is a poem that is crucially aware of the trials of the Camarch Valley landscape, the politics behind its coniferous overrunning and the cultural significance of trying to hold onto the stories of a particular place. Moreover, its urge to re-animate the life of the past is fundamentally indicative of the restorative direction of Bidgood's poetic thought from the very first. Indeed, in its scope, this early poem captures a number of themes which are primary to her entire poetic endeavour: forest, valley, ruins (or stones), memory and, of course, the eponymous 'Given Time' of the present.

This final notion of the importance of the present arguably needs particular emphasis, given that Bidgood is perhaps best known as a poet of the past. In response to Jason Walford Davies's observation of her use of modern images (he cites 'windscreen wipers, mini-television screens, jet planes, westerns, oil spills, even Jimi Hendrix, the Doors and Joni Mitchell'), she has remarked that 'I'm glad you pointed that out because some people seem to think that I'm entirely a poet who writes about history' ('HW', 53). Thus, responding to Bidgood's 'first sight of Abergwesyn' (RB), 'Roads' emphasizes how 'nowhere but this here and now / Is my true destination' and rejects any speculation about what other directions life might have taken in its refusal to 'wonder what heron-guarded lake / Lay in the other valley' (GT, p. 16).[15] Indeed, in lines that suggest very precisely Bidgood's newly found poetic commitment to the area radiating out from Abergwesyn – the poem is characterized by her typical mid-Wales topographical notes of valley, lake, forest and river – 'Roads' concludes with the simple declaration that 'all the steps of my life have / brought me home'. To put it another way, the mid-Wales present is, for Bidgood, emphatically the centre-point. Indeed, 'Little of Distinction' underlines this very clearly (GT, p. 18). The speaker's visit to the village on which the poem is centred may have been driven by a certain antiquarian urge:

> Little of distinction, guide-books had said –
> A marshy common and a windy hill;
> A renovated church, a few old graves
> With curly stones and cherubs with blind eyes:
> Yews with split trunks straining at rusty bands;
> And past the church, a house or two, a farm,
> Not picturesque, not even very old.

However, the emotional impact of the piece derives precisely from the current moment in mid-Wales place. Whilst acknowledging the fact that life 'breaks / So many promises', the poem's speaker observes that the array of unexpected beauty she discovers in the supposedly undistinguished village 'gave me a present / It had not promised.' Thus, she notes the 'fantastic curlicues' of a veranda throwing 'a patterned shadow on the grass', the delicacy of ash-leaves stirring 'Against a sky of that young blue', and the 'exact statement' of 'Trees and grey walls'.

But most striking of all is the sheer pleasure that she finds in the wide view of the surrounding land, 'the miles on hazy miles / Of Radnorshire and Breconshire below, / Uncertain in the heat – the mystery / That complements precision.' The mid-Wales experience of 'Little of Distinction' is, then, one of immediate aesthetic enjoyment: it is significantly about responding to the patterns, colours and physical impressions of the present moment. The 'present' of the poem is thus both gift and time.

However, 'Little of Distinction' is also about rendering Radnorshire and Breconshire as places of mystery, to balance the 'exact statement' of trees and walls immediately to hand. It is about seeing the wider vistas of these two counties as what the geographer Yi-Fu Tuan has called 'mythical space', one version of which arises from the fact that what lies beyond the immediate world of 'pragmatic activity' is precisely 'hazy'.[16] In 'Little of Distinction', the shimmer of the heat-haze is actively used by Bidgood to render the broader mid-Wales area in just this way: it is 'fuzzy', blurred, imprecise.[17] The sweep of Radnorshire and Breconshire is thus offered up as a space of what Bidgood much later called 'fertile uncertainty' ('Not the Pathetic Fallacy'; FM, p. 58). In other words, it is a space that, in its lack of clarity, stands as an arena of generative potentiality. (Significantly, Bidgood raises this notion of 'fertile uncertainty' in relation to the precisely generative influence of Edward Thomas's poetry: 'HW', 50.) Depicted in this way, mid-Wales becomes a place not only of present aesthetic response, but also of future possibilities – of what may emerge out of the 'fertile uncertainty' of its mythical, hazy space. Indeed, even though the poem 'Stone' (GT, p. 40) begins with the bluntly anti-pastoral contention that 'Arcadia was never here', and observes both how 'Ice-needles tortured the thin soil' and how 'spring snow lay long by the north wall', it still sees mid-Wales as a place of potential. 'Stone' thus recounts how 'Waves of life receding left / jetsam of stone', with ruined cottage and 'half-sunk' megaliths alike marking human existence now departed from both valley and surrounding hills. The poem thus details the demise of life at the cottage:

The rushes cut each autumn
to mend the thatch, one year
were cut no more; over the centuries
the path was lost.

By contrast, the poem declares, 'Only stone lasts here'. Such stone may be mystifying in the sense that it 'baffles questioning' and withholds from the speaker its history of 'so many summers'. However, it is not indicative of some sort of defeat. Rather, and in a crucial moment of affirmation, Bidgood contends that:

Stone proclaims life, affirms a future
by virtue of so many pasts

What stone perhaps most obviously declares is ruins. However, this poem suggests that it also declares the vitality of the past, which may spring forth again in the future. Bidgood's mid-Wales may be a place of physical decay. But, equally, it is far from being a place whose life should be consigned to history. Responding to a ruined house in the Irfon Valley just upstream from Abergwesyn, 'Hennant' makes this absolutely clear (GT, p. 45).[18] 'Stones are memorials', this poem declares, 'but in their disarray / and littleness against green wilderness / speak of beginnings'. Moreover, whilst 'Hennant' acknowledges that such beginnings may not take place precisely where the old life ceased, the poem contends that they will nonetheless be a fundamental renewal of it: 'the walls that rise', Bidgood observes, 'will be these walls'. As Jeremy Hooker puts it, Bidgood's work has 'a quiet, strong faith in the future'.[19] More than this, indeed, Bidgood's 'faith in the future' is crucially restorative, seeing the potential for the departed life of mid-Wales to begin again.

However, not all of the mid-Wales work in *The Given Time* emphasizes the restorative potential of the land; nor is the aesthetic pleasure of 'Little of Distinction' necessarily a dominant note. Rather, Bidgood's vision of the territory radiating out from Abergwesyn is often strikingly dark. This is suggested not only by aspects of pieces such as 'The Given Time' and 'Tree-felling', but also by two of the major poems in the collection – 'Cardigan-shire Story' and, perhaps Bidgood's single most important early piece, 'Burial Path'. Both these poems emerged from Bidgood's local history research, the former from word of mouth and the latter from an early twentieth-century Welsh-language essay that gives an account of the incident in question.[20] 'Cardigan-shire Story' (GT, pp. 34–5), then, narrates the hill journey of a 'girl' who has given birth to a child that night, after months of 'hiding and lies'. Setting out from what Bidgood has identi-fied as the hill-farm of Blaen-Glasffrwd (RB), which lies some two miles south-east of Strata Florida in Cardiganshire at an elevation of around 1,200 feet, the girl's intended destination is 'her mother's house'.[21] However, the poem makes brutally clear from its opening lines that the story will not end with a happy welcome home:

> The baby died, of course,
> his first night was his last.
> Night was the murderer,
> using all its weapons for the kill.

Specifically, the weapons that actually achieve the killing are the weather and topography of the mid-Wales hills. The poem notes that just one such weapon 'would have done' the job: 'the cold / on those hills'. But there is also the rain ('to soak the ragged blanket'), the wind ('to drive home the cold and wet') and the roughness of the ground over which the pony stumbles in the 'moonless dark', 'jolting the weak newborn'. Indeed, the girl is even 'mocked by an unseen river', which continues both to laugh at her and to function as a source of murderous temptation:

> The river went on laughing
> and voices spun giddily
> telling her a river could wash away
> a year, drown all its secrets –
> saying Who would know, who?
> ride home alone, let him sleep, sleep.

The mid-Wales land through which the poem's protagonist rides is thus bluntly antipathetic to humanity, and far from being a hallowed space (as it was in 'Mid-Wales') becomes actively malign. Whilst its temptations are resisted by the suffering girl (she holds the child 'closer' rather than consigning him to the river), her apparent moral fortitude is no defence against the attacks of her environment, as the poem's closing lines reiterate:

> The baby died, of course,
> but night was the only murderer,
> a killer with excessive strength
> and no motive whatsoever.

The brutality of the land, figured here in the persona of the night, is overwhelming and utterly motiveless. It kills, in effect, simply because it does. Quite clearly, this is no 'tranquil' or merely 'pleasant picture' of mid-Wales space, as John Tripp's review of *The Given Time* would have suggested.[22] Moreover, rather than presenting any sort of easy pastoral retreat that effectively functions as what the ecocritic Greg Garrard calls 'an evasive or mendacious depiction of rural life', Bidgood's poetic here acknowledges the very particular challenges to humanity offered by the mountainous mid-Wales territory out of which she writes.[23] Indeed, such is the extent of the anti-Arcadian note struck in this particular poem that 'Cardiganshire Story' might well be linked to the environmental lineage of Charles Darwin, whose 1876 autobiography observes 'the struggle for existence which everywhere goes on'.[24] Thus, the environmental commentator David Pepper observes that:

> Darwin's early experiences inclined him to an 'anti-arcadian' hopeless view of nature. In the Galapagos Islands he saw a bleak, depraved and hostile landscape. In South America he saw fierce competition for space, the decimation of indigenous species by European invaders and a fossil record that attested to much extinction.[25]

The description 'bleak, depraved and hostile' might very well apply to the physical space of Bidgood's 'Cardiganshire Story', with its topographical and meteorological harshness, its temptations and its actively destructive tendencies.

The tough mid-Wales of 'Cardiganshire Story' is certainly related to that of 'Burial Path' (GT, pp. 73–4). This latter poem, which is essentially a miniature epic, is a dramatic monologue that offers up the reactions of a widower to the long journey which he takes with fellow members of Soar y Mynydd chapel (on the banks of the Camddwr, in the hills to the west of Abergwesyn) in order to bury his wife, Sian, in what the poem calls 'the burial place of [her] people'.[26] The journey itself starts from a house called Pysgotwr (RB) in 'the mountainous parish of Llanddewi Brefi' and ends at the church of Llanddewi Abergwesyn.[27] It was, according to Bidgood's source, twelve miles long.[28] The route crosses punishing mountainous terrain, travelling over 'four rivers and four mountains' as the poem puts it, whilst climbing a total of more than 2,300 feet and descending more than 2,450.[29] The poem is rich in particular environmental markers, all of which emphasize the challenges of the terrain through which the burial party carries Sian's coffin:

> it was not the dark rocks of Cwm-y-Benglog
> dragged down my spirit,
> it was not the steepness of Rhiw'r Ych
> that cracked my heart.

What is striking, however, is that whilst the land itself may be forbidding ('the sinew-straining tracks, / the steeps of Rhiw Gelynen and Rhiw'r Ych'), the communal ritual that is being undertaken is manifestly sustaining. Although the widower notes that 'forty times and more / I put my shoulder to the coffin', and although he acknowledges that 'Carrying you, there was great weariness', he also observes that he took 'pride in an old ritual well performed':

> And at the grave, pride too in showing
> churchmen how we of Soar knew well
> ways of devotion, fit solemnity.

Perhaps what left the female protagonist of 'Cardiganshire Story' especially vulnerable was the fact that she was, even if only temporarily, out of her community, caught in loneliness between the farm where she had hidden and her mother's house. She was, in the poem's terms, 'afraid to bring [the baby] out of night / after nine months' hiding and lies'. Or, to put it differently, the fear of social stigma had undercut her existence within a communal context – and the challenges of the environment seemingly overwhelm her as a consequence. By contrast, whilst the speaker of 'Burial Path' is amongst his people, he remains uplifted, recalling 'the coffin riding / effortlessly the surge of effort'. However, as soon as he is alone – as soon as the community disappears from round about him, its collective duty done – any such sense of being uplifted vanishes abruptly:

> Now as I went down Rhiw'r Ych alone . . .
> It was then my heart cracked, Sian, my spirit
> went into that darkness and was lost.

Ending on this point of emotional devastation, the dispersal of community seems to have shifted the mountainous mid-Wales of the Abergwesyn area from being primarily a physical challenge to being a state in which the land is nothing less than the locus of damnation, a place in which the spirit descends into 'darkness' and is 'lost'. The difference between this finally cursed mid-Wales of 'Burial Path' and the sacred space of 'Mid-Wales' or the aesthetic pleasures of 'Little of Distinction' is thus striking. Specifically, such difference should make abundantly clear that even Bidgood's earliest poetry of the Abergwesyn area is complex and varied – and that any attempt to present it as uniformly (and merely) 'tranquil', 'gentle' or 'pleasant', as John Tripp did, is fundamentally misdirected.

*   *   *

It is perhaps easiest to align Bidgood's mid-Wales-rooted work with the Welsh-language tradition of *canu bro* (poetry of place). However, the way in which both 'Cardiganshire Story' and 'Burial Path' raise issues to do with community suggests that elements of her work can also usefully be thought of in relation to the Welsh-language tradition of the *bardd gwlad* (folk poet) whom W. Rhys Nicholas pertinently describes as 'a poet in a rural community, reflecting the character of his society, its personalities, and its varied activities, its crafts and its diverse interests'.[30] Within this context, both 'Cardiganshire Story' and 'Burial Path' are manifestly poems that narrate specific 'person-alities' within specific mid-Wales communities – even if both pieces are, in part, to do with exclusion from or loneliness within such communities. Jeremy Hooker has suggested that 'the *idea* of the *bardd gwlad* . . . is still powerful for some English-language poets in Wales', and has proposed that Bidgood is one such poet.[31] This is a contention that would seem to be supported from the very start of Bidgood's poetic output, with her first three collections emphatically offering up not only the sense of *a poet of place* but also of *a poet of a community in its place*. From the first, in other words, Bidgood's poetics of Abergwesyn – and of mid-Wales more widely – are not just to do with particular physical localities; they are also fundamentally to do with the ebb and flow of community within these localities.

Not Without Homage (1975) and *The Print of Miracle* (1978) thus continue to build on the initial movement towards both place and community that was established in *The Given Time*. Of course, as with her very earliest work (see chapter 1 above), it would be wrong to suggest that all of the pieces in these two volumes are to do with the mid-Wales locality or its people. In *Not Without Homage*, for example, 'Boy in a Train' describes a journey on a 'suburban line' – the suburban note recalling the Coulsdon setting of 'In the Suburbs' – during which the poem's speaker sees the eponymous child reading a horror story, his 'avid eyes . . . tak[ing] in the pictured beast, / black and alone on a storm-lit plain'.[32] Noting the boy's glance 'for reassurance' towards the normal life of 'cluttered gardens, sheds and washing-lines' beyond the train window, the poem suggests that escape from the monster he has seen is now impossible: 'The beast of loneliness / looked at you too', the speaker declares, 'and saw his host' (*NWH*, p. 5). 'Witness' is also based on a train, with the poem positioning the journeying poet-speaker as the chance observer of a father–daughter relationship that is much more distant than the father would wish it to appear:

> He laughs often,
> but his eyes call
> 'My daughter, my daughter',
> after a ghost that dwindles
> down-wind. (*NWH*, p. 34)

In their portrayal of people at moments of psychological pain (or its inevitability), such pieces very much suggest that bleak human vision with which 'Burial Path' so emphatically ended. They should thus not be considered as somehow alien to Bidgood's early poetic, notwithstanding their lack of mid-Wales geography. Similarly, 'Film, Aran Islands' responds to the eponymous Irish islands in terms that very much recall the concern with ruins that Bidgood's mid-Wales poetry displays:

> Man's life rooted, spread, gripped
> on this hard island till sap dried.
> The walls he left go on
> uselessly resisting the salty wind. (*PM*, p. 30)

Moreover, in 'Bullingham, Hereford' (*PM*, p. 45), the resonant interplay of colours (white and red) and the poem's almost heady response to physical patterns ('high white notes of cider-apple trees, / line after line, in fullest bloom') constitute a very similar sort of environmental response to the aesthetic pleasures of 'Little of Distinction'.

Such pieces are clearly not out of place within the context of the early work that I am considering here. However, Bidgood's poetic centre of gravity within *Not Without Homage* and *The Print of Miracle* nonetheless remains the mid-Wales that radiates out from Abergwesyn, with her diverse response to landmarks, narratives, characters and traditions in the area significantly suggesting the concerns of both *canu bro* and *bardd gwlad*. Admittedly, the ambiguous poem 'Stateless' (*NWH*, p. 8) might be read as a statement of caution about the potential of mid-Wales to offer 'real / identity cards' to a speaker who declares herself to have 'no papers': 'Forgive me', she remarks, 'if till they arrive / I think it too early to rejoice'. What 'Stateless' seems to suggest, in other words, is that its speaker is only ever temporarily in place, and that even the possibility of genuine identification must be treated with scepticism. However, the difficulties of human engagement with mid-Wales are, it seems, precisely a part of what draws Bidgood's poetic so emphatically towards this place and its communities. Thus, for example, 'Thirst' (*NWH*, p. 10) is a very sharp rejoinder to a too-easy declaration of love for 'our' valley. Noting how the 'love' that the land 'accepted once' was rooted in work of an 'instinctive' sort ('the dumb tending of beasts and crops') rather than any feeling of 'sweetness in the heart', the poem warns against the 'conscious devotion' of its addressee, which sees the land 'eulogised, courted, remembered, returned to'. There is a clear sense here of Bidgood seeking to offer up something of what W. Rhys Nicholas calls 'the character of [the *bardd gwlad*'s] society' in the poem's suggestion of instinctive agricultural commitments which have been fundamental to the historic life of the valley.[33] By contrast, the poem's addressee – whose response to the land appears to be both 'shaped in the brain' (thus not instinctive) and fundamentally idealized – is crucially out of step with established patterns of local life. The consequence is that the addressee is left open to the destructive potential of the land that has been apparent elsewhere:

> Beware!
> Something lives here that has an unquenchable thirst.
> The bones of your life, drained dry of love,

would hardly be noticed in the rushes
of our insatiate valley.

'Thirst' seems to be a direct critique of that aspect of pastoral
vision which Terry Gifford describes as a 'comfortably complacent'
response to rural life, in which (for example) a landscape is
'celebrated . . . as though no-one actually sweated to maintain it
on a low income'.[34] More than this, the poem seems to exist as a
warning that such an attitude is nothing less than dangerous,
leaving those who subscribe to it vulnerable to the draining
power of an 'insatiate' land. A few pages later in the same
collection, 'Settlers' (NWH, pp. 12–13) continues the debate. This
more substantial piece considers incomers to the mid-Wales area
– here identified explicitly through the poem's reference to
'Daren hill', which rises to over 1,700 feet above the upper
Camarch Valley – whom the poem's speaker sees as knowing
'Nothing of the land, or beasts, nothing of us / and our ways.'[35]
Representing the voice of the established community, the speaker
notes how the 'pretty girl' of the newly arrived couple wants to
'coax' the sheep-dogs 'like pets' and he reacts with scorn:

> Yard dogs they are, for working, not for the house.
> She knows no better. Wait till winter comes! –
> These young ones will be friends with that too, I suppose,
> Like they think Daren is a friend.

The incomers' attempt to be friends with the land (and perhaps
even with winter itself) suggests to the rooted speaker that they
misunderstand the place fundamentally, and thus put themselves at risk of the sort of destruction outlined in 'Thirst'.
Daren, says the speaker, is just a hill – but one that has 'killed
more than beasts in its time'. The point of the poem at this
moment is that a romantic (Gifford's 'comfortably complacent')
response to the land is fundamentally incompatible with the
established attitudes of the old community which, in its
familiarity with work and death in the hills, is much more aware
of the dangers of the area. However, the poem's final stanza

crucially changes the picture. Whilst observing that the incomers 'have not the language, / nor knowledge of farm and chapel and the net / of family in which we are held safe – / or choked, whichever way you think of it', the speaker lets his scepticism rest for a moment and he recognizes their possession of another, older sort of knowledge that the settled community of the area does not have:

> Very old things they know, that were thought more of
> many years ago – like when to go
> up Daren ridge to that old stone
> like a signpost pointing west:
> which track to take from there to the other stones
> that lurch in a crooked circle on Bryn Du:
> what time of the moon to tread that path

Acknowledging the sensitivity of the eponymous settlers to the pre-Christian and pre-historic remnants within the land, the speaker concedes that 'There is a lot we have forgotten' – that 'we' specifically being the established community of the area. Moreover, recognizing that 'this country / is many different lands', the poem ends by conceding that to 'one Wales' – essentially a pagan one – these seemingly romantic, naive incomers 'are not strangers, perhaps, but have come home'. What is important about 'Settlers', then, is that it is a poem of various communities within one place – indeed, of various places within one place. Thus it acknowledges the Welsh-language life that has revolved around farm work and chapel, but it also seeks to recognize a life that long ago responded to and now responds again to standing stones, to 'the stars' and to phases of the moon. As such, Bidgood's poetic response to mid-Wales community at this point does not merely deal with those long-established in the area; it is also, and crucially, an engagement with changing community. In her position as *bardd gwlad*, responding to characters within the locality, the poem's settlers are just as much a part of Bidgood's scope as is the poem's rooted speaker.

This is emphasized again in the poem 'Invaders' (*PM*, p. 22), which is a further addition to the same debate. Here, however, there seems to be far less equivocation about the new arrivals, who are seemingly a manifestation of that restorative urge which was suggested by 'The Given Time'. In 'Invaders', then, a house 'which its builder's kin / gave up for dead twenty years ago' finds a family of new inhabitants, whose wary three-year-old daughter the poem's speaker disturbs whilst 'walking the muddy track by her new home'. Where the addressee of 'Thirst' seemed focused on love for the land, the incomers here appear to be focused on work:

> From inside the stockade of hedge there came
> staccato phrases – a brush sweeping,
> rattle of curtain tried on rail,
> creak of new cupboard doors where china
> was mustered clattering into its planned array.

Far from the romantic posture critiqued in 'Thirst', this response to existence within rural Welsh space is fundamentally practical; and it is out of such practicality, the poem seems to suggest, that a 'thin smoke' rises from the 'resurrected house', a smoke which 'scribbl[es] an alphabet of life upon / the wet encircling empty hills'. The land may still present its challenges (it is both wet and empty), the poem declares, but life may begin again through a commitment rooted in simple work. What is clear, however, is that whilst such commitment mirrors the patterns of the old community (as indicated in both 'Thirst' and 'Settlers') this new life is indeed a different one from that which went before: as the poem's speaker observes, 'Someone shouted, cheerfully, / *but not in the old language*' (emphasis added). Restoration, it seems, may still involve primary cultural loss.

Whilst Bidgood's acknowledgement of present communal change is clear, her response to the past patterns of life within mid-Wales space – to both their physical landmarks and the characters who contributed to them – is just as important. For example, 'Huw' (*NWH*, p. 28) tells of an old man, no longer in full possession of his mental faculties, whose mind is 'far on the driftways of his youth'. As the very start of the poem makes clear, the eponymous Huw is a local character who emerges from generations of remembering:

An old man, dead now, told me once (said an old man to me)
that boys on their long way to school . . .
used to see Huw, his white hair dank with rain,
picking up stones beside the road he mended once

Huw is important, however, not just as a colourful individual. He is also significant in the way that his drifting memories reach back to the droving life of the area, the impact of which, Bidgood herself argues in *Parishes of the Buzzard*, was 'undoubtedly great' on Abergwesyn, in a relationship between village and drovers that lasted 'From mediaeval times for centuries' (*PB*, p. 189).[36] Thus, the poem describes the way in which Huw's mind is full of 'barking, bellowing, / shouts of "Ho tarw!", thudding of beasts / in doomed processions up Cwmdyfnant track'. As such, this poem not only responds to a particular personality; it also engages with an important aspect of one of those communal 'activities' or 'interests' that W. Rhys Nicholas describes as central to the work of the *bardd gwlad*.[37]

A slightly different response to the past life of the area is taken in 'All Souls'' (*PM*, p. 12), which focuses on old buildings in an attempt to bear witness to the now uninhabited houses of the Gwesyn Valley. 'All Souls'' thus describes how the poet-speaker walks out of her house 'into a black All Souls'' night and sees the lights from the valley's few surviving houses calling to one another and 'speak[ing] / for others that lie dumb'. It is this latter note that is crucial, as the following lines make clear:

From the hill Clyn ahead
Glangwesyn's lively shout of light
celebrates old Nant Henfron, will not let
Cenfaes and Blaennant be voiceless.

In its recognition of houses that have fallen silent, this poem manifestly acknowledges the changing patterns of land and habitation in the Gwesyn Valley: for example, the ruins of Blaennant (home of the man on whom the eponymous character of 'Huw' is based) are to be found at the edge of a coniferous plantation.[38] 'All Souls" is, in other words, premised on the sense of landscape as fluid – as 'process', to use the useful description put forward by the anthropologists Pamela J. Stewart and Andrew Strathern.[39] However, in the notion of living houses giving voice to abandoned ones, Bidgood simultaneously refuses to let such change, such 'process', erase past lives. Indeed, for the speaker of the poem, this refusal is a fundamental personal commitment. Thus, in the poem's final lines, she declares of the abandoned houses:

> For them tonight when I go home
> I will draw back my curtains, for them
> my house shall sing with light.

Against the uncompromising and 'deafening darkness / of remotest hills' – a phrase that again construes mid-Wales in terms of a tough, antipathetic physicality – the commitment of the speaker here is to offer 'speech to the nameless, those / who are hardly a memory'. In such offering of speech, 'All Souls" is precisely a counterbalance to the near-loss of geo-cultural memory to which the poem refers at this point. Admittedly, this is a poem that recognizes Bidgood's own status as a sort of outsider within the Abergwesyn community: 'I am a latecomer', concedes the speaker. And this arguably puts Bidgood herself at odds with the insider status of the traditional *bardd gwlad* to which W. Rhys Nicholas points when he talks of the response of the *bardd gwlad* to 'his native *bro*'.[40] Nonetheless, 'All Souls" is still manifestly a poem that seeks to preserve the particular knowledge of the community in which the poet-speaker finds herself. It is, to put it differently, a joyous and defiant act of cultural memorial, an active remembering of place.

*   *   *

In its bringing together of memory, the responsive present, ruins and valley – as A. M. ('Donald') Allchin shrewdly observes, the house names in the poem form 'a kind of roll-call of valley names'[41] – 'All Souls" is a significant poem in terms of those driving motifs within Bidgood's entire poetic which I noted in my earlier discussion of 'The Given Time'. So, too, is 'Standing Stone' (*PM*, p. 26), although this piece adds to the dynamic on display in 'All Souls" a considerable emphasis on trees. As in 'The Given Time', then, the speaker of this poem observes a historic act of human building – here, a simple standing stone. Crucially, this stone is about to be overwhelmed by 'new firs'. It is, however, not just the stone that is about to be choked by aggressive coniferization; rather, it is the whole valley. Thus the speaker's mind jumps ahead to when the trees will have been 'cleared', the valley 'freed' and the stone able to 'offer again / the ancient orientation'. I have argued elsewhere that 'Bidgood's use of waterways and the valleys which they create is a returning motif in her work'.[42] Thus I have proposed that her work is responsive to that environmental mode of literary thinking that the ecocritic Lawrence Buell has called 'Watershed Aesthetics', by which he means literary works which display 'an ecocultural understanding of peoples defined by waterways'.[43] Bidgood's urge to root her thought in 'Standing Stone' in terms of the life of a valley, precisely as she does in 'All Souls", is clearly part of such a tendency. Just as important here, however, is the way in which the valley is also the site of a primary contest between stone and trees. Placing her hands upon the standing stone in an act of what the poem calls 'dumb love', the poet-speaker observes that 'The stone stores, transmits.' The stone, in other words, is a figure of memory within the valley. As Donald Allchin puts it, standing stones are, for Bidgood, 'carriers of tradition, conveying a message which is not less true despite our difficulty in putting it into words'.[44] The trees, by contrast, suggest forgetting, cultural erasure, silencing, as it is only when they are gone that the stone is able to perform again its 'ancient' act of orientation. As such, that the coniferous plantation of 'Standing Stone' is culturally (and thus politically) malign is abundantly clear from the poem. But Bidgood's position here is not one of quiet acceptance. Rather, as the poem concludes, the poet-speaker observes:

> I walk down-valley
> on an old track. Behind me
> the ephemeral trees darken.
> Among them, the stone waits.

Describing the trees as 'ephemeral', Bidgood declares her faith in their ultimate demise. By contrast, memory, in the form of the stone, is seen as biding its time, waiting for the moment of its eventual return. Cultural memory, the poem seems to suggest, will ultimately triumph over the erasures of afforestation. As such, the poem's description of the future clearing of the trees in terms of *freeing* the valley is a highly politicized vision of cultural liberation to come. Indeed, seen in this light, the poem thus stands as a direct gesture of defiance aimed at that insensitive UK afforestation policy, to which I have previously referred, that was visited upon Wales in the mid-twentieth century.[45] More than this, it is also a vision of the ultimate undoing of such policy.

However, it is the unpublished poem 'The Zombie-makers' (written between late 1969 and mid-1970) that perhaps makes Bidgood's early opposition to such landscape policies most explicit.[46] This piece suggests that those who are responsible for afforestation (as well as for the creation of reservoirs, an issue to which the poem also refers) are guilty of having 'violated' mid-Wales space, and that subsequent attempts to 'prettify' the 'body / with labelled forest trail and picnic area' create nothing more than 'a ghoulish animation / that is not life'. The preponderance of ruined and abandoned houses in her early work suggests that Bidgood is acutely aware of that twentieth-century 'crisis of depopulation in rural areas' of Wales to which Kirsti Bohata refers in her own discussion of the Welsh literatures of afforestation. However, at the point of 'The Zombie-makers' at least, Bidgood clearly had no faith in the notion of forestry as a viable solution to this problem – contrary to the position of the Forestry Commission itself which, as Bohata points out, 'la[id] emphasis on bringing work to those areas suffering from economic decline'.[47] In this sense, aspects of Bidgood's early work are manifestly part of that stream of Welsh literary production which registers its political opposition to what Bohata calls 'the ambitions of the Forestry Commission and Ministry of Defence, not to mention the Water Board' (in other words, the appropriative mid-twentieth-century attitude of such bodies towards Welsh land) and their consequent 'threat' to established Welsh cultural life.[48] For Bidgood, as 'The Zombie-makers' indicates, the consequence for land thus appropriated is 'not life' at all. Rather, what is left is mere 'animation' that is not even given the dignity of a genuine death. It is pertinent to note that the horror-movie scenario that Bidgood creates here is almost diametrically opposed to the sense of quiet, 'complacent' pastoral that John Tripp's review of *The Given Time* sought to suggest.[49] However, the more important point is this: in such work, Bidgood's poetics of Abergwesyn (and of the mid-Wales space which radiates out from it) are nothing less than a bluntly defiant commitment to the region's memory and to its yet-surviving life.

3

Myth and the Sacred

Following her first three collections, Bidgood's next major work was the radio poem 'Hymn to Sant Ffraid' which was 'commissioned by BBC Radio Wales in conjunction with the Welsh Arts Council, and broadcast on 5 April 1979' (*SoP*, p. vii). Running to 465 lines and divided into three sections, this remains Bidgood's longest individual poem to date.[1] After its broadcast, 'Hymn to Sant Ffraid' went unpublished in its complete form until 2006 when it appeared in the Canterbury Press volume *Symbols of Plenty* (Bidgood's *Selected Longer Poems*, as the volume's subtitle has it). Using the spelling 'Hymn to Sant Ffraed',[2] a substantial extract from the poem had appeared in 1981, in *The Anglo-Welsh Review*. Subsequently, the piece as a whole had been scheduled for publication with Gwasg Boase (Monmouth) towards the end of the 1980s, but this press ceased to run before the planned book came to fruition.[3] The poem received fairly extended critical attention in Kenneth R. Smith's 1989 *Poetry Wales* article 'Praise of the past: the myth of eternal return in women writers'.[4] However, Bidgood herself was clearly sceptical about aspects of Smith's critique and took what was, for her, the unusual step of writing a substantial riposte (reproduced in this volume as Appendix C) which she sent to *Poetry Wales*. As she has put it subsequently, 'when we [she and Smith] were chatting at lunch, I thought we were communicating', yet 'when I read what he had written,' Bidgood recalls feeling that Smith 'had made up his mind about what he would say before coming to see me!' (RB). Bidgood's riposte was not published by *Poetry Wales*, so her specific concerns about Smith's reading – such as her sense that he fundamentally misreads the orientation of the poem's second section (see p. 53 below) – have, until this point, remained out of the public domain. However, even setting to one side such issues of contested interpretation, the letter is an important document in the sense that, as an extended piece of authorial self-reflection, it constitutes a manifestly valuable companion piece to the poem as a whole.

*   *   *

Despite Bidgood's concerns about his particular reading of the poem, Smith was nonetheless right to point out that 'Hymn to Sant Ffraid' (to adopt Bidgood's later spelling) was intended 'for recitation'.[5] Written specifically as a commission for a thirty-minute radio production, the poem is split between three voices – spoken in the 1979 broadcast, as the BBC's typescript of the poem makes clear, by Margaret John (first voice), Olwen Rees (second voice) and John Darran (third voice).[6] The same typescript also includes Bidgood's directions regarding music and sound effects (the latter including wind and church bells), these suggesting that the whole was clearly conceived by the poet in terms of performance rather than simply as poetry for the page. Stylistically, the poem is certainly more various than the bulk of Bidgood's output. On a very basic level, it mixes poetry and prose, which is not typical of her work. Moreover, although the 'Hymn' makes much use of Bidgood's signature winding, conversational sentence, it also adopts linguistic patterns that are manifestly more stylized. For example, the following lines from the poem's seventh stanza display a striking combination of alliteration, internal rhyme and syntactic parallelism:

> Blood blots the Bridestone,
> flame springs, fire supplicates –
> Bride, goddess, bring now
> the breaking, the slaking,
> the flowing, the growing! (*SoP*, p. 5)

As my analysis below indicates, the piece as a whole is also very heavily 'sourced', in the sense that it draws its themes and images quite clearly from various volumes which Bidgood consulted in her research for the poem.[7] Indeed, following Kenneth R. Smith's interesting suggestion of a connection between the 'Hymn' and the work of David Jones (with which Bidgood's letter to *Poetry Wales* concurs),[8] Jones's declaration of compositional principles in the 'Preface' to *The Anathémata* might also be seen as fundamentally applicable to 'Hymn to Sant Ffraid': 'Part of my task has been to allow myself to be directed by motifs gathered together from such sources as have by accident been available to me and to make a work out of those mixed data.'[9] Of course, in terms of any indebtedness to Jones, it is also interesting that 'Hymn to Sant Ffraid' displays that mixing together of prose and poetry which is so familiar from the earlier poet's work. But identifications between the 'Hymn' and Jones's poetic should not be pushed too far. Whilst Bidgood notes that the subject-matter of her poem 'brings it into an area which is . . . not inimical to David Jones's preoccupations' (RB), the 'Hymn' simply does not try to approach that idiosyncratic and restless inventiveness of language which constitutes such an important part of Jones's literary achievement.

Thematically, then, 'Hymn to Sant Ffraid' is centrally concerned with the complex and various mythology associated with the late fifth/early sixth-century Saint Brigid of Kildare, known in Wales as Sant Ffraid, and the altogether older pan-Celtic deity of the same name, much of whose 'cult legend', as Anne Ross suggests, was 'taken over into Christianity' in the traditions which grew up around the Irish saint.[10] This sense of an intertwined heritage to the Brigid figure is made explicit in Bidgood's prefatory note to the poem, which declares the work to be an 'ode to a concocted Celtic Saint':

> concocted in that a real person of whom little is known took on some of the attributes of a previous fertility goddess cum muse, and became the centre of a cult which expressed a number of perennial human preoccupations. (*SoP*, p. 2)

The variousness of its central figure as outlined here is fundamental to the 'Hymn' as a whole. However, it is the first section
of the work (usefully titled 'Saint and Goddess' in the 1981
extract)[11] that perhaps makes particularly overt the poem's roots
in a combination of Christian and pre-Christian myth. 'Hymn to
Sant Ffraid' thus starts with 'February, / month of Sant Ffraid'
and the earth which has 'long lain white, rigid, / locked into
lifelessness', with ice on river, field, byre, hill and heart (*SoP*,
p. 3). Of course, February is particularly associated with Saint
Brigid in the sense that her feast day takes place on the first day
of the month.[12] However, the poem's second stanza goes on to
greet the Ffraid figure ('Brigid of Ireland, Ffraid of Wales') as the
force that begins to warm the winter-frozen land:

> We call her now to walk on the riverbank,
> Brigid of Ireland, Ffraid of Wales, the saint, the golden one
> who breaks the ice, dipping first one hand, then two hands
> freeing the river to flow into time of seed,
> time of ripening, time of harvest. (*SoP*, p. 3)

Whilst explicitly calling Ffraid 'the saint', the connection made
here between the Ffraid figure and the warming year crucially
relates to Brigid's ancient 'rôle as goddess of fertility',[13] particularly in terms of her association with '*Imbolg*, the pagan festival
of spring' (which falls, like the saint's day, on 1 February).[14] This
is, in other words, the Scottish sense of Brigid as 'the Fair Woman
of February' which Fiona Macleod (William Sharp) records in his
volume *Where the Forest Murmurs: Nature Essays* – an identification
that Macleod pertinently suggests reaches back 'Long before the
maiden Brigida . . . made her fame as a "daughter of God".'[15]
Indeed, in his study *Scottish Folk-lore and Folk Life* (1935), which
Bidgood consulted in her research for the poem, Donald A.
Mackenzie quotes Alexander Carmichael's seminal work of
Scottish folklore, *Carmina Gadelica*, to explain that:

> The winter is the 'dead season', when nature is asleep, and Bride
> [Brigid], who has a white wand, 'is said to breathe life into the

mouth of the dead Winter and to bring him to open his eyes to the tears and the smiles, the sighs and the laughter of Spring. The venom of the cold is said to tremble for its safety on Bride's Day (1st February, old style), and to flee for its life on Patrick's Day.'[16]

Brigid is, in this sense, the force by which fertility returns to the land, her revivifying power operating through a two-stage process which the start of Bidgood's poem expresses very precisely in the dipping of first one and then two hands into the water to free the river from ice. Yet more specifically, Bidgood's intertwining of saint and goddess at this point appears to draw on particular traditions that are remembered in the poem 'The Birth of Spring' – a rendering of various fragments from the *Carmina Gadelica* that was published in G. R. D. McLean's *Poems of the Western Highlanders* (another volume that Bidgood consulted in her research for the 'Hymn'):

> On her Feast Day Saint Bride bending low
> A finger dipped in the river-flow;
> Off the cold-hatching mother did go . . .
>
> On Saint Patrick's Day Bride bending low
> Both her hands bathed in the river-flow;
> Off the cold-bearing mother did go[17]

Significantly, whilst the reference in McLean's poem is overtly to 'Saint Bride' and whilst the sense of timescale is likewise linked to the Christian calendar of saints' days, Bride's characteristic as bringer of spring manifestly draws from the myths of the earlier fertility goddess.

It is, then, precisely such doubleness that drives the opening of 'Hymn to Sant Ffraid' and which constitutes the dominant note of the poem's first section. As such, part of Bidgood's procedure is to draw quite explicitly on Christian tales of the saint's life. Thus, for example, the third stanza describes Brigid in terms which relate directly to the Welsh version of the saint (i.e. Sant Ffraid), as found in the *cywydd* of the late fifteenth-/early sixteenth-century poet Iorwerth Fynglwyd.[18] In the summary given by Anita Tregarneth (whose volume *Founders of the Faith in Wales* was also consulted by Bidgood in preparation for the 'Hymn'), Fynglwyd's poem tells how Ffraid 'procured honey for the poor by miraculous means, and gave away many cheeses from the Steward's store without diminishing the stock'.[19] Bidgood's 'Hymn' renders these tales thus:

> Hers was a magic of giving,
> honey for the poor, and cheeses,
> yet the shelves were never emptied.
> No beggar went from her gate
> with unfilled hands or heart. (*SoP*, p. 4)

Such ideas also relate directly to Irish renditions of the saint's life. The trope of giving produce away or having it taken without 'diminishing the stock' is found in the 'Life of Brigit' that appears in the fifteenth-century *Book of Lismore* – Whitley Stokes's translation of which is quoted directly by Bidgood at the very end of Part I of the 'Hymn'.[20] Indeed, the notion of Brigid never turning away those who come to her for help is emphasized strongly by that particular 'Life', which notes that (in Stoke's translation) 'Of her father's wealth and food and property, whatsoever her hands would find or would get, she used to give to the poor and needy of the Lord.'[21] Thus, on one level, Bidgood's Brigid is quite explicitly the saint of Kildare:

> White-veiled she led her white-robed monks and maidens,
> blessing Kildare with her living and her dying. (*SoP*, p. 4)

Here, of course, the veil refers to Brigid's taking on the life of a nun, the detail of its colour being recounted, for example, in Sabine Baring-Gould and John Fisher's account of the saint's life ('Macchille invested her with a white cloak, and placed a white veil on her head').[22]

However, whilst such explicitly Christian elements are manifestly strong within Bidgood's poem, they do not overrun

the pagan myths – a point that my remarks about the poem's
first two stanzas should also suggest. Part I of the 'Hymn' thus
crucially goes on to observe how 'Behind that gentle form [i.e.
that of Saint Brigid] we dimly see are other shapes that shift in
the mist' (*SoP*, p. 4). Such shapes recall 'Brigid the Goddess, the
Mother', in whose worship Bidgood imagines blood-sacrifice
('Blood blots the Bridestone'), and whose characteristics she
details as 'muse, healer, goddess of fire' (*SoP*, pp. 4 and 5).
Within Celtic mythology, as Anne Ross has pointed out, Brigid
'was mother-goddess *par excellence*', whilst her triune nature was,
according to *Cormac's Glossary*, rooted in the myth of the three
daughters of 'the Dagda', all of whom were called 'Brigit': one 'a
poetess' and 'female sage', one 'the female physician' and one
'the female smith'.[23] Drawing on traditions cited in Robert Graves's
The White Goddess (another of Bidgood's sources), which notes
that 'It was in [the goddess's] honour that the ollave [master-
poet] carried a golden branch with tinkling bells when he went
abroad', Bidgood thus declares Brigid the goddess to be:[24]

> Poet and patron of poets, for her
> a golden branch all hung with bells
> was carried in procession. (*SoP*, p. 5)

Bidgood's goddess is also 'Mistress of skills', presiding over 'the
merrily-beaten anvil' and the 'forge-fire' (*SoP*, p. 5); and, again
drawing on Graves, she is the 'High One' and the 'White Swan'
(*SoP*, pp. 5 and 6) – the latter being, as Graves makes clear, her
symbol in 'Gaelic Scotland'.[25] Moreover, the aspect of Brigid
as fertility goddess which was suggested at the very start of
the poem emerges again in Bidgood's description of Brigid as
'bringer of corn' (*SoP*, p. 5). Thus she is precisely rendered as
'the pagan mother goddess, whose symbolic "belly" or "womb"
was envisioned as producing the season's crop', as Pamela Berger's
discussion of the Celtic goddess puts it.[26]

The first section of 'Hymn to Sant Ffraid' is, then, particularly
concerned to detail negotiations between myths of goddess and

of saint. Indeed, its closing passages explicitly consider the process of Christianization which saw the latter take on the roles and symbols of the former. Thus, observing that 'Magic fought magic', Bidgood declares that 'Christ's was the strongest' and notes that 'A Church took root and spread.' For Bidgood, however, this is not an act of cultural destruction; rather, it is a gentle redirecting of traditions. Although 'Ancient words of power were silenced', the poet suggests that:

> Yet here in the Celtic lands, the new faith dealt gently with the old. Sometimes it twined about the primitive stones, enriching them with the name of Christ and the mark of his cross. (*SoP*, p. 6)

As such, the poem sees the mother-goddess as being given back to the people 'as Mary the Mother of Christ, or as his foster-mother, St Brigid of Ireland, Sant Ffraid of Wales' (*SoP*, p. 7).[27] Nonetheless, as the opening lines of Part II make clear, the 'fiery shape' of the goddess is never far away:[28]

> Sometimes we scarcely knew
> which Brigid we saw.
> When we invoked you,
> our words were shadowed by older words
> of older prayers. Your emblems
> were laden with ancient meanings. (*SoP*, p. 8)

Donald Allchin's warmly appreciative 'Afterword' to *Symbols of Plenty* declares 'Hymn to Sant Ffraid' to be 'a poem that involves a major statement of the meaning of "Celtic Christianity"' (*SoP*, p. 67), and suggests that the poem as a whole 'has as its substance the central matter of the whole Celtic poetic tradition – praise: the praise of God above all, expressed in and through the praise of his whole creation, all the elements of the goodness of things' (*SoP*, p. 80). However, whilst conceding the driving significance of the Christian saint to Bidgood's poem, as well as the notion of the praise-poem in general,[29] it is manifestly just as important to acknowledge the 'fiery shape' of the goddess which Bidgood figures as walking behind the saint. This is not, in other words, an uncomplicatedly Christian poem.

Nonetheless, Part II of the 'Hymn' is significantly focused on the saint – although the whole section is stalked by its opening caveat about her devotees being at times unaware of 'which Brigid we saw' (*SoP*, p. 8). Interestingly, Kenneth R. Smith saw Part II (called simply 'The Legend' in the 1981 extract) as 'dedicated to the Mother goddess'.[30] This is something that Bidgood's letter of riposte rejects with a blunt 'No',[31] and the second stanza of the section would certainly seem to suggest a focus on the Christian(ized) element of the Brigid myth in its emphasis on the build-up of 'a fabric of living fantasy' to create 'a shrine for the saint' (*SoP*, p. 8). Indeed, one part of this section appears to go so far as to support Allchin's reading of the poem in terms of 'praise of God above all', with the fifth stanza taking on the voice of Saint Brigid's devotees to declare:

> Eagerly we enriched your legend
> with golden traditions; you wore them,
> like torques and armlets, for our joy
> and the glory of God. (*SoP*, p. 9)

In this context, then, Part II recounts the specifically Welsh tale of Sant Ffraid's provision of fish for the people of north Wales during a time of famine:

> We told of your fishes, the little brwyniaid –
> how you filled the seas of Môn
> with shoal after shoal, leaping to the nets
> of starving fisherfolk who called on Sant Ffraid. (*SoP*, pp. 9–10)

The 'We' here remains the devotees of the saint. As such, the point of this particular story, which is again related in Anita Tregarneth's *Founders of the Faith in Wales*, is to offer up tales of the power of the saint on whom the people had called.[32] This is, in other words, part of that enriching of Saint Brigid's legend 'with golden traditions' which the poem has previously described.

Similarly, later in the same section, Bidgood recounts the tale of the saint touching the leg of a church's altar-table:

> Power sprang in you
> like flame, unwilled.
> The wooden altar-pillar
> you touched in kneeling
> grew green, took root, lived for ever,
> sustained by your invisible
> and unconsuming fire –
> a useless miracle, a glory. (*SoP*, p. 12)

There is much bound up here. Primarily, the passage recalls the legend told in Herbert Thurston and Donald Attwater's edition of *Butler's Lives of the Saints* (1956) in which (translating 'from the lessons in the *Breviarium Aberdonense*') 'it happened that [Brigid] touched with her hand the wooden pillar on which the altar rested':

> In memory of that maiden's action long ago up to the present hour this wood remains as it were green, or, as if it had not been cut and stripped of its bark, it flourishes in its roots and heals cripples innumerable.[33]

However, the passage also picks up two further motifs, both of which are identifiable in the *Book of Lismore*: first, the sense of unwilled flame (at the point of Brigid's taking the veil, the *Book of Lismore* notes that 'A fiery pillar rose from her head to the roof-ridge of the church'); and secondly, the association of Brigid with fire which leaves unharmed that which it seemingly burns.[34] In tune with the declared intention of the speaking 'we' earlier in Part II of Bidgood's 'Hymn', such events are proclaimed 'a glory' by the poem. Thus, the saint – and, by extension, God himself – is venerated in the telling.

However, the concluding lines of Part II shift away from the Christian(ized) story and return to the overt doubleness of Part I and the opening stanza of Part II. Of course, the fire-tales of the saint certainly recall the 'fiery shape' (*SoP*, p. 8) of the goddess.

So it is perhaps unsurprising that the closing stanza of Part II makes sure that the section ends with the notion of complex origins, rather than with any one articulation of the Brigid figure:

> We cannot say of you
> ' she is exactly this or that,
> or name with certainty your origin,
> or set limits to your meaning. (*SoP*, p. 13)

The rich complexity of the poem's mythology continues into Part III, which is called 'The Saint Invoked' in the 1981 rendition.[35] This section thus draws variously on Irish and Scottish folk customs, specifically the fishing-related practices recounted in Seán Ó Súilleabháin's volume *Irish Folk Custom and Belief* (1967) and the rituals of 'Bride's Eve' described in Mackenzie's *Scottish Folk-lore and Folk Life*. It also engages with an array of Welsh geography, especially chapels and churches dedicated to Ffraid.[36] Indeed, in what appears to be an original addition to the Brigid myth on Bidgood's part, this latter concern with Welsh places even pulls in the seventeenth-century poet Henry Vaughan, who is buried in the churchyard at Llansantffraed (i.e. Saint Brigid's church) on the eastern bank of the Usk. Thus the poem effectively dedicates Vaughan to Brigid as 'her Swan' (*SoP*, p. 15).[37]

However, what seems to me to be the heart of the entire poem comes in the eleventh stanza of this final section:

> Now it is we, Sant Ffraid,
> we of a later age,
> who by your ancient symbols,
> by their perennial meaning,
> invoke your aid in all things,
> changed and unchanging. (*SoP*, p. 16)

Paralleling the trajectory of the early poem 'Little of Distinction' (*GT*, p. 18), the point of 'Hymn to Sant Ffraid' is not the originating exploration into ancient symbols and tales of the past, however strong that urge may be. Rather, the poem's primary concern is with drawing such elements of the past into the present.

The invocation of Ffraid which constitutes much of the final section of the 'Hymn' is thus precisely a plea for help in the current moment – or, in Bidgood's earlier terms, 'this given time' (*GT*, p. 11). As the second half of the eleventh stanza of Part III declares:

> Feed us, we are hungry!
> Warm us, we are cold!
> Enlighten us, we are foolish!
> Mother us, we are lonely!
> Fashion us, we are incomplete! (*SoP*, p. 16)

These primal concerns – food, warmth, wisdom, care, completeness – are presumably the 'perennial human preoccupations' which Bidgood's prefatory note to the poem gestured towards. Over the course of the poem's final section, then, Ffraid is invoked to help a variety of people in need of such things: those, for example, 'who cannot move lovingly' (*SoP*, p. 17); 'all who are slow' (*SoP*, p. 18); 'the unwanted' (*SoP*, p. 20); even 'scholars, / bent over curly manuscripts' (*SoP*, p. 19). It is thus in this precise sense of a call for help in the present moment and to address present needs that one should understand Kenneth R. Smith's more general suggestion that 'Bidgood's praise of Ffraed or Brigid is in the form of a prayer, invocation, or offering, which invites the deity into the presence of the poet/reader.'[38] Or, to put it another way, as 'Brigid the Goddess' (*SoP*, p. 4), 'saint of fire' (*SoP*, p. 19), 'Protectress of the peat-stack' (*SoP*, p. 20),[39] 'Hymn to Sant Ffraid' ultimately construes the figure it invokes as nothing less than a potent spiritual force whose myth – rendered by Bidgood as inherently various, as both pagan and Christian – is available in the present, at least as an idea, as a source of restorative power. Indeed, alongside such striking concerns with myth and the sacred, in drawing so diversely on Irish, Welsh and Scottish traditions, 'Hymn to Sant Ffraid' also crucially stands within Bidgood's poetic oeuvre as an alternative, more broadly conceived Celtic vision to set alongside her highly Wales-specific poetry of the Abergwesyn area.

*   *   *

Alongside its importance as Bidgood's longest poem to date, part of the significance of 'Hymn to Sant Ffraid' is the way in which it highlights Bidgood's concerns, apparent at various points across her work, precisely with myth (broadly understood here in Don Cupitt's sense of 'traditional' stories 'recounted in a certain community')[40] and the sacred (whether figured in terms of the transcendent 'saint of fire' or the more immanent, everyday 'Quiet Brigid of the kine': SoP pp. 19 and 18).[41] 'Carn Cafall', in Not Without Homage (NWH, pp. 20–1), provides one example of the tendency towards myth. Here Bidgood engages with mythic Welsh material that is recounted in the notes to the tale of Culhwch and Olwen in Charlotte Guest's translation of The Mabinogion. Specifically, Bidgood's concern is with a story drawn from the Mirabilia Britanniae[42] which tells of how Arthur's hound Cafall, when hunting 'the swine Troynt' (Twrch Trwyth in The Mabinogion itself), left a paw print in a stone 'in the region called Buelt' ('the district of Builth', as Guest explains).[43] Having described 'Arthur's great hound . . . / nosing and lolloping through the hills / over against Rhayader', Bidgood tells how:

> His warrior master built a cairn,
> crowned with the stone message
> set there to wait – how many centuries? –
> high on Carn Cafall in Buellt –
> a cryptogram crying for its decipherer.

Continuing to draw on Guest's notes, Bidgood goes on to explore the tradition that people who take away the paw-printed stone find that it has vanished the next day, the stone having gone 'back to its rough home / to wait another year or century'. As was the case in the poem 'Stone' (GT, p. 40), so here too stone refuses to give up its meaning: those who remove Cafall's stone and try to understand it either 'knew themselves / ignorant, baffled' or 'thought they saw lines of meaning' but wake to a memory swept clean 'of yesterday's half-understanding'. As 'Carn Cafall' puts it, 'the enigmatic stone endures unread'. However, and again following the pattern of 'Stone', whilst Cafall's stone itself 'baffles questioning' (to use the words of the earlier poem), its very persistence hints at some sort of future, as Bidgood suggests that its mythic counterparts likewise persist:

> Arthur sleeps, with Cafall at his feet . . .
> Troynt, his gashes healed,
> snuffles and stirs, and only half-asleep
> scents the old swine-paths over waiting hills.

In an interesting echo of 'Settlers' (from the same collection: *NWH*, pp. 12–13), Cafall's stone exists to suggest a mythic past that somehow retains a potential hold over an ignorant and unremembering Welsh present ('The cairn is unvisited now, the hill-name garbled'). In other words, for Bidgood here, a mythic Wales hangs over the present as an unfinished narrative which may yet be stirring. Or, to put it in different terms again, this is all a part of Bidgood's concern with the ongoing vitality of the past.

On a very basic level, 'Carn Cafall' recounts a mythic tale which is intended simply 'to explain' – a process that Don Cupitt suggests is one basic element of what he calls 'the work of myth'.[44] Specifically, in this case, the tale of Cafall's paw print provides a narrative that gives an explanation for a pattern in a rock. According to Cupitt, however, another aspect of 'the work of myth' is its ability to function as a form of legitimation. And it is precisely this latter sort of myth that is primarily explored in the poem 'Safaddan' (*PM*, pp. 52–3). In 'Safaddan', then, Bidgood's main concern is with the tale told by Giraldus Cambrensis of how Gruffudd ap Rhys ap Tewdwr is recognized as the 'natural prince of the country' by the birds of Breconshire's Llyn Safaddan (Syfaddan)[45] – birds that, as Bidgood's headnote to the poem explains, 'sing only for the rightful heir to the throne of Wales'. However, the poem crucially engages with other myths about Safaddan, as the opening stanza makes clear. Thus, the speaker of the poem – an anonymous figure in a boat who is presented as witness to the events narrated – declares that:

> In the depths
> Llyfni [*sic*] coursed, eternally separate,
> spurning the lake-waters beyond
> intangible banks of its own force.
> Silent lay the drowned city of legend
> with its aqueous colonnades.

Arguably, these mythic tales of the extraordinary separateness that is sustained between Safaddan's waters and those of Afon Llynfi which flows through it,[46] and of the fabled existence of 'the town at the bottom of the lake'[47] are also used by Bidgood as forms of legitimation: they effectively establish the remarkable quality of the place in which the poem's main narrative is to take place. Interestingly, that main narrative is presented through the eyes of a chance onlooker (the figure in the boat) who is too far away to be able to hear the words of the three horsemen who order the birds to sing. Moreover, and by contrast with the tale as told by Giraldus Cambrensis, the narrator of the poem at no point knows the identities of the participants – either those of the two 'Anglo-Normans' (as Bidgood's headnote identifies them) to whom the birds do not respond, or that of Gruffudd himself. Rather, having 'thrust' his boat through reeds and into 'open water', the speaker is right out amongst the lake's birds, whose responses are consequently far more of a focus in Bidgood's poem than they are in Giraldus's narrative. Thus, the poem's second stanza declares that:

> I had never seen the lake so thronged with birds
> or known them so quiet. Hundreds there were,
> out on the water, on the island,
> and secret among the reeds.

Such quietness continues after the first two horsemen have 'shout[ed] over the water', with the narrator declaring that 'From all / that intricate pattern of stilled wings / and watchful eyes, not one bird startled up.' By contrast, after the third man (Gruffudd) has 'called' over the water, the entire mythic landscape

– birds, Afon Llynfi and drowned city – appears to erupt in joyful recognition of what the narrator subsequently calls the 'kingly rider':

> All round me, suddenly, were wings
> beating the water, rustling the reeds,
> and a thousand songs of homage rose.
> My boat rocked on the joyful surge
> of Llyfni's [sic] invisible stream, my ears
> were dazed with triumphant proclamations
> of sunken bells, and louder and louder
> the All Hails of Safaddan's birds.

Bidgood crucially embellishes Giraldus's narrative here and, in so doing, significantly extends the remarkable quality of the tale. Thus, it is her addition that numbers the birds' songs into 'a thousand' (Giraldus does not specify the number of birds involved), just as she adds the 'joyful surge' of the Llynfi and the ringing of 'sunken bells'. Perhaps more importantly, however, by bringing the whole array of birds, river-flow, legendary city and Gruffudd himself into a complex and interlinked whole, Bidgood seemingly keys into the heart of the myth-making process itself. As Don Cupitt explains, myth-making 'seeks a more-or-less unified vision of the cosmic order, the social order, and the meaning of the individual's life'.[48] Thus, as the poem's speaker puts it in the closing lines of the penultimate stanza, 'Lake and kingly rider and host of birds, / and I with them, were caught up into the sun.' Bidgood's mythic Safaddan, in other words, creates a space in which human and non-human orders are brought together in a dramatically unifying moment of social recognition – specifically, of course, the recognition of Welsh royal identity over and against illegitimate claims to such identity. Indeed, the mythic framework of the poem seems to suggest that such recognition having been given to a genuine Welsh claim to Welsh space, the world both present and past (the latter figured in the submerged city) is elevated in a moment of transcendent joy.

However, Bidgood's concern with the mythic does not necessarily turn on stories of wide social significance. 'Drinking Stone' (*PM*, p. 21), for example, recounts a purely local tale of a standing stone that 'each midsummer cockcrow / goes thirsty down to the stream'. This seems to engage with that function of myth which Laurence Coupe describes as 'possibility' and as 'stimulus to speculation' – notions which he explains more fully by quoting Paul Ricoeur's suggestion that myth can be 'a disclosure of unprecedented worlds, an opening on to other *possible* worlds which transcend the established limits of our *actual* world'.[49] Indeed, it is precisely this sense of 'possibility' that seems to attract the speaker of 'Drinking Stone' who, being told the tale by a local man who is 'wary of my response', reacts not with scepticism but by 'thirstily drink[ing] / wonders'. 'Gigant Striding', from Bidgood's 1996 collection *The Fluent Moment*, draws on a similarly local fragment of John Leland's *Itinerary* which recounts how, in the region of Afon Claerddu (some nine-and-a-half miles to the north of Abergwesyn), the residents of the area 'fable that a gigant striding was wont to wasch his hondes' in the river 'and that Arture killid hym'.[50] Bidgood's poem speculates on why Arthur might have killed the giant:

> Perhaps it was just for his gigantic
> striding, that diminished the moor;
> his great hands commandeering the stream –
>
> for being huge, anarchic; sharing
> ancientness and threat
> of the desolate land. (*FM*, p. 34)

As a kind of flipside to the invigorating possibility of myth, Bidgood here imagines that the giant symbolizes threat to Arthur, precisely through opening up the possibility of that which extends beyond typical human limits, and must therefore be removed. As the poem's final line has it, in what may be read as a small lament for the destruction of mythic scope, 'A vast shadow hovers and is gone.' But it is perhaps 'Hoofprints', the opening poem of *The Print of Miracle* (*PM*, p. 11), which expresses most precisely Bidgood's engagement with this sense of myth as possibility. Here, the poet draws on another local legend, the genesis of which she explains in her volume of local history, *Parishes of the Buzzard*:

> On a rocky outcrop of the hillside above Alltyrhebog are two impressions in the shape of hooves, made, so local tradition tells, by a magic pony that leapt across the Irfon from Llwynderw mountain, and landed with fore-hooves against the rock. The fact that one of the Pentwyn people in years gone by is said to have carved the first hoofprint, and the second one is known to have been added by one of the Hope family, has not affected the handing down of the classical story of the magic horse, one of many which performed such feats in various parts of Wales.[51]

'Hoofprints' is also concerned with the way in which the magical tale became attached to the carvings, although it takes a very different approach from *Parishes of the Buzzard* by counter-intuitively suggesting that the story 'was always here', 'poised' and ready to be recognized. Thus the prints of the 'magic horse' had 'waited in the rock / till guided hands revealed them'. In other words, the poem's suggestion is that the carvings revealed the truth about the waiting legend, rather than the legend having been merely a response to them. In this sense, Bidgood constructs myth here precisely as that which may draw out the inherently remarkable from the ordinary – as that which may open up vistas of possibility. As the poem's closing lines put it, 'In the rock of our days / is hidden the print of miracle.'

*   *   *

The notion of the miraculous at this point recalls Bidgood's engagement with the sacred which 'Hymn to Sant Ffraid' clearly involved in its evocation of the potent spiritual force of inter-twined deity and saint. Such a sense of the sacred is significant to a variety of Bidgood's poetry – and by 'sacred' here I mean to suggest Mircea Eliade's ideas of either differentiated space (what he calls 'strong, significant space' or, quoting the biblical book of Exodus, 'holy ground') or an experience in which '*Something* that does not belong to this world has manifested itself apodictically.'[52] In chapter 1, for example, I proposed that the early poem 'Llanddewi Hall, Radnorshire' constructed its eponymous house as a sort of spiritual haven (in other words, as sacred space), sanctifying the various lives that had been centred upon it over the centuries. Similarly, I have elsewhere suggested that the later poem 'Chwefru' (from the two-part sequence 'Emblems', in *The Fluent Moment*: *FM*, p. 55) 'makes upland Welsh space holy in [its] rendering of butterflies as angels . . . and, more importantly, in [its] evocation of Christ's ascension'. The upshot in that particular case, I have argued, is that Bidgood seemingly places a mid-Wales valley 'in communion with heaven itself'.[53]

Such intrusion of the heavenly into human life is engaged with especially sharply in the poem 'Iconoclast' (*PM*, p. 25). Here, Bidgood uses found material – in the same manner as she does in 'Gigant Striding' – to imagine the seventeenth-century destroyer of religious images William Dowsing, from whose journal she quotes in the poem. Drawing variously from his records of iconoclasm at St Peter & St Paul in Clare (Suffolk), Little St Mary's in Cambridge and the college chapel of Peterhouse in Cambridge, Bidgood initially portrays Dowsing's 'soberly exultant' testimony to the work that he carries out.[54] However, in the second stanza, whilst listing the day's destructions on what the poem pertinently calls 'the smug page' of his journal, Dowsing is disconcerted to find 'images unbroken in his mind's tabernacle'. In other words, that which he has destroyed physically survives in his imagination. The poem's third and final stanza thus portrays an especially dramatic example of what Mircea Eliade calls an 'irruption of the sacred', as the iconoclast succumbs to sleep:[55]

> Battered by a thousand wooden wings, he lay
> broken, listening in terror, understanding nothing,
> while the great Angels he had left for dead

> still cried aloud God's message
> in the forbidden language of beauty.

Here, then, Bidgood imagines a vast display of divine beauty breaking through into the human mind – divine beauty that, utterly incomprehensible to the iconoclast, both survives his attempts to destroy it and utterly overwhelms him. That there is, for Bidgood, some sort of challenge provided by engagements with the sacred is also suggested by the early poem 'Carreg Clochdy' (*GT*, pp. 41–2). The context for this piece is again provided by *Parishes of the Buzzard*:

> Chapels high on mountains were not uncommon in the Middle Ages, when unlettered worshippers learnt the lessons of atonement – 'the repentant soul's painful return', as O. [*sic*] Hartwell Jones called it – by acting out the upward struggle out of sin. One such tiny church is locally rumoured to have existed centuries ago in Llanddewi Abergwesyn on a craggy summit above the Tywi, near an outcrop called 'Carreg Clochdy' ('Belfry Rock').[56]

In an evocation of the penitential journeys that G. Hartwell Jones describes when he notes 'the hill sanctuaries on the steeps or craggy heights scaled by the shepherds of Wales',[57] Bidgood thus imagines one such shepherd climbing barefoot 'to the Church of Penitents':

> Shepherds only, not skilled in the churchmen's tongue,
> we prayed as best we could when the stones bit deep,
> till the path's last dizzy turn showed us
> the little church, figuring forth Heaven and safety.

In line with the notion of penitent struggle, Bidgood figures the landscape as dangerous (the 'path's edge' falls 'abruptly' to one side, 'sheer to the gorge below / where foam gleamed white through treetops') and punishing on the body. However, when the 'ancient place' of destination is reached, the shepherd's experience suggests precisely what Mircea Eliade calls the 'strong, significant space' of 'holy ground' as the poem figures its protagonist touching 'the strength / of the church door' to quell his fear.[58] At this point, the world seems to blossom, with the sun itself figured as an agent of consecration:

> Then seeing the sun's hand of blessing
> laid on the mountain tops, and hearing from far off
> the tiny well-known voices of my flock,
> I smiled, and willing to live
> what God should send to be lived, went down the hill.

Coming into contact with sacred space, in other words, seems to open up both landscape and human life to the presence of the divine.

However, it is perhaps in the nine-poem sequence 'Encounters with Angels' – printed in full in *Symbols of Plenty* (2006; pp. 55–63) but drawing in part on material that had appeared in earlier collections (*SP*, p. 34 and *SW*, pp. 28–30) – that Bidgood's engagements with the sacred reach their most intriguing. Here, the presence of '*Something* that does not belong to this world' is the basic premise of the sequence, in the sense that sacred intrusions are simply a given.[59] However, for much of the sequence, Bidgood's point appears to be to offer up such 'irruption[s] of the sacred' in forms that are fundamentally unexpected.[60] Thus, for example, the opening poem ('Angel with Orrery': *SoP*, p. 55) presents a 'relaxed, / a rational angel' who is just as comfortable 'spin[ning] the children's orrery' as travelling through the vastness of eternity, 'through black depths / and towering flames, passing unharmed / back to the adored source'. Similarly, drawing from Francis Kilvert's diary,[61] 'Resurrection Angels' (*SoP*, p. 57) presents angels 'at play' after 'the watch at the tomb, / the giving of good news':

> Stolid-seeming villagers stared
> enchanted, watching sun dance and play,
> light-slivers splinter water's dark.
> In dazzle they half-saw

> great shining shapes swoop frolicking
> to and fro, to and fro.

Their work done, these angels are, it seems, simply enjoying themselves; indeed, as the poem puts it, they are basically 'serving / no purpose'. Such questions about purpose are brought up again by the next piece, 'Atheist Angel with Message' (*SoP*, p. 58), in which Bidgood figures an angel who declares that 'God is an unnecessary concept'. But why, asks the poem's speaker, bother delivering messages if there is 'no God':

> 'Do you just like
> travelling? I mean – all those messages
> from no-one, for nothing?' 'It's my nature',
> he said, preening. 'That's what an angel does'.

Within this context, even the angel's message seems to be relatively unimportant: 'It's only a message!', he declares, with the apparent consequence that the poem's speaker simply 'put[s] it away / for later'. Nonetheless, although shorn of an originating divinity, the angel of this poem still trails 'undiscriminating glory' as he soars away. By contrast, the 'Angel of Death' (*SoP*, p. 56) is utterly unremarkable. Recalling a dying man, the poem observes that:

> He lay waiting his time. It was no surprise
> when the angel was suddenly there
> by the weary bed. But I had expected
> a splendid solemn being to lead him away.
> Were it not for her wings (and even they
> were unspectacular) this girl
> might not have been an angel at all.

Struck by her very mundanity, the poem's speaker reacts with incredulity, asking 'Are *you* the Angel of Death?' (emphasis in original). This angel, whom the poem ends by describing as an 'unfrightening guide', crucially recalls one aspect of Bidgood's Ffraid who, as 'Quiet Brigid of the kine' (*SoP*, p. 18), is a similarly modest figure. This is, in other words, a very different sense of the sacred from that which bursts over the terrified form of the protagonist of 'Iconoclast' or which appears in the 'fiery shape' of Brigid the goddess. For Bidgood, in other words, the sacred may well trail 'undiscriminating glory', but it may also simply appear as a part of what 'Angel of Death' pertinently calls 'the ordinariness of it all'.

4

The Necessity of Darkness

Set against the 1970s, Bidgood's collections published during the 1980s and 1990s seem to suggest something of a reduction in output: between them, *Lighting Candles: New and Selected Poems* (1982), *Kindred* (1986), *Selected Poems* (1992) and *The Fluent Moment* (1996) brought together no greater sum of new material than the total contained in her 1970s volumes alone plus 1979's 'Hymn to Sant Ffraid'.[1] Considering why this might have been the case, Bidgood has speculated on the impact of her early 1980s idea to find a publisher beyond Wales (RB). At the time, this project came to nothing, although 2006's *Symbols of Plenty* saw it come to fruition when it had long since ceased to be an issue for the poet herself. Similarly, she has also tentatively pointed to her early 1990s adjustment to working with what she has called 'a hands-on editor' following the arrival of Amy Wack at Seren (RB).[2] Bidgood was to develop a much valued and clearly important professional relationship with Wack, in the latter's position as Seren's poetry editor. However, Bidgood has conceded that, having previously been used to having more or less 'a free hand', it initially took 'quite a time for me to work . . . out' the new dynamics of 'hands-on' editorial engagement (RB). Within the context of such observations, then, it is significant that it was specifically during the period from the start of the 1980s to the earlier 1990s that Bidgood's poetic output seems to have been temporarily reduced.[3] Nonetheless, the 1980s and 1990s were also the years during which Bidgood's reception was most emphatically secured. Two collections were shortlisted for Wales Book of the Year (*Selected Poems* in 1993 and *The Fluent*

Moment in 1997);[4] the end of the 1990s saw her honoured as a
fellow of The Welsh Academy;[5] and critical responses to her
work became increasingly warm. Thus, reviewing *Lighting Candles*
for *The Anglo-Welsh Review* in 1983, David Annwn suggested that
Bidgood's poetry 'makes its points and achieves its effects "from
every angle"', and praised her work for its 'precision and compassion which touches thought and feeling'.[6] Katie Jones (now
Katie Gramich), considering *Kindred* for *Planet* in 1987, described
Bidgood's work as 'mature, controlled, understated' and free
from both 'popular pretentions' and 'academicism'.[7] More
emphatic yet, in her assessment of *Kindred* for *Book News from
Wales/Llais Llyfrau*, Hilary Llewellyn Williams suggested that
whilst she would read the two other books in her review (by
Douglas Houston and Sheenagh Pugh) for 'intellectual stimulation'
and 'general interest' respectively, it was to Bidgood that she
would turn 'for pure pleasure'.[8] In the same publication in 1993
Douglas Houston himself was to observe about *Selected Poems*,
and in manifestly impressed tones, that 'I couldn't find one
wobbly enjambment in the book, each line tipping gently into
the next, each statement and image extending the sense, with an
incisive air of integrity and control.'[9] Referring to the same
volume, Merryn Williams suggested in the October 1992 edition
of *Poetry Wales* that the *Selected Poems* could 'only add to
[Bidgood's] high reputation', having offered up work which
simply 'does not date'.[10] Moreover, Donald Allchin, writing in
Planet in 1993, argued that the same volume should 'assure for
[its author] a central place in the canon of the Anglo-Welsh poetry
of this century'.[11] Indeed, Don Dale-Jones went even further
in his review of *The Fluent Moment* in 1997, suggesting that
Bidgood's work should function as a fundamental corrective to
late twentieth-century problems:

> Her poetry, with its mature historical perspectives and wise,
> compassionate insight into enduring human nature is a wonderful
> corrective for the increasingly hysterical, increasingly distorted
> world-pictures that the late twentieth century seems unable to live
> without.[12]

More succinct but just as striking was Eddie Wainwright's reaction to the same volume: 'I admired it and savoured it', he wrote in *Envoi*.[13] But perhaps the highest praise came from Paul Groves, in the winter 1997/8 edition of the leading British journal *Poetry Review*. Again considering *The Fluent Moment*, Groves's assessment was ultimately very simple: 'This is', he suggested, 'poetry at its purest, unpolluted by dross'.[14] Of course, there were some dissenters from the prevailing opinion. Gareth Owen, writing in *BWA: Bulletin of the Welsh Academy*, found what he saw as the 'sombre world' of *Selected Poems* to be rather too bleak to bear at length ('Five or six of these poems would suit me very well but a whole book has me . . . booking the next flight to Arcadia').[15] And Caroline Sylge, in *PN Review*, thought that *The Fluent Moment* took insufficient risks 'to make the desired impact'.[16] Such assessments were, however, distinctly in the minority and, overall, the degree of praise from both critics and fellow poets over the course of the 1980s and 1990s was striking – especially for a poet who was, as Merryn Williams's review of *Selected Poems* acknowledged, 'less well-known than she deserve[d]' beyond Wales.[17] To put it in somewhat different terms, these two decades saw Bidgood emphatically acknowledged as one of Wales's most important literary secrets.

*   *   *

Dai Griffiths's review of *Selected Poems* (1992) for *BWA: Bulletin of the Welsh Academy* is valuable for its attempts to sketch developments across a range of Bidgood's poetry. In this piece, Griffiths effectively proposes *Kindred* as something of a turning point in her career, notable for 'a deeper compassion' (by which he appears to mean a willingness to come face-to-face with those he calls 'ordinary people') and 'an expansion of theme'.[18] Such 'ordinary people' had, of course, always been important to Bidgood: the nameless woman and her baby in 'Cardiganshire Story' spring readily to mind, as do the protagonist and the chapel community of 'Burial Path', as well as the children of

'Invaders'. Admittedly, it must be conceded that the residue of such people (typically, the stones their homes have left behind) are, as my analyses in chapter 2 suggested, seemingly just as significant for Bidgood as the people themselves. Nonetheless, whilst Griffiths's suggestion perhaps overstates this issue in terms of a general shift, he certainly puts his finger on an important element within Bidgood's poetic: her concern with ordinary or day-to-day lives and with typically uncelebrated human detail. A variety of poems in *Kindred* make this tendency clear, as Griffiths's remarks would suggest. 'Hawthorn at Digiff' is a particularly significant example (*K*, pp. 32–3). Here, Bidgood characteristically engages with the ruins of the eponymous house – located in the Irfon Valley, near Abergwesyn (figure 12)[19] – with the poem's fourth stanza reflecting on human life in the valley across time:

> I bring a thought into this day's light
> of Esther and Gwen, paupers:
> Rhys and Thomas, shepherds: John Jones,
> miner of copper and lead:
> who lived here and are not remembered,
> whose valley is re-translated
> by holiday bathers across the river,
> lying sun-punched: by me:
> by men who keep a scatter of sheep
> on the old by-takes.

The point of the poem here is, precisely and self-consciously, to *bring into the light of day* lives that are now 'not remembered'. Specifically, of course, Bidgood's concern at this point is with those either at the margins of economic survival (paupers) or those whose business is manual, land-based work (shepherds, a miner). But whilst such socio-economic characteristics are important, Bidgood's poetic motivation towards 'ordinary people' is not necessarily driven by a concern with a specific class or economic grouping. Rather, in 'Hawthorn at Digiff', her response seems to be primarily about drawing out of obscurity the lives of those who have formed the everyday pattern of the Irfon

Valley. As such, whilst 'Cae Newydd' (also from *Kindred*) deals with a very different economic class from that suggested by 'Hawthorn at Digiff' (in this case, landowners), Bidgood's poetic motivation is seemingly still the same – to recount the near-forgotten detail of essentially unremarkable human lives in a particular place:

> The quill sputtered; he stopped to mend it.
> 'Your brother has set sixty perches of woods.'
> Beyond wet panes, rain sleeked the grass,
> slid off bare February boughs.
> 'He has doubled the ditch about them
> on Cae Newydd, and made a sled-path
> down to the house.' (*K*, p. 19)

This, then, is the primary sense in which the characters that people Bidgood's poems are 'ordinary': they are otherwise uncelebrated and little remembered, even if their economic circumstances are not always lowly. Of course, it is perhaps unsurprising that the poor and manual workers (particularly land-based workers) find a place in Bidgood's poetic, given her particular concern with the economically marginal and rural area of mid-Wales. But the more important point is Bidgood's 'bring[ing] . . . into this day's light' the detail of obscure local lives.

It is this impetus that seemingly underpins Bidgood's drama-tization of the shifting personal circumstances of two tough north Breconshire women in 'Banquet' (*K*, pp. 10–11), from their sexually bereft and economically reduced youth to unexpected religious flowering in old age. Thus, Bidgood recounts how, whilst 'Their youth was poor and barren as the land':

> They were strong, though.
> Fighting their stony patch
> on its shelf of rock, they won.
> The mound-encircled garden was rough, plain,
> growing food, not flowers

It is into such tough, plain circumstances that religious revival comes, in the person of a preacher who brings the two women into what the poem calls their 'banqueting-time', which Bidgood characterizes in unusually heightened language as 'wine of God, and gold, and bath / of sweetest milk, damask tent / and bed of silk'. Whilst the closing stanza indicates that 'The dark time came again', with the women left merely 'catching at the rags of a memory' of their spiritual fervour, the reviewer Keith Silver does the poem few favours, in his otherwise insightful response to *Selected Poems*, by seemingly reducing it to a narrative about religion which leaves 'a bitter aftertaste'.[20] The place of religion within the poem is undeniably ambiguous: the women seem as lonely after their brief period of spiritual richness as they did before its advent. However, the point of the poem is ultimately less to do with religion than it is with telling the tale of two women's lives, in all their various, contrasting phases of bleakness and colour.

Of course, Bidgood's willingness to engage with day-to-day lives is not merely expressed in terms of historic characters. Rather, as 'The Blessing' and 'Magic' make clear (both also from *Kindred*), contemporary figures receive similar attention. 'The Blessing' (*K*, pp. 21–2) responds to a landscape which Bidgood presents as almost grotesque: the grass 'is violent green over black pools'; the stream is 'shrivelled'; one of the 'contort[ed]' oaks that the poem observes is host to 'the bright cancer of an orange fungus'. The poet-speaker is abundantly clear that she 'could never' have 'chosen this place / . . . for happiness'. But the point of the poem is that someone else *has* set their life here, and the speaker encounters the small textures of everyday happiness in 'toys on the lawn, a doll / spreadeagled' and in the 'little girl' who runs out to play. As a direct counter to her own intensely negative response to this particular landscape, Bidgood offers up the future reaction of the girl that she sees:

> Her memory is growing,
> cell by cell, tiny yet, but already
> embracing everything here,
> blessing the land. 'A lovely place,'

> she will say when she is grown,
> 'I used to live in a lovely place.'

It is precisely this urge towards overturning apparent degradation that characterizes 'Magic', the much briefer poem with which 'The Blessing' is effectively paired. In 'Magic' (*K*, p. 23), then, Bidgood finds herself again confronting everyday and ostensibly unremarkable life – in this case a 'baby' and her parents on a train. When the child says 'Magic', the poem's speaker observes how 'Her laughing parents / egg her on':

> 'Go on, love, say Magic!'
> and she does, over and over,
> putting all the richness back
> into the thin spoilt word.

Bidgood here does not merely engage with Griffiths's 'ordinary people'; rather, she goes so far as to offer them up as figures of transformational power. Just as the nameless girl in 'The Blessing' effectively gives beauty to what the poem had previously presented as a place of grotesque decay, here, too, a world of meaning that is, for the speaker, otherwise degraded (the notion of magic as 'thin' and 'spoilt') is revivified by the simple language-games of a similarly anonymous baby and her parents. Indeed, it is not just 'richness' which is given back here; it is '*all* the richness' (emphasis added). This is, in other words, restoration to absolute fullness. And it is precisely this which should alert us to the sense that, in Bidgood's poetic, 'ordinary people' are ultimately not ordinary at all: even the smallest or least remarkable of lives, some of which may have left barely an echo in history, are worthy of recall and note. Moreover, in 'The Blessing' and 'Magic', Bidgood's suggestion appears to be that such lives may even have the potential to transfigure the world around them – precisely to show 'how different is real from ordinary', as the later poem 'Driving Through 95% Eclipse' puts it (*SW*, p. 40). Indeed, as 'Speech' demonstrates (one of the small number of new poems in 1982's *Lighting Candles*), even the most mundane marks of such small human lives can be transformational, as a line of washing suddenly gives 'a transient, trivial, cheerful speech' to the previously 'inarticulate' and 'dark valley' of the poem's attention (*LC*, p. 73).

In the sense that 'The Blessing' and 'Magic' arguably suggest a degree of faith in the restorative or transformative power inherent in ordinary human lives which had perhaps not been achieved in Bidgood's 1970s collections, these two poems also have a bearing on Dai Griffiths's second main contention about *Kindred* – that it displays a 'tendency . . . towards an expansion of theme'.[21] Of course, both pieces are manifestly inheritors of earlier celebratory or partially celebratory work such as 'Llanddewi Hall, Radnorshire', 'Carreg Clochdy' and 'Mid-Wales'. Moreover, the notion of transformative human blessing appears strikingly in the early piece 'The Bee Keeper' (*GT*, p. 22), although unlike 'The Blessing' and 'Magic' the central human figure of this poem is crucially remote and 'priestly', 'enacting a mystery', rather than encapsulating ordinariness. However, the redemptive power of everyday humanity is undoubtedly a striking force in the two pieces from *Kindred*. Moreover, 'Girls Laughing' (*LC*, p. 67) suggests a closely related impulse, in its depiction of overflowing and overwhelming delight. Here, then, the poet-speaker watches two girls folding a sheet. 'Tugged off-balance' by the 'bulging unstable exuberance / stretched between them', the girls are reduced to staggering, weeping laughter. In the terms of 'Magic', this is life precisely pulled back to richness. More particularly, it is richness that is delivered out of an entirely mundane human moment.

Notwithstanding the fact that such material builds on established celebratory impulses in her work, this small group of poems from *Lighting Candles* and *Kindred* arguably offers up an important extension of Bidgood's emotional reach at this point – an extension that is also apparent, over the course of the 1980s and 1990s, in terms of subject-matter. This tendency is perhaps most noticeable in an (albeit modest) increase in both geo-cultural scope and contemporary cultural adventurousness, with the latter taking Bidgood beyond (for example) the telephone boxes, trains and lorries that have been a part of her poetic since its beginnings.[22] Thus, Dai Griffiths appropriately points to the poem 'Oil-spill, 1991' (*SP*, p. 27) which is significant for its contemporaneity not only in terms of its response to recent environmental disaster but also in its references to technology and pop culture (a zooming camera lens; the 'punk-spikes of oiled feathers' which characterize a dying cormorant). Likewise, *Kindred* travels far beyond Bidgood's central mid-Wales concerns by offering up a poem formed out of her response to a television documentary about the Inuit ('Elders': *K*, pp. 27–8); similarly, in *Selected Poems*, Egyptian mythology provides the starting-point for '"Amon Ra Wakes for Us When We Sleep"' (*SP*, p. 12), and in *The Fluent Moment* the sequence 'Into the Dark' (*FM*, pp. 65–71) draws on the period spanning the withdrawal of Roman power from what is now Wales – although all of these poems are, in their extended geo-cultural reach, effectively developments of the early poem 'Hennant' (*GT*, p. 45), which was notable for its Mayan references. Again in *The Fluent Moment*, the poem 'Party Night' finds itself close to what is seemingly a rave at a commune. Moreover, through the speaker's narration of a television documentary ('a two-hour time-warp'), this piece simultaneously recalls the 1970 Isle of Wight festival. The poem thus draws in 'Hendrix, Baez, the Doors' and Joni Mitchell, as well as Bob Dylan's 'Desolation Row' (the latter from the documentary's soundtrack):

> Hope, chicanery, muddle, disillusion –
> it all ended in tears. The camera showed some
> on Joni Mitchell's face, the microphone
> picked up the shake in her voice as she pleaded
> with explosive hordes for 'a little respect',
> a chance for her music. (*FM*, p. 59)

The same collection also explores the poet's response to an installation by the video artist Gary Hill in '"Tall Ships", Gary Hill Video Exhibition' (*FM*, p. 50), an ekphrastic piece which is important for its disorienting exploration of perspective. Hill's *Tall Ships* installation was, as Robert C. Morgan explains, 'like an isolation chamber':

> Upon entering the darkened corridor, eyes had to adjust to the dim light of the video projections. Moving along the corridor, black-and-white images of people, spaced equidistantly on either side, advanced toward the viewer, then turned away.[23]

Bidgood's poem responds precisely to the images cited here. However, the speaker ends up unable to determine whether she or what she sees is actually the image, with such disorientation even extending to a sense that the installation's video footage takes on an agency of its own. Thus, the poem observes that:

> Far off, there is a man sitting on the ground.
> He sees me watching him; unfurls,
> moves heavily, deliberately nearer.
> Always a little blurred, he looms, confronts me.
> Which of us is the moving image?
> When I go on, he turns at his leisure,
> swings dwindling into distance. He, it seems,
> chose when to veer away.

Here, then, the poet-speaker gives the impression that it was the man in the video image, just as much as her, who chose to move. Indeed, by contrast with the apparent decisiveness and freedom of the image, the poet-speaker subsequently declares that 'My mind / is unfree still.' Ekphrastic poems are something of a rarity within Bidgood's overall oeuvre. ('Encounters with Angels' (*SoP*, pp. 55–63) was intended, in part, as an ekphrastic project, though '[I] didn't stick very consistently to plan!', Bidgood concedes (RB).) Moreover, such a detailed and apparently personally responsive poem is especially unusual in the sense that it effectively approaches a confessional mode. However, more obviously personal poems such as 'Drums' and 'The Ferret' (*K*, pp. 15 and 30–1), which both emerge out of Bidgood's childhood (RB), begin to increase in frequency from the 1980s onwards – a tendency that I shall consider in the next chapter – so '"Tall Ships", Gary Hill Video Exhibition' can be usefully understood as a part of this trend.

Dai Griffiths's contention about a thematic broadening-out that is specifically identifiable in *Kindred* is, thus, perhaps too precisely tied to one particular collection. Nonetheless, what might be taken to be his general sense that Bidgood's poetic concerns start to expand from the 1980s – albeit modestly so and with no startling innovations – is clearly helpful. However, whilst increased range is manifestly an issue worthy of note, Bidgood's friend Donald Allchin offers an alternative reading of her development during this middle period of her work that is arguably of greater significance than the identification of simple extensions in reach. In his *Planet* review of *Selected Poems*, Allchin suggests that some of the new work in this volume 'makes possible a re-evaluation of Ruth Bidgood's earlier writing':

> It is not that radically new themes are taken up, but rather that old themes are treated with a new force and immediacy. The adjectives used to describe Ruth Bidgood's early collections – quiet, perceptive, understated – seem to be only partly true.[24]

Allchin's argument is thus that there is an upsurge in the overall potency of Bidgood's work at this point which, 'suddenly encapsulat[ing]' aspects of her poetic character, reveals the insufficiency of earlier critical assessments of her poetry. Along-side 'Oil-spill, 1991', Allchin especially identifies three longer poems as a focus for this, with the advent of such longer material during this period being an issue which both Allchin and Griffiths observe.[25] Of course, the long 'Hymn to Sant Ffraid' significantly predated *Selected Poems*. However, Bidgood had incorporated little extended work into earlier collections, with the only previous example being the sequence 'Seven Found Poems' (*NWH*, pp. 22–6). Moreover, the sort of multi-part longer poems that Allchin identifies ('Carreg yr Adar (Rock of the Birds)', 'Rhyd y Meirch' and 'Valley-before-Night') had simply not appeared in prior volumes, however much they may reflect the patchwork form of the 'Hymn'. Allchin's particular contention, then, is that these three poems demonstrate an 'intense sense of the conflict between darkness and light, dying and living' – such potent expression of these primordial oppositions seemingly being a primary articulation of the 'new force and immediacy' that he had also identified.[26] Indeed, Allchin's remarks here are especially significant in the sense that Bidgood's engagements with such primal concerns are of fundamental importance to her collected output during the 1980s and 1990s as a whole. As such, it is to Bidgood's expressions of light and dark during this period, and to what Allchin describes in terms of her increasingly direct confrontations with 'the hard, mortal side of human experience', that I shall turn for the remainder of the current chapter.[27]

*   *   *

Bidgood's choice of the title *Lighting Candles* for her 1982 volume of new and selected poems perhaps most obviously suggests the thematic importance of light and dark to her work by this point. (By contrast, she had named her three prior collections after poems which are primarily rooted in stone.) The title poem itself (*LC*, p. 59) – which was the closing piece in the preceding collection, although there named simply 'Candles' (*PM*, p. 54) – ultimately sets the lights of the poet-speaker's own house against the darkness of the surrounding mid-Wales night:

> Standing outside, I see
> upon a dark and turbulent sky
> my house launched, with a freight of light.

The poem had begun as a consideration of 'Indian women at night / launching candles on leaf-boats' to carry prayers 'into the dark' upon 'the sacred river'. Thus, at the end of the piece, the poet-speaker's house full of light similarly becomes a sort of prayer launched into the surrounding darkness of the non-human world. Of course, the thematic concern with light and dark can be traced back to the very beginnings of Bidgood's work: although primarily a poem of stones, as I have suggested, 'The Given Time' certainly contrasts the future darkness of the tree-swamped ruin with the imagined brightness of the living house in years gone by ('Winter brightening the low rooms / With snow-light and spark-spattering logs': *GT*, p. 11). Moreover, 'All Souls" – a major piece emerging from this theme – had, like 'Candles', already appeared in *The Print of Miracle* (see chapter 2 above).[28] By the new material of *Lighting Candles*, patterns of light and dark are thus firmly established as key modes of Bidgood's poetic thought. 'Flying Kites' (*LC*, p. 62), the first of the new poems in this collection, makes their importance clear from the start. Here, then, a tattered and 'dingy' kite caught 'between fence and tree' effectively characterizes the winter dusk with which the poem begins. The kite is a memory of the Dutchman who had made it when visiting the Abergwesyn area with 'His girl' during the previous summer.[29] The poem thus ends with the imagination of a future summer in which the man's kites may again vanish upwards into dazzling brightness:

> Faan, Marion, come again
> when, colours taut on a braced frame,
> another year's adventure takes the skies
> on cord so fine it vanishes into blue
> from summer-dazzled eyes.

In nearly all cultures, as the geographer Yi-Fu Tuan explains, 'the right side is regarded as far superior to the left' – a symbolic pattern onto which the light/dark dichotomy is crucially mapped. Thus, for example, 'The right side is that of the living, a world of daylight; the left side is the dark underworld of the dead'; similarly, 'Christ, in pictures of the Last Judgment, has his right hand raised toward the bright region of Heaven, and his left hand pointing downward to dark Hell.'[30] As such, the light/right side of this binary divide constitutes 'everything that is

Figure 1 *Ruth Jones with her parents, Revd William Herbert Jones (1874–1945) and Hilda Jones née Garrett (1887–1971), in Seven Sisters (Blaendulais), Glamorgan, c.1924.*

Figure 2 *Ruth Jones aged eleven (1933/4), in Aberafan, Port Talbot.*

Figure 3 *Ruth Jones, WRNS, 1943.*

Figure 4 *Ruth Bidgood, with her children (left to right) Anthony, Janet and Martin; August 1960, near Rhayader.*

Figure 5 *David Edgar Bidgood, 1966.*

Figure 6 *Tŷhaearn, Abergwesyn, March 1967.*

Figure 7 *Abergwesyn, April 1999. Tŷhaearn is the house towards the right-hand side of the picture.*

Figure 8 *Ruth Bidgood receiving applause on her award of the 2011 Roland Mathias Prize; The Guildhall, Brecon, 8 April 2011.*

Figure 9 *Clearance of Coed Trallwm, Cnyffiad Valley, December 1966.*
This was the scene that inspired the early poem 'Tree-felling'.

Figure 10 *Llanddewi Hall, Radnorshire, April 1972.*

Figure 11 *Cluniau-fawr, Camarch Valley, August 1967.*

Figure 12 *Ruins of Digiff, Irfon Valley, June 1984.*

Figure 13 *On Rhiw Garreg-lwyd, above Tyhaearn, February 1986.*

Figure 14 *View up the Camarch Valley, March 2004.*

good and legitimate', as Tuan puts it. The closing summer brightness of 'Flying Kites' expresses precisely this, its contrast with the poem's opening winter dusk signifying the pleasure of friendship's potential return.

Patterns of physical light and dark continue in the next two poems of *Lighting Candles*, 'Blizzard' and 'Heol y Mwyn (Mine Road)'. However, in these pieces assumptions of a clear contrast between the two sides of the divide are interestingly undercut. As Bidgood has indicated, 'Blizzard' (*LC*, p. 63) responds particularly to the high land over the Gwesyn to the immediate south-east of the poet's then-home Tŷhaearn (figure 13) and to the Gwesyn Valley itself, in which Tŷhaearn is situated (RB).[31] The poem's opening two stanzas set ominous dusk and a furious night-time blizzard ('come shrieking down in darkness [from the high land above] / to batter at our safety' in the valley) against the world of the next day, which the poem characterizes in terms of 'sun, sun and snow'. However, whilst darkness is manifestly dangerous in this poem in the sense that it is effectively being presented as the carrier of the brutal storm, the bright world that has emerged from it is not necessarily comfortable either. Rather, it constitutes a potentially disorienting erasure, as the 'ruts / of an obscure track' on 'the boggy plateau' which the poem had considered in its opening stanza are now utterly lost. Thus, the poem's speaker declares that:

> all tracks [are] gone but those
> our seeking footsteps make upon the hill.

Whilst these lines in part imagine walking up into the brightness of a seemingly pristine land, long-standing markers of orientation have crucially disappeared. In this sense, brightness is not necessarily an easy solution to the threats of darkness within the particular challenges of mid-Wales space. In Yi-Fu Tuan's terms, the experience of 'Blizzard' is that the side of darkness – signifying that 'which is maleficent and to be dreaded', that which is 'ambivalent' – is no longer entirely distinct from the side of light, which appears to have taken on some of the characteristics of the dark world.[32] 'Heol y Mwyn (Mine Road)' (*LC*, p. 64), which also uses the notional light/dark dichotomy to respond to the mid-Wales landscape, arguably extends this idea.[33] The opening of this piece is again set in unsympathetic weather, as the speaker and her unnamed companion battle along the eponymous path through 'the wet wind' until 'Soaked, blinded, we crouched for refuge / in an old adit'. From this location, the friends can hear the sound of water within the hill, which the poem describes as 'the unceasing enigmatic speech / of depth and darkness'. The impact such sound makes upon the speaker and her companion is made clear in the final stanza:

> The wind veered,
> the sky drew in its nets, empty.
> Freely we walked up a sunny valley.
> Our lightest words had now
> more gentleness, since we had known,
> together, the chill uneasy sound
> of the hill's hidden waters, falling,
> falling, for ever into dark.

Here, then, the revelation of the land's underpinning dark otherness crucially transforms attitudes within the now-sunny world of the surface. In this sense, light is not an escape from darkness; rather, the darkness inescapably shadows the bright world and is, moreover, the force which transforms it. From this perspective, darkness might well be seen as the dominant element within Bidgood's rendition of the light/dark equation. Indeed, even the relatively simple binaries of 'All Souls'' and 'Lighting Candles' point in this direction, with both poems figuring what are effectively small points of light shining out, in however determined a fashion, against a much wider background of darkness. Moreover, in 'Flying Kites', too, it is significant that whilst darkness is current and actual, brightness is merely a possible future; to put it differently, darkness is the present tense into which one must keep hope that returned brightness will come. Thus, in such work, Bidgood's poetic is ultimately tied to what is, for Yi-Fu Tuan, the 'underworld', the realm of the dead.[34] In this context, Jane Aaron's analysis of both 'Heol y Mwyn (Mine Road)' and 'Slate-quarry, Penceulan' (from *Kindred*) is especially pertinent, and is worth quoting at length. Aaron contends that these two poems – which both contrast the darkness of mine workings with what 'Slate-quarry, Penceulan' calls the upper world of 'sunny grass' (*K*, p. 49) – respond to attitudes which would have characterized the life of the mining village of Seven Sisters in which Bidgood spent her earliest years. Thus, Aaron declares of 'Heol y Mwyn (Mine Road)' that:

Dread knowledge of the hollow darkness in which men had worked far down below adds depth and gentleness to the friends' surface exchanges. To me this poem speaks of what it must have meant to an imaginative child to know that the men and boys of her locality were daily living and working in dangerous dark tunnels, far below the ground's surface. The knowledge of how their daily bread was earned may well have pressed upon the imaginations of the female inhabitants of the coal villages more hauntingly than it did on the miners themselves, precisely because the women had no actual experience of pit work. The strangeness of the men's daily disappearance down the mine-shaft was not for them demystified and rendered 'normal' by the day-to-day routine and camaraderie of the workplace. Certainly, Ruth Bidgood, for one, returns again and again in her poems to the contrast between life in the light, on the surface, and the never-to-be-forgotten darkness below.[35]

This note of darkness as 'never-to-be-forgotten' is crucial: darkness is, in Bidgood's work, recurrently the essential ground against which the figures of light must work to set themselves; to put it another way, darkness is the overriding context within which light must make its way. 'Slate-quarry, Penceulan' (*K*, p. 49) makes this point with particular force. Here, then, Bidgood opens the poem by contrasting the darkness of the quarry ('dark hills of broken slate' and 'a black / unfenced shaft down by the river') with the hill above it, which she initially describes as 'a strip of untroubled green catching the sun'. However, having talked to a man who knows the land from the inside, the poem's speaker explains that under the sunny green hill there is a 'chamber whose functional hugeness / amazes, whose dark hollowness / rears up close under sunny grass'. Thus, by the end of the poem, the previously 'untroubled' stretch of sunny grass has crucially become 'the green brittle hill': the security of the bright world has been irreversibly shattered by the knowledge of the huge darkness beneath, into which the world of light might seemingly collapse at any moment. Perhaps it is thus not surprising that the new work in *Selected Poems* begins with 'Breaking Bowls' which, considering the Mayan practice of breaking the possessions of the dead 'to let their souls go free / into the owner's eternity', finds itself precisely within Tuan's deathly underworld of darkness:

> We crunch and stumble
> through a dark archway, over shards,
> splinters, rags of a life, taking
> (as we were warned) nothing with us,
> except an idea of completeness, an intuition
> of light, perhaps a welcome
> for the little souls of things
> flying free to meet us. (*SP*, p. 9)

Certainly, this poem offers up some consolations in the face of mortality: the 'idea' of wholeness; the possibility ('perhaps') of things returned to us from life; and a feeling of light ('an intuition'). But this sense of light as essentially nothing more than a hunch seems very small against the concrete actuality of the poem's 'dark archway' of death. In other words, if there is light here it is just a hint, just potential indeed, in the surrounding gloom. In this context, it is important to recall Bidgood's observations, made in an interview published in 1990, which suggest that she sees in the outworking of life 'a pattern in the sense of light and shade, and the shade being necessary for the picture'. Asked by her interviewer to confirm that 'You see the shade as necessary', Bidgood's answer is an unequivocal 'Yes'.[36] Bidgood's poetic vision, in other words, is one in which darkness is a fundamental necessity.

In the same discussion, however, Bidgood is clear that 'Nothing is simple' and that 'There is a lot of paradox, and contradiction' surrounding the light/dark dichotomy. As such, it is important to acknowledge that the potential for light which 'Breaking Bowls' suggested is sometimes unequivocally realized in her work. 'Stop', for example (*LC*, pp. 70–1), ends with the poet-speaker emerging from a church into daylight:

> I go out into low sunlight,
> content to be dazzled, momentarily
> knowing no stop, momentarily
> seeing in that bright blindness,
> plain to read as a child's alphabet,
> the hieroglyphs of beauty.

Here, even if only 'momentarily', brightness appears to be embraced without reservation, specifically as a revelation of beauty. The poem's headnote quotes 'The Mountain of the Lord' by Abhishiktananda (the Benedictine monk Henri Le Saux) to observe that 'no beauty ever stops the monk, "for he knows something more beautiful than all beauty"'.[37] Within this context, the unequivocal acceptance of light at this point ('knowing no stop') seems to constitute a moment of astonishing spiritual elevation, in which the poem's speaker moves beyond the restrictions of normal life to approach the precisely paradoxical realm of beauty beyond all beauty. This is light, in other words, expressing Yi-Fu Tuan's right-hand, blessed side of 'sacred power', or what 'The Mountain of the Lord' later calls 'the mystery . . . beyond all thought'.[38] Although rather more down to earth, 'The Spout' (from the new material in *Selected Poems*) similarly celebrates a work of brightness, which emerges in a generally dreary world of 'rutted' fields that are 'grey-brown, / a mess of plashiness':[39]

> Just before the gate, we saw grasses
> gleam and part. A newborn spout
> sprang up, sparkled, flowed.
> It spoke to the children. They laughed, screamed,
> bathed muddy hands, patted the spout,
> attacked it, tried to force it back down,
> jumped on it, over it, into it. (*SP*, p. 14)

Rather than this gleaming sparkle of water being qualified by some underpinning darkness as the green field was in 'Slate-quarry, Penceulan', the joy that it generates in the children seems to confirm a similar joy in the earth itself. Thus, not only is the otherwise dismal mid-Wales landscape seen as being 'redeemed / by the small eager spout', but the poem also sees what it calls 'the thrusting, humorous creature of water' as having 'irrepressibly proclaimed / upwardness, happy intransigence, / in the depth of things'. For 'The Spout', then, the 'depth of things' is not dark; rather it is the source of a determined cheerfulness, an uncompromising bubbling up of good humour. Moreover, it is nothing less than a commitment to the pursuit of light which seemingly drives 'Chwefru', in which the poet-speaker explicitly sets out to fashion an emblem 'from wings and light' to set against her companion's tendency towards 'the mind's dark' (*FM*, p. 55). The consequence, as I suggested in chapter 3, is a dazzling communion with heaven itself.

Nonetheless, it is the burden of darkness that seems to bear down most heavily on four of the key poems in this period – namely the three long pieces that Donald Allchin identified ('Carreg yr Adar (Rock of the Birds)', 'Rhyd y Meirch' and 'Valley-before-Night'), plus the sequence 'Into the Dark' from 1996's *The Fluent Moment*. Such darkness is articulated both in terms of the light/dark dialogue itself and through that brutal engagement with mortality which Allchin also noted. Of these poems, 'Valley-before-Night' (the title piece of the new material in *Selected Poems*) is especially important in the sense that it constitutes the most extended single treatment to date of a number of Bidgood's primary concerns: houses, valley, and the life of a place through time (memory and the 'given time', or the co-existence of past and present). The basic premise of this long piece is that what Bidgood's headnote describes as the 'upper Camarch Valley (figure 14) in the old parishes of Abergwesyn and Llanafan' is a threatening and problematic place, known locally as Cwm-cyn-Nos (the 'before-night valley'). Thus, the poem's opening stanza begins by asking:[40]

> 'Why Cwm-cyn-Nos?' No-one's answer
> seemed complete. 'It was best
> to be home in that valley, or out of it,
> before night', one said, adding 'perhaps'.
> Another, 'There was never a road
> up the Camarch, till the Forestry came'.
> One man quietly said 'That is a dark valley'. (*SP*, p. 45)

Such a sense of the danger involved in being out in the valley at night-time interestingly reflects the ancient Celtic beliefs expressed by Alwyn Rees and Brinley Rees in their volume, *Celtic Heritage: Ancient Tradition in Ireland and Wales* (1961), which notes that 'Fairies and other spirits become active after sunset; night, in a very real sense, belongs to them, and it is fitting that mortals should withdraw to the security of their own firesides.'[41] However, the narrator's initial perception of the valley is in the notional safety of the daytime and is thus suffused in light, as she sees the Camarch 'river danc[ing] / with brilliant daytime candles, omens / of nothing but heat'. Nonetheless, in a movement that echoes the undercutting of light by darkness that I have identified elsewhere in Bidgood's work, the narrator observes that, even in such brightness, 'there seemed a darkness of obliquity, / enigma' about the valley (*SP*, p. 45). Indeed, as the poem progresses, light often seems to serve on the side of darkness itself, as Bidgood engages with stories from the valley's past in which omens of death appear in the form of corpse-lights (harbingers of death). Thus, the first of the poem's prose passages (the mixture of poetry and prose seemingly learnt at the point of

'Hymn to Sant Ffraid') finds light shining in the darkness. But this is not light that equates to life:

> Coming home late one evening from shepherding, William Arthur of Blaencwm saw a light dance on the river between Carregronw and Fedw, and hurried on.
> Near that spot the next day was found the body of Griffith Thomas. (*SP*, p. 46)

For the ancient Celts, as Rees and Rees make clear, 'night is the propitious time for divination, witchcraft, wakes for the dead, and the telling of supernatural tales'. Those night-time manifestations of the supernatural which are a feature of 'Valley-before-Night' are inheritors of just such traditions, in which 'the dead of night is felt to be nearer to the Other World than is the light of day'.[42]

However, as a direct contrast to the omen-haunted deaths which three of the prose sections of the poem narrate, part of Bidgood's concern in 'Valley-before-Night' is with the few remaining children of the valley – specifically, some of her own grandchildren ('Robin, Hazel, Tomos and Gwyn', as the poem's headnote declares: *SP*, p. 45), who were living at the house Coedtrefan at the time.[43] However, whilst the children may signify the potential for ongoing life in a valley otherwise decimated by depopulation ('Only Llednant is still a working farm. Most of the houses are ruined or demolished', declares the poem's headnote) even these symbols of hope are potentially haunted by darkness here. Thus, Robin comes back 'chastened' from watching 'the ritual kill' of a hunt, and whilst he is soon restored to good humour, the poem makes it very clear that darkness and death remain stamped upon him:

> The younger ones jostled and laughed;
> soon he was laughing with them,
> the still moment with its burden of death
> given to the river flowing always
> through night at the back of the mind. (*SP*, p. 47)

Here, then, night always lurks 'at the back of the mind'; darkness, in other words, is offered up as a background inevitability of the human condition. Indeed, whilst the literal night-terrors of two-year-old Tomos are soothed by his father bringing him out into the valley's night to see the moon, Bidgood views the child as having been prey to even greater darkness than that which might lurk in the upper Camarch itself:

> slowly
> he slackens and nestles, even smiles,
> finding this valley night kinder
> than the dreamed one, where who know [sic] what
> old savageries had claimed him
> as victim, participant. (SP, p. 50)

Moreover, although the poem is quite clear that seven-month-old Gwyn is 'totally given up to laughter' and is 'not vulnerable / to the ambiguities of dusk', the window panes above him are 'darkening' all the same (SP, p. 52), whilst the four stanzas that follow all deal with death in various forms (SP, pp. 52–3). This moment is particularly unnerving within the broader context of Bidgood's work, in the sense that it recalls 'Girls Laughing' (LC, p. 67) but seems to erode the potential for unqualified laughter suggested by that particular poem by hedging it about with darkness and death. Thus, in describing baby Gwyn, Bidgood observes that 'He does not yet know / ordinary from strange' (SP, p. 52) – that 'yet' bleakly, if pertinently, suggestive of the way in which the ease of Gwyn's own unqualified laughter will inevitably cease to be.

The final section of 'Valley-before-Night' is entitled 'Coedtrefan: Dechreunos', the latter term referring to a practice that Bidgood has described as follows:

In this area there was a custom that in each valley, every evening, most people wouldn't light up their houses at all: they would simply bank the fire up and meet at one house, which would light all of its candles. This was *dechreunos*. They would spend a few hours there . . . And then they would go back to their own homes for their bowl

of cawl, or whatever, and stoke the fire for a little bit of light so they
didn't have to light their own candles, and go to bed early . . .[44]

Dechreunos thus articulates that tendency for a house to be lit
against the wider darkness of the mid-Wales landscape which
has appeared as an important motif elsewhere in Bidgood's
work. As such, at the poem's closing, light seems to reassert
itself in opposition to darkness, in the manner of 'All Souls"
and 'Lighting Candles', offering a 'sheltered hour / of talk in a luxury'
of brightness. However, even here, whilst light flows outwards
into the night, whilst it 'pours like benediction', Bidgood still
asserts that 'Dark finds its entrance, speaks / to dark of each
heart'. Indeed, in this sense, it is significant that the human
figures which go into the light-bearing house are depicted as
'shape[s] of darkness'. Thus, although the poem's final articulation of the light/dark dialogue would suggest a possible
beating back of the darkness in the observation that 'On spilt
light, shadows stretch and shrink', darkness is still crucially
located in the shape of humanity itself (*SP*, p. 54).

The darkness that presses down upon 'Valley-before-Night'
runs strikingly through the long poems 'Rhyd y Meirch' and
'Carreg yr Adar (Rock of the Birds)' (both also from the new
material in *Selected Poems*), but is here expressed in terms of
that blunt engagement with 'the hard, mortal side of human
experience' which Donald Allchin has observed as being of
particular importance to this stage of Bidgood's work.[45] 'Rhyd y
Meirch' (*SP*, pp. 38–40), then, is overrun by blood and slaughter:

> All names in this quiet valley
> speak of war –
> Rhyd y Meirch, ford of war-horses:
> Rhiw Felen, blood-coloured hill;
> Maes Galanas, field of slaughter.

Bidgood's source material for this poem was D. C. Rees's *Tregaron:
Historical and Antiquarian* (1936). Under an entry for 'Castell
Camddwr', which he locates 'on the west side of the river

Camddwr', Rees notes a ford in the area that 'bears the name of Rhyd-y-meirch ("ford of the cavalry")':[46]

> Near by the men-at-arms of Gronow and Llewellyn, the sons of Cadwgan ab Bleddyn, being joined by the soldiery of Caradoc ab Gruffydd ab Rhydderch, made ready for a fierce onslaught, in the year 1073, against the army of Rhys ab Owain and Rhydderch ab Caradog, Princes of South Wales, to avenge the murder committed on the late Prince, their grandfather. They gained a complete victory over the Southern Princes.[47]

The poem acknowledges that 'the battle that bloodied grass', the battle of Camddwr, was fought 'nine hundred years ago' – such broad gestures fortunately not replicating Rees's mistakes about this particular event (he misdates it and has the wrong side winning).[48] Nonetheless, however long ago the battle may have been, Bidgood presents its historic slaughter as having direct and devastating impact on a much more recent inhabitant of the valley who 'turn[s] sick / at the gush and smell of the blood' that is the everyday matter of his farming life. Seeing how animals 'leaked blood' in their 'tortured births / and messy deaths' on the family farm, the young man acknowledges his 'disgust' at such processes. Crucially, however, he blames the valley itself for his sensitivity, declaring that 'Something / in the place itself had stained my mind.' Thus, fleeing in terror from the chapel in which the preacher had been expounding notions of the 'blood-washing of sins', the young farmer finds himself pleading for an altogether different kind of cleansing:[49]

> Hunched in drizzle
> on wet grass, I saw again the painted words
> over the pulpit, 'Duw cariad yw';
> and muttered like a fool
> 'Wash me in rain, my God, my God,
> Wash me in rain'.

However, it is not just the young man who seeks the cleansing of water from the valley's blood-stained history. Rather, as the poem concludes, it presents the very place as still trying to scrub itself clean of its ancient but persisting narrative of blood, declaring that 'The valley's windblown rain / washes and washes at the stain.'

In 'Carreg yr Adar (Rock of the Birds)' (*SP*, pp. 16–19), by contrast, the death is that of just one man – a hiker whose corpse is not found until 'the rags of his body had long begun / their measured rot towards / clean bone, blown dust'. Moreover, the body here seemingly leaves no long stain, and is soon 'gathered up and gone', with the place given over to 'New grass' which will know 'only air, rain, dew, the excrement / and paw-press of the hill's creatures'. However, the man's death seems to echo into the past, with the walker and his dog seen by a woman whose dwelling is one of the 'Little crumbled houses' which are, in the present, merely 'shapes of an old summer life'. (Bidgood has suggested that the woman and her 'man' are 'possibly inhabitants of a medieval dairy-house' (RB).) Moreover, the death of the hiker also seems to conjure up a figure of destruction, which Bidgood refers to as a 'shaman' (RB) and which appears to grip the valley just as surely as did the centuries-old battle in 'Rhyd y Meirch':

> I wear the feathered cloak
> I am beak-faced.
> I range the valley
> to tear and gorge.
> I do not spare the half-born lamb
> or the still-breathing ewe.
> I do not spare the body of a man.

Under the sign of this particular character, who is figured in the contemporary narrative by 'the rasping cry of a crow, / calling its mate to carrion', death is presented as inexorable, with Bidgood ending her poem by having the hiker and his dog 'follow[ing] their appointed way' to where the man's body is subsequently found near the eponymous Rock of the Birds. From this brutal perspective, humanity is ultimately nothing more than food for scavengers. As Donald Allchin suggested, this is now a world away from work that is merely 'quiet, perceptive, understated'.[50]

*   *   *

Bidgood's collections from the 1980s began with *Lighting Candles*. Those published during the 1990s ended with 'Into the Dark' – the closing sequence of *The Fluent Moment*. As its headnote makes clear, this sequence imagines the reactions of six individuals during the 'uneasy years spanning [the] departure' of the Roman legions from what is now Wales. Notwithstanding its title, 'Into the Dark' is as much concerned with Donald Allchin's 'hard, mortal side of human experience' as it is with the light/dark dialogue. Thus, for example, the second poem of the sequence, 'Leaving the Villa' (*FM*, p. 66), imagines a Roman woman who has to leave her beloved home in 'the misty western land' as both safety and economic viability decline:

> The farm was dying. Market roads
> had roughened to pot-holed tracks,
> and our men hung back, hearing
> too many tales of plunder. Death
> could pounce from any thicket,
> lurk round any bend.

Again, Bidgood conjures up a brutal vision of human existence; indeed, the poem ends with the notion of 'death waiting on every road'. Moreover, such brutality is present in equal measure in the third poem of the sequence, 'Change' (*FM*, pp. 67–8), which faces up to the departure of the legions by asking rhetorically 'Master from here, master from off, / what difference?' For the speaker of this poem, a change in human mastery makes no difference precisely because humanity is fundamentally subject to ultimately more inexorable forces:

> All are mastered
> by hill's weather,

93

by body's forcing,
years' withering.

Nonetheless, the final poem of the sequence ('Supplication': *FM*, p. 71) engages directly with darkness. However, this is not darkness as the symbolic equivalent of the profane, impure, ambivalent or feeble (to cite Yi-Fu Tuan's various associations on this side of the binary).[51] Rather, facing the cultural upheaval that is to take place beyond the vanished power of Rome, the poem's speaker declares:

Into this dark
I pray we go down
as into a holy well,
as into black waters
of healing.

As the poem's speaker goes on to say, 'In this ending / I pray we know / newness' – that 'we' crucially catching the sense that this 'Supplication' is not primarily about the fate of individuals, but is rather to do with the outworking of a shared future in the face of a common crisis. Here, then, in a moment that typifies the richness of Bidgood's engagement with this theme, the necessity of darkness offers up nothing less than the possibility of communal restoration.

5

Other Histories

Although Bidgood's poetic output apparently declined for a number of years over the 1980s and 1990s, *Singing to Wolves* (2000) demonstrated that her capacity for sustained productivity had manifestly returned by the latter part of the 1990s.[1] Here, after all, was a full-length volume of new poetry only four years after the previous one (*The Fluent Moment*, 1996). Admittedly, it took another nine years for the next such publication to appear (*Time Being*, 2009). However, the three volumes of primarily 'selected' work which intervened (*New & Selected Poems*, 2004, *Symbols of Plenty*, 2006 and *Hearing Voices*, 2008) still contained, between them, a substantial amount of new material. (The 'New poems' section of *New & Selected Poems*, for example, stretched to over forty pages.) Moreover, another full-length volume, *Above the Forests*, is scheduled for publication in the summer of 2012 with Blaenau Ffestiniog's Cinnamon Press.[2] Following on from *Time Being* in 2009, this will represent the shortest period between books wholly dedicated to new work since the three-year gaps of the 1970s. The rhythm of Bidgood's poetic output has obviously shifted over the years, and did appear to slow down substantially for some considerable time after the initial energy of the late 1960s and 1970s. Most notably, the 1980s saw fewer than fifty new poems brought together in *Lighting Candles* and *Kindred*. However, and bringing her to the age of eighty-nine, the most recent decade of Bidgood's poetic life – the decade of *New & Selected Poems*, *Symbols of Plenty*, *Hearing Voices*, *Time Being* and now *Above the Forests* – has emphatically confirmed the return to sustained energy that had been initially suggested by *Singing to Wolves*.[3] It has also, of course, been a decade that has contained some important moments of public recognition, both within Wales and beyond: *New & Selected Poems* was shortlisted for the inaugural Roland Mathias Prize in 2005,[4] an award that *Time Being* went on to win in April 2011 (figure 8), whilst *Time Being* was, in addition, a Poetry Book Society recommendation. Speaking within the context of her award of the 2011 Roland Mathias Prize, chair of the judges Glyn Mathias suggested that *Time Being* 'packs such an emotional punch. The quality of writing is sustained throughout, and yet she makes it look so easy.' For Mathias, in other words, this was a poet writing at a consistently high level and with impressive assurance. As such, *Time Being* was, he declared, 'the crowning collection of [Bidgood's] long career'.[5] However, it says much about Bidgood herself that she found the win 'hard to believe' and that, having started to read the other books on the shortlist in the aftermath of the prize-giving itself, she made a point of stressing that 'I think I have been very lucky; the others are all so good' (RB).[6] Such a self-effacing attitude might well suggest one reason for her generally low profile over the years, recent recognitions notwithstanding: she has never pushed herself into the limelight of literary celebrity, as her undeniably slight total (to date) of three printed full-length interviews also surely indicates. However, that comparatively low profile is, of course, also to do with her particular approach to poetry itself – especially within a wider British context. Thus, whilst Bidgood was establishing herself as a poet of measured, conversational verse with few fireworks, the British poetry scene was, during the late 1970s and early 1980s, being briefly dazzled by the pyrotechnic imagery of the so-called Martian school. Bidgood's work manifestly did not sit comfortably alongside such material; nor does it alongside the various and still-fashionable inheritance that Martianism has bequeathed to a range of subsequent British poetry (the primacy of the defamiliarizing image; quasi-surreal tendencies).[7] As Merryn Williams has put it, very pertinently in this respect, 'there is nothing in Ruth Bidgood's poetry that is flashy or fashionable'.[8] Indeed, it might be fair to say that, apart from her early stylistic links with the Second Flowering, Bidgood's poetry has found its successes almost in the face of headline literary fashions.

*   *   *

Singing to Wolves was, of course, not just an indication of a return to sustained energy, however important it might have been in that respect. It also seemed to confirm the increased importance to Bidgood, by this point in her career, of what the title of this chapter calls 'other histories' – by which I mean histories of places and people (the latter significantly including Bidgood herself) that lie beyond her signature mid-Wales concerns. It is, then, these 'other histories' that will concern me for much of this chapter. However, acknowledging the importance of such interests is not meant to suggest that a mid-Wales focus is in any way absent from *Singing to Wolves*. Indeed, work in this collection and in the new material from *New & Selected Poems* adds significantly to Bidgood's overall poetics of her geographical and cultural centre-ground. One especially important poem is the fascinating 'Felling-machines' (*SW*, p. 46), which seems to hint at a new ambivalence towards the coniferous forests that earlier work had so unambiguously rendered as a blight on the mid-Wales landscape. Certainly, there is manifest relief that the forests themselves are being felled, as the poem begins with the blunt declaration that 'At last the spruce-trees were coming down.' This, it seems, is something for which the poet-speaker has long waited, given her simple assessment that the trees were 'never likeable'. As such, she remarks, 'I thought forest-felling machines / were benign' – the machinery, in effect, constituting a ready cure for the geopolitical sickness of that aggressive afforestation which I have previously noted (see chapters 1 and 2 above). However, in observing the felling process itself, the speaker's emotional reaction is distinctly muted:

> Yet when one [felling-machine]
> swung again and again its ripping claw
> to uproot tree after thin tree,
> I didn't want to cheer, though wouldn't have opted
> for changing the outcome.

There is, in other words, something in the process of destruction that seems to worry the speaker, even if she is not at all sad to see the demise of the trees themselves. Thus, she concludes the poem by observing that:

> I just wished
> their silly bare skinny crammed-together trunks,
> with the engine of death swinging again
> towards them, would stop reminding me
> of something human, doomed.

The expression of environmental unease here is clearly articulated in anthropomorphic terms, with the 'bare skinny crammed-together trunks' of the felled trees disturbingly suggestive of thin human limbs crowded together. (Bidgood herself observes that the image of the trees was 'vaguely connected in my mind with holocaust victims' (RB).) Indeed, it might thus be argued that Bidgood's unease is not environmental at all, and that she is, as Lawrence Buell puts it in a useful assessment of the contrary implications of anthropomorphism, 'mak[ing] nature sympathize with humankind' in the sense that what ultimately worries her is that latter thought of 'something human, doomed'. However, Buell also acknowledges that anthropomorphism may be used 'in the interest of dramatizing the claims or plight of the natural world'.[9] And within this context, I would suggest that there is an interesting sense in which 'Felling-machines' recognizes what environmental philosopher Val Plumwood has called 'non-human claims to the earth' in its disquiet about the mechanized destruction of living things – notwithstanding the speaker's preference for the environmental consequences of such destruction and her dislike of what is actually being destroyed.[10] Such comments are not intended to construct 'Felling-machines' as a primarily or explicitly environmentalist poem. However, they do aim to acknowledge that, on one level, its concluding anthropomorphic image reaches towards some sense of what Plumwood has called the 'ethical consideration' that our non-human 'planetary partners' should attract.[11] Indeed, the significance of such 'partners' becomes especially clear in the very next poem from *Singing to Wolves*, 'Polluted', with which 'Felling-machines' forms a pair – both poems referring to the same hill, south-east across Afon Gwesyn from Tŷhaearn (RB).[12] Here, then, Bidgood's concern is not with a living thing; rather, it is with matters of geology and the water cycle, as the Abergwesyn water-supply is abruptly disturbed:

> Suddenly the spring, never known to fail,
> ran dirty. Whatever the flaw,
> it was deep in the hill.
> Water came clouded from the rock,
> yellow-grey from tap to glass. (*SW*, p. 47)

The importance of the non-human is made bluntly clear in the speaker's observation that 'It seemed the great sow of a hill / that suckled the valley-dwellers / had fallen sick.' Clearly, these lines as a whole key into what Kate Soper calls the 'coding of nature as feminine', which she describes as 'deeply entrenched in Western thought'.[13] However, it is interesting that the poem goes on to shift its initial zoomorphic figuring of the hill as mammalian female to specifically human female in another moment of striking anthropomorphism. Thus, the valley's human inhabitants begin to fear that the hill 'might inadvertently / feed them poison, or worse, might *will* / this perilous lactation, *wishing* them gone' (emphases added). The ascription of human scheming to the hill here gives to an inanimate form a sort of agency that dramatizes a profound sense of continuing human subjection to the non-human world. This is, in short, an abrupt undoing of what Plumwood has called the 'weakened sense of the reality of our embeddedness in nature' that is, again, deeply rooted in Western culture.[14] However, it is perhaps in 'Camarch in Sun' (*SW*, p. 31) that Bidgood's anthropomorphic renditions of mid-Wales space are used to most dramatic effect. Here, then, the poem concludes by presenting the eponymous valley as facing annihilation and as 'pleading / a little longer to be spared' (an acutely human reaction). The point of this, however, is not to articulate some message of environmental crisis – that trope of planetary apocalypse which, as the ecocritic Greg Garrard usefully notes, has 'provided the green movement with some of its most striking successes'.[15] Rather, by reducing the valley to the scale of human life and fragility, the poem works to undercut any sense of land itself as permanent, unchanging. Thus, in one of her familiar drawn-out sentences – such stylistic notes remaining clearly identifiable over the course of her career – Bidgood observes how:

> It seemed glinting river, alder-shade,
> heat-firmed mud of worsening track,
> ruffling spread of old hedges,
> fields below forest, still spelling
> (in rich grass or thistle)
> good land, bad land,
> ploughed or never-ploughed,
> a life's mixed fortune –
> all could go, a valley vanish
> at wing-flash, light-strike.

Superficially, this seems to echo the sort of environmentalist thinking that Val Plumwood suggests when she talks about 'the fragility of ecological systems and relationships'.[16] But although the sense of fragility is shared, for Bidgood this is all to do with the impermanence of the valley itself: as she goes on to assert, 'The land seemed a sojourner / no less than its people had been, / soon like them to go hence, / soon to be no more seen.' The long geological timescales of the Camarch Valley are, in this sense, no more permanent than the transitory stories of its human inhabitation. As such, at this point, the entire physical basis of Bidgood's mid-Wales – its very geological underpinning – seems to become as insubstantial as breath. Indeed, this sense of mid-Wales land itself as inherently temporary is made absolutely explicit in the poem 'Bugeilyn' (the second piece of the sequence 'Into the Wind', which deals with the area of the Cambrian Mountains to the south-east of Machynlleth). Here, then, Bidgood considers the eponymous lake itself:[17]

> The lake
> is no more eternal than rock,
> could go gliding in a final slide of ice,
> or hiss into a gulf of cinder and flame (*SW*, p. 60)

Admittedly, Bidgood immediately goes on to acknowledge that Bugeilyn 'may have many millennia yet'. But its ultimate fate is clear: however substantial it may seem, however long its geological past and future, it will certainly disappear. Although the poem may end with the 'overpowering glory' of what its speaker sees, that glory is significantly 'transient'. The land offers high beauty but is, nonetheless, inherently fleeting.

'Omen', from *New & Selected Poems* (pp. 248–9), is a return to perhaps more familiar mid-Wales themes, emphasizing the gothic darkness of the place by drawing on the tales of 'phantom funerals' which, presaging death, have been associated with the 'lonely' house Blaennant.[18] Here, then, Bidgood narrates the grim demise of a father and mother from tuberculosis, both deaths being prefigured by supernatural manifestations. Thus, as her father approaches his end, the poem's speaker relates how:

> One night my mother and I
> saw the funeral lights.
> All down the track from our yard gate
> the lantern-line, dwindling, dipped and swung.
> In mid-procession twin brightnesses,
> a gap of dark between,
> marked where the horse-bier journeyed,
> carrying him away.

In its engagement with death omens, such work clearly builds on the earlier 'Valley-before-Night'. However, it is also a bleak overturning of the positive assessment of historic mid-Wales community offered by 'Burial Path' (see chapter 2 above). For that poem, the community was a source of strength. Here, by contrast, following the death of both parents, it is the community's neglect of the daughter that is emphasized: 'I have been alone two years, / with little help from those / who, it seems, crowd here only / for that churchward trudge.'[19] However, 'Fields of Force' (*N&S*, pp. 240–3) operates as a sort of counter to such harsh renditions of mid-Wales life (amongst which must be included the heartbreaking death of a young boy in 'Cries': *N&S*, p. 239). In this four-poem sequence, various Abergwesyn locations seem to generate life that is either particularly intense or that is somehow capable of survival beyond the destruction of its physical structures. Thus, for example, in the third poem ('Chapel': *N&S*, p. 242), the communal existence of the eponymous chapel pulled down ninety years before is somehow channelled into the memorial trees that were planted, 'as was the custom', at 'each corner of the site':[20]

> It was as if
> in this place there was still
> something needing years to grow,
> slowly, slowly reaching up;
> as if all the prayer and singing,
> all the love and observance,
> had to have somewhere to go

The trees are, the poem seems to suggest at its close, both testament to and manifestation of 'a rooted power' which survives into the present. Countering the darkness of 'Omen' and 'Cries', as well as the sense of transience captured by 'Camarch in Sun' and 'Bugeilyn', 'Chapel' thus points to the way in which Bidgood's Abergwesyn area is, by this point in her career, an intricately rich locus of ideas and forces – its poetic depth rendered precisely through the complex interactions that exist across the now-extended range of her mid-Wales work.

*   *   *

It was, however, those 'other histories' which I noted above – both of places beyond mid-Wales and of Bidgood herself – that *Singing to Wolves* perhaps brought to particular prominence, and such material was also undeniably important to the volumes that followed immediately on from it. (I leave *Time Being* for consideration in my final chapter.) Of course, work of this sort had been apparent in Bidgood's output from the first, as my analyses in chapters 1 and 2 acknowledged, whilst 'Hymn to Sant Ffraid' also constituted a broadly conceived poetic (see chapter 3 above). However, Bidgood's attention to 'other histories' is arguably more consistently focused and substantial in her later work than was the case earlier on. Thus, for example, *Singing to Wolves* has as its title sequence a series of five poems that are 'rooted in the area of three interconnected waterways on the Wales–England border (Afon Honddu, River Monnow and Escley Brook)', whilst this collection also contains the short, north-west Wales sequence 'Llŷn'.[21] Alongside a number of freestanding pieces that are geo-culturally diverse, *New & Selected Poems* returns to the broad area of 'Singing to Wolves' in the seven-poem sequence 'Gerinou'. *Symbols of Plenty* collects together the 'Pennant Melangell Poems' which have as their focus Cwm Pennant, in the northern-most tip of Montgomeryshire, as well as the important autobiographical sequence 'Riding the Flood'.[22] Indeed, the found poetry which makes up *Hearing Voices* (2008) perhaps articulates this concern with 'other histories' most sharply, albeit from a slightly different perspective, in the sense that it offers up the histories of other people 'from the inside' as it were. Thus, its poetry is formed directly out of Bidgood's engagement with archives of historic letters and diaries. Moreover, given that *Hearing Voices* draws on work from the 1970s onwards (whilst also including more recent material, some of which was previously uncollected),[23] this volume is perhaps the single most obvious demonstration of the way in which there has always been a centrifugal aspect to Bidgood's work – by which I mean a tendency to leave the immediate behind. Indeed, in the case of strict found material, what is left behind is nothing less than the originating perspective of the poet herself.

The borders sequence 'Singing to Wolves' (*SW*, pp. 7–11) takes Bidgood down into Monmouthshire and Herefordshire (plus the very eastern limits of Breconshire), to the east of the Black Mountains, and thus emphatically beyond her central ground in the Cambrian Mountains. The first poem of the sequence, 'Llanthony' (*SW*, p. 7), is all about human relationships with wildness:

> 'Why should we stay here
> singing to wolves?' said Llanthony monks;
> and left for soft living at the daughter-house,
> finding themselves unloved by the Welsh,
> and jaded with beautiful desolation –
> just what the first anchorites had loved,
> such wildness a treasure

Here, then, Bidgood's focus is on the monks of the remote Augustinian house of Llanthony Priory, in the Vale of Ewyas, who left in the 1130s for around forty years under pressure from local unrest.[24] For Bidgood, this departure symbolizes a rejection of what the poem (drawing on Giraldus Cambrensis) presents as the attraction of the location for 'the first anchorites' who had simply wanted 'to contemplate heaven, / and the hills (almost as high), with herds of deer / ranging their tops'.[25] Greg Garrard pertinently remarks that the 'Judeao-Christian conception of wilderness . . . combines connotations of trial and danger with freedom, redemption and purity'.[26] If it is the latter association that Bidgood suggests drove the initial anchorites towards wildness, it is at least something like the former which causes the subsequent monks to turn away from it: 'soft living' is infinitely preferable, it seems, to the challenges of existence in Welsh remoteness. By contrast with the monks, however, the poet-speaker subsequently observes a little girl in the present who, 'kneel[ing] on grass, / in the shade of the chapter-house wall, / carefully picking daisies', is distinct from all the other children playing energetically amongst the priory ruins. Contemplating this quiet figure, the poem concludes by considering that perhaps here is one who, 'in her generation', will give her love to 'the remote, solitary, / trackless':

> to risk-encircled beauty;
> deer on the marches of heaven; the sweet
> unprofitable singing to wolves.

Given her own originating decision to move to a place of remoteness (by which, of course, I mean Abergwesyn), it is tempting to see this little girl as a figure for Bidgood herself. The literal singing of the monks at the poem's beginning would thus, by its conclusion, become figurative – specifically, a metaphor for writing poetry. Indeed, from this angle, the notion of unprofitability is interesting, too. Most obviously, it seems to suggest a commitment to poetic activity on Bidgood's part irrespective of its lack of material reward – from which perspective it simply does not matter if one is only singing to the unresponsive non-human world. But the notion of '*sweet* / unprofitable singing' (emphasis added) also implies that the unprofitability itself might be part of the attraction. Poetic 'singing to wolves' is done emphatically for its own sake. Indeed, this is a notion that is not entirely unrelated to Bidgood's apparent disinterest in courting literary celebrity which I noted earlier. However, any parallels with the poet herself should not be pushed too far: Bidgood's artistic commitment is certainly not to places that are 'trackless', with her work being focused so persistently on the constructions of human culture. As I have put it elsewhere, 'Bidgood's sensibility tends towards the built rather than the natural'.[27] Moreover, nearly the entire range of her poetic output is set against any such rhetorical simplification of remote rural places as entirely free of human imprint. Thus, it is interesting that, in this poem, an idea/1 of solitariness generates a construction of remote space which, the bulk of Bidgood's work would suggest, is actually not available in practice – at least, not within the geographies that are her dominant concern.

Indeed, the subsequent four poems of the sequence are typically populous or full of human marks. 'Capel y Ffîn' (SW, p. 8) considers a gravestone that gives 'nothing but a name, / initials, dates of birth and death, / and then a verse about the sweetness, / depth, of laughing'. In a sort of memorial version of 'Girls Laughing', Bidgood associates the person buried with the twisted trunks of the nearby yew-trees which, in their various dramatic shapes, 'seem / compatible with deep, wild, joyously / contorting laughter'. Moreover, the poem's final lines go so far as to suggest that the 'laughter of survivors' is ultimately shallow by comparison with that of the dead. The notion of laughter is again crucial to the third poem of the sequence, 'Cwmioie' (Cwmyoy or Cwm-iou, in Monmouthshire; SW, p. 9).[28] This piece also considers memorials, albeit inside a church rather than in a graveyard, in order to bring into the light small lives, little celebrated (a process I highlighted in chapter 4). Thus, the poet-speaker's living companion who 'lies asleep on a pew' finds the 'dust' of 'Thomas Price, who "takes his nap / in our common mother's lap"', as a 'compatible neighbour' within the cool of the church. However, it is a memorial to three young girls 'of one house [who] came home / early from play' which provides the poem's ultimate focus:

> The sleeping man wakes up. Outside,
> the sunbathers have gone. A breeze mutes heat,
> scampers over the graves, and starts
> a susurration of grass, not unlike
> whispers or stifled laughter.

Having been preceded by the association between laughter and the dead in 'Capel y Ffîn', the ending of 'Cwmioie' suggests a similar pattern. Here, seemingly, the three dead girls are imagined at pleasurable play once again, with laughter thus being offered up in defiance of death itself.

The final two poems of the sequence ('Merthyr Clydawg' and 'Michaelchurch Escley: Christ of the Trades') are again both centred on churches, the whole sequence having arisen out of what the poet has described as a day of 'church-crawling with three friends' (RB).[29] Crucially, these two pieces take Bidgood over the border into England. However, 'Merthyr Clydawg' (*SW*, p. 10) somewhat disputes such territorial transition:

> Clodock; it sounds rustic, and English.
> Clydawg; the lost Welsh is back.

On one level, this borders area is, for Bidgood, a place of what this poem calls 'shifting boundaries', a contested space of 'strife, loss, perpetual haunting, garbled names' – a situation which the lines above figure precisely, with their shift between English and Welsh place names.[30] However, by the poem's conclusion, Bidgood seems to go much further than this. Thus, she declares that this is a place with:

> Welshness in the soil's depth,
> unacknowledged riches,
> uncomprehended power.

Bidgood's suggestion is clear: that this now-English space is underpinned by Welshness, in which its depth, riches and power are to be found. This is not to suggest that there is, to quote Ian Gregson's sharp critique of Gillian Clarke, some 'primordial, fully authentic Welshness waiting under the surface' of the land in this place.[31] Rather, Bidgood is here gesturing to the cultural roots of the region in which the sequence as a whole is set – the historic Welsh commote of Ewias, an area that was substantially incorporated into England in 1536.[32] Bidgood's poem thus reconnects Clodock with its Welsh heritage – both with Saint Clydog himself who, as a descendant of Brychan (the 'Traditional founder of Brycheiniog'),[33] had ruled the area in the sixth century,[34] and also with the long-standing importance of the Welsh language to the region. (John Davies observes that Ewias was one of those districts where 'the Welsh language would continue to be spoken for centuries' following 1536 and 'which it would not be wholly fanciful to consider as *Cambria irredenta'*.)[35] The upshot of Bidgood's poem is, it seems, something close to a reclaiming of formerly Welsh territory, suggesting that the roots of the area in which Clodock is to be found link the place more fundamentally to Wales than they do to England. 'Merthyr Clydawg' is, in short, a striking act of cultural-political cartography. Nonetheless, it is the closing poem of this diverse sequence, 'Michaelchurch Escley: Christ of the Trades' (*SW*, p. 11), which seems to me the most remarkable of the five. Here, in a vibrant example of one of her occasional ekphrastic poems, Bidgood considers the mural at the eponymous parish church which depicts Christ surrounded by implements of manual labour.[36] Bidgood's poem is concerned in part to dramatize the ambiguity of the image. Thus noting how 'Scissors, shears / overlap the line of his arm', it asks 'is he cut?', and then responds similarly to Christ's hands:

> One hand, the right, presses his breast; the other
> is raised, palm out – warding off, or giving
> a left-handed blessing?

Joan Evans has refused the entire artistic category of 'Christ of the Trades', suggesting instead that the intrusion of implements around the body of Christ in images of this nature 'symbolize[s] . . . the injuries inflicted upon Christ by all manner of people' – most particularly those who are guilty of 'profanity and sabbath-breaking'.[37] Bidgood's poem appears to reflect precisely such notions, suggesting that the Christ-figure 'seems / menaced by aggressive sharpness' and figuring the proximity of the tools as 'encroachment'. However, Bidgood takes the idea of assault even further, rendering the mural as an image in which 'the things of everyday / [are] banding [together] to shear, scrape, gash, destroy / the extraordinary'. In Bidgood's hands, in other words, the image of the mural is transfigured from moral lesson into the expression of a fundamental conflict between the mundane and the remarkable. And it is the latter that emerges triumphant at the poem's close as the body of Christ, notwithstanding the assault upon it, becomes a point at which nothing less than 'invulnerable light' enters the world.

Alongside poems such as 'Burial Path', 'Hymn to Sant Ffraid', 'Rhyd y Meirch' and 'Valley-before-Night', 'Singing to Wolves' is one of Bidgood's most important achievements and is a fascinating combination of conceptual scope and geographical focus. (The whole sequence is bound together by both physical and human geography: all of the poems emerge from sites within one group of interconnected waterways as well as from the area of the historic Welsh commote of Ewias.) The shorter 'Llŷn' sequence, also from *Singing to Wolves*, may be less substantial and rather more geographically diffuse but it nonetheless offers some strikingly evocative renditions of various points around the eponymous north Wales peninsula. Thus, from Clynnog Fawr (on Llŷn's north-western coast), the stretching peninsula to the south-west appears as follows:

> All slender Llŷn lay beyond,
> reaching westward into rain,
> rocking with autumn winds. (*SW*, p. 43)

Ynys Enlli (two miles off the south-western tip of the peninsula itself) is 'that shape far out in spume and rain, / beyond the silent waves that leap and leap' (*SW*, p. 45). And at Aberdaron, looking out over the sea to the south, Bidgood's experience is fundamentally one of the sublime:

> From the edge of day
> an unstable plain,
> grey-green and white,
> came tilting, sliding towards us.

> High-tide breakers
> exploded just below.
> I realised how much fear
> there is in awe. (*SW*, p. 44)

These are manifestly readings of the Llŷn region which approach it in terms of grand scope, and there is thus no concern with environmental detail here. Indeed, in the emphasis on potent non-human forces – the fierceness of the sea, the island wrapped in mist and waves, the peninsula itself as a thing of wind and rain – Bidgood seems to be constructing Llŷn as precisely the sort of wild space to which 'Llanthony' gestured. Llŷn, in other words, becomes a sort of wilderness – that notion of land which Greg Garrard explains as being construed as 'beyond the boundaries of cultivation'.[38] However, contrary to the idea/l of the 'trackless' articulated in 'Llanthony', and however wild Bidgood may suggest that Llŷn is, she also crucially places it within a human context. Thus, 'Clynnog Fawr' (*SW*, p. 43) acknowledges those many people who had come to the 'great empty church' in the past, particularly those 'who struggled, failed, returned' – to the extent that, as the poem finishes, 'there seemed to rise, / within the thin wind's meagre celebration, / difficult praise from the uncomforted'. Similarly, 'Enlli' (*SW*, p. 45) significantly forms its subject as 'the holy island', thus placing it firmly within the discourse of human culture (recognizing, in other words, its status within religious tradition). And, perhaps most notable of all, the sublime power of the sea in 'Aberdaron' (*SW*, p. 44) is distinctly offset by the poet-speaker's nonagenarian friend who:

> looked out at the waves
> with a friend's acceptance,
> and, glass in hand, turned back
> to conversation, laughter;
> as little daunted by the years,
> by journeys or soaking weather,
> as by that great uneasy sea.

Whilst these closing lines do not seek to deny the brutal power of the sea, the undaunted acceptance of it by the poet-speaker's elderly friend rather blunts the conventional wilderness associations simultaneously suggested by the rest of the poem (danger; the awe and terror of the sublime). Like time and distance (the years, the journeys), the wild sea off the southern reaches of Pen Llŷn is seemingly just another of those potent physical forces within the context of which one old woman has learnt, cheerfully, to live.

*   *   *

Whilst Bidgood's poetry is typically built around the observational 'I' of a poet-speaker, overt self-examination (the 'I' as the primary object of poetic attention) has been much rarer. Poems have undeniably emerged over the course of her career that echo her own circumstances. Cases in point are the early pieces 'Shoes' (*GT*, p. 50), which Bidgood describes as 'a poem directly from my life' (RB), and 'Roads' (*GT*, p. 16) which responds to Bidgood's first 'sight of Abergwesyn' (RB) and is precisely a reflection on her own journey ('all the steps of my life have / brought me home'). But it is not really until her later work that her own history has become a focus of particular scrutiny. Indeed, it took until *Symbols of Plenty* (2006) for such a tendency to find concentrated form in the sequence 'Riding the Flood', which is pertinently subtitled 'A Memory Sequence' (*SoP*, pp. 47–54). However, material in both *Singing to Wolves* and *New & Selected Poems* (2004) certainly paved the way for this. Alongside the appearance of two poems from 'Riding the Flood' itself in the latter volume (*N&S*, pp. 250–1), a number of other moments in these books reflect Bidgood's sharpening interest in the poetic formation of her own past. (I use this particular notion advisedly – i.e. that of Bidgood poetically *forming* her past – to recognize Claire Boyle's description of autobiography, summarizing the position of Georges Gusdorf, as 'a performative act which brings into being a subject that does not pre-exist the text'.[39] In Bidgood's

111

own terms, this is precisely the sense that, in writing about the self, 'the only thing one is totally faithful to [is] the poem' (RB).) For example, the splendid and witty 'Cucullatae' (*SW*, p. 23) considers images of the poet's 'English grandmother' (on the beach at Tenby), her mother and herself at 'Six years old'. Each of the poem's three stanzas focuses on one of the figures, whom Bidgood's headnote brings together as 'aspects of the Triple Goddess' – in other words, as she explains, 'Maiden, Wife and Hag'. Thus, Bidgood's grandmother is 'draped / in uncompromising black', having 'lost her husband / thirty-seven years ago'. However, she remains a figure of power: as the poem observes, 'One sees / she is accustomed to rule.' By contrast, the poet's mother, who 'risks / a bright note' in a scarf around her hat, is 'dignified' but appears 'a little anxious'. Seemingly distracted by her child ('judging by the direction of her gaze', the poem's speaker observes, 'her chief worry is me'), there is no comparable sense of power here. Finally, considering her own image in the poem's closing stanza, and with what seems to me to be dead-pan humour, Bidgood initially comments on her 'thoroughly swathed' appearance, creating the drily comical image of a 'beehive hat / of indeterminate stuff, / that encases my head / from crown to eyebrows'. However, the closing three lines are again all about power:

> My faint smirk may be saying
> though hitherto I have been
> unempowered, that won't last.

It is pertinent to observe that the single family portrait suggested by the poem is, in fact, a fictional composite: as Bidgood has explained, 'while there were photographs of all of us hatted . . . I made up the one where we all appeared together' (RB). Thus, in what is emphatically the creation of her own past here, Bidgood crucially dramatizes changing power-relationships within an extended family setting. In particular, she sharply figures a child's dawning sense of her own potential to challenge existent authority structures in the move from swaddled infant to more independent, knowing individual. Ways of thinking in childhood are also the focus of 'Not Heaven, Perhaps' (*N&S*, p. 227). Emerging out of Bidgood's own history, this is significantly the opening poem of the new material in *New & Selected Poems* – this primacy of position suggesting the growing importance of such work. Here, Bidgood recounts her attempt 'not to miss' a spot near her childhood home in Aberafan when travelling on the train to Cardiff:

> a glimpse of red roof,
> and the dark spread of pine
> I used to climb into.

The poem's particular point of remembering is the thin poplar tree which had grown next door. Recounting how she used to see this tree from the attic of her home, Bidgood notes the way in which it was 'topped by a long twig that might seem / to indicate aim or destination'. Such interpretation of the tree's shape is, however, precisely what the poet-speaker suggests was alien to her childhood way of thinking. Thus, the poet's younger self was crucially 'free of compulsion / to translate shape as message', and instead took pleasure in the *thisness* of the tree – its 'slenderness, leafiness or starkness, / dizzy tallness'. Rather than filling it with human meaning, the tree seems to be left to exist as an entity in its own right, as the young poet-speaker 'saw / too much to interpret'. For the child she was, in other words, Bidgood suggests that the point of the tree was, precisely, its physical qualities and not what it might be made to stand for, as metaphor.

However, it is in the nine-poem sequence 'Riding the Flood', from *Symbols of Plenty* (an earlier, six-poem version having been published in the magazine *Scintilla* in 2002),[40] that Bidgood's attention to her own past comes into particular focus. The opening poem, 'First' (*SoP*, p. 47), draws on her earliest youth in Seven Sisters and considers the part that she played in the construction of memories within a house as the first child born there. Thus, figuring herself in the third person, Bidgood tells how, as an infant, she 'pulled herself up by the sill, / started to see shrubs, railings, the long / faraway shapes that were hills'. Much of the poem is precisely given over to forming recollections of this sort, suggesting simple pleasure in things as a child's awareness of her surroundings builds up. But Bidgood's point is not just the production of childhood memories. Rather, as the poem concludes, her suggestion is that the child's early life is intimately intertwined with that of her immediate environment and that those early experiences crucially 'made for the house its first memories / of childhood'. Memory, in this sense, is some-thing that Bidgood wishes to extend from herself to inanimate objects. Similarly, and like early poems such as 'Stone' and 'Hennant' (*GT*, pp. 40 and 45), the third poem of the sequence, 'Links' (*SoP*, pp. 48–9), proposes the memory inherent in stone:

> And I
> in a windbitten valley have laid my hand
> on stone of old walls, and felt a held life,
> all the remembering there is
> of what was made in that starved place[41]

This is what the poem goes on to call 'material memory' which, even if it is 'barely accessible', points very clearly towards the importance of the physical, for Bidgood, in the process of remembering. Indeed, it is arguably the materiality of memory that is one of the most striking features of 'Riding the Flood'. For example, in 'Pattern' (*SoP*, p. 48), another Seven Sisters poem, the traces of earliest youth centre around the image of a wall, the recollection of which creates a feeling of 'dark mild happiness', but which is most clearly articulated through the sensation of the infant poet 'liking / the difference between dank stone, / plushy moss, on my pudgy hands'. Similarly, the unlocatable memory of 'Inward Eye' (*SoP*, pp. 49–50) is also heavily reliant on textures:

> I'm not dreaming, but briefly seeing
> the lowest foot or two of a broad
> greeny-brown tree-trunk, heavily ridged;

> knobbly root-spread, and beyond,
> rusty, collapsing, the corrugated roof
> of a shed.

As if to confirm such focus on the textural (this is a world that is 'ridged', 'knobbly', 'corrugated'), the poet-speaker goes on to observe that 'I know the scrapy feel, / on my hand's flesh, of the bark.' What is remembered, in other words, is precisely to do with sensation. However, this is not always a matter of touch. In 'Shards' (which draws on Bidgood's time in the Women's Royal Naval Service; *SoP*, pp. 50–1) it is colour that is dominant, in the recalled image of a:

> white lane angled sharply
> down to a wall of sea
> extreme in its blue.
> Across the fierce colour
> crept one white ship.

In the opening poem, by contrast, some of the memories are bound up with smell ('the mellow cardboard smell of the box'; *SoP*, p. 47). This is also the case in 'Investment', another WRNS poem (*SoP*, p. 51). Recalling a 'waterfront café' in the Ayrshire town of Largs near where Bidgood was stationed (RB), the poet-speaker here notes the way in which 'Mixed with our coffee / were motor-boat smells, oily, metallic, hot.' For Bidgood, in other words, memory is an intensely physical process. Indeed, it is telling that the final (and title) poem of the sequence (*SoP*, p. 54) emphasizes precisely this point, in its metaphorical construction of the very experience of remembering:

> There are days when waves of unremembered life
> tumble in, one upon another, almost
> irresistibly. You can feel the thuds
> through the soles of your feet, through blood and bone,
> all the channels and sluices of the body.

In short, memory is something that is *felt* in the body. From this perspective, memories may even lift you away, the poem suggests, as Bidgood's extended metaphor imagines the eponymous need to 'ride the flood' of incoming recollection, and 'voyage to countries / you had given up hope of revisiting'. Whilst this poem clearly ends the sequence by having shifted away from the particularities of her own past, it nonetheless seems to me the most developed example of (an otherwise rare) confessionalism in Bidgood's career. This is, I would suggest, a poem all about the experience of being subject to eight decades of memories and is thus a deeply moving expression of the sense that their immense, collective power may ultimately take one away into the furthest-flung corners of the mind, from which point a person may never return. As the final lines of the poem put it, 'Don't ask / whether that high tide of remembering / will ever carry you home.'

*　　*　　*

As I indicated above, however, Bidgood's concern with 'other histories' has perhaps been most obviously expressed through her interest in found poetry. Significantly, moreover, such interest dates from an early point in her career. Whilst she has generally avoided making herself the centre of her own poetic attention, she has conspicuously embraced the idea of observing other individuals from (as I put it earlier) 'the inside', through her creation of poetry out of historic, personal documents – predominantly letters and diaries, many of which have been drawn from the Hanmer collection in the Shropshire Archives.[42] The most important early example of such work is to be found in the sequence 'Seven Found Poems', which appeared in *Not Without Homage* (1975). However, *Hearing Voices* (2008) brought together this sort of material from the breadth of her career. Taken as a whole, this collection constitutes what is perhaps the most striking demonstration within her poetic output of the way in which Bidgood's 'other' identity as a researcher in local history has fed into her life as a poet. Indeed, in this sense, it is significant that *Hearing Voices* is dedicated to 'the late R. C. B. Oliver of the

Radnorshire Society, in gratitude for much generous help with local history' (*HV*, p. [7]).

Bidgood's brief introduction to the book (*HV*, p. [6]) provides the technical context for such work. Here, she explains that she understands found poems as 'passages from . . . any prose source' (although she specifically cites 'letters, diaries, wills, deeds') which, 'without their writers' knowledge or intention make themselves known as poems':

> Their form is free, but their rhythm (different from, stronger than, that of what we think of as prose): their unity: and often an intensity, an emotional charge: have encouraged me to 'lift' them from their setting and edit them into lines of verse which I hope bring out their poetic qualities. Editing is often minimal; sometimes it entails abbreviating, cutting unnecessary repetition; but in a true found poem one should not invent or add.

Hearing Voices is divided into two parts, and whilst Bidgood's closing definition here applies to the first of these ('Found Poems'), she makes it clear that it does not apply to the second ('Poems Using Some Found Material'). In this latter section, by contrast, the poems are 'partly inventions' and make use of found material as a 'key element' within, but not as the entirety of, any given piece. As such, it is the first of these poetic types in which Bidgood's commitment to other voices seems to find its most concentrated expression and which I thus consider here. In this sort of work, in other words, the poet is essentially an editor rather than an author and, as a consequence, the *heard voices* themselves remain dominant. The three-part poem 'Elizabeth Lochard Grumbles to her Sister' (*HV*, pp. 28–9) draws on the very strong female characters in the Hanmer material. (As The National Archives summary of the collection puts it, 'The women of the family seem to have been dominant characters'.[43]) One of the relatively few previously uncollected pieces in the volume, this poem is a sharp dramatization of various expressions of familial ill-feeling.[44] Thus, for example, Elizabeth is heard to complain about alleged poor treatment of her clothes ('I would not a put anything / in such a dusty cloth! / It was not fit to carry anything / but shoes or foul linen'). She also provides the following strongly rhythmic evidence of a squabble about an heirloom:

> I desire to know
> what it is of my Mother's
> that is in my keeping
> that you demand.

Here, then, Bidgood's own poetic voice is fundamentally put to one side for the task of bringing out the aggrieved emotional dynamics of her historic speaker. Thus, the repeated line-endings of 'anything' in my first extract ('I would not a put anything'; 'It was not fit to carry anything') are used to empha-size the extremity – indeed, the absoluteness – of Lochard's emotions, whilst the line-divisions of the second extract break up the speaker's sentiment into its fundamental phrases (the challenge; the object of contention; the accusation; the contention itself). By contrast, 'Herbal' (from 'Seven Found Poems'; *HV*, p. 19) is a celebration of words almost for their own sake:

> Mint, saladin, clare,
> Fennel, sweetfern, sage red,
> Pillotar of the Wall,
> Angilliere, wormwood,
> Dragones, scabious, rue

This poem may emerge out of nothing more elevated than a list, the original having been drawn up by another of the Hanmer women, Frances Eyton, who 'commanded considerable respect' and was thus known as 'Madam Eyton'.[45] Nonetheless it renders the processes of domestic management as bravura linguistic display. The mundane, in other words, appears as the remark-able. Female production, moreover, is rendered as high art, thus overturning what Kate Soper suggests is the traditional exclusion of female work from the category of art itself.[46] Admittedly, 'Herbal' is something of an oddity within Bidgood's oeuvre and almost recalls sound poetry such as Bob Cobbing's classic text 'Alphabet of Fishes'.[47] More typically, the emphasis of her found material is on the creation of emotional impact – precisely in the manner of 'Elizabeth Lochard Grumbles to her Sister'. In this vein, then, the previously uncollected 'Renegade', which Bidgood describes as 'one of the newest' pieces in *Hearing Voices* (RB), offers up a moving portrait of the complex relationship between the eighteenth-century preachers Howell Harris and John Powell of Abergwesyn.[48] Drawn from Harris's diaries, the three parts that make up this particular piece chart the movement between his initial affection for Powell (in the first part) –

> Oh! how dear is now
> John Powell of Abergwesyn,
> who once was despised by all. (*HV*, p. 33)

– to a state of disenchantment (in the second):

> but how can God
> have sent this man,
> with his pride in clothes,
> resentment, boasting, passions dreadful,
> disturbing spirit, censuring,
> drinking, lightness, rashness –
> no awe, no sight of God
> in His works? (*HV*, p. 34)

In the third part, the two men achieve some sort of rapprochement, as Harris is made 'to tremble before God' in a dream and becomes aware of both 'John Powell's fall / and my own corruption'. However, not only does the poem thus hint towards some significant spiritual crisis on Harris's part, but as it concludes, Harris observes of Powell that 'He has written to me / and his letter has broken my heart' (*HV*, p. 36). No further details are forthcoming, and the power of the poem's finish is thus substantially in the idiomatic simplicity of this final statement. Whilst the list of Powell's supposed faults in the second part of the poem perhaps recalls the building word-power of

'Herbal', the near-anguished but utterly unadorned conclusion to the poem as a whole encapsulates the fundamental importance to much of Bidgood's found work of what her introduction to *Hearing Voices* called 'emotional charge' (*HV*, p. [6]). Indeed, such points of ringing emotional openness demonstrate unequivocally that, as the back cover notes to *Time Being* so usefully suggest, Bidgood 'avoids sentimentality but not sentiment; an observation can engender joy or sorrow or fear uncluttered by irony'.

6

A Mid-Wales Epic

At the end of 2002, shortly after she had turned eighty, Bidgood finally left her home in Abergwesyn and moved four or so miles to the east, to the main-road village of Beulah in the Camarch Valley. In her most recent published volume to date, *Time Being* (2009), the poem 'Back' (*TB*, p. 35) emerges out of precisely this shift, as the poet-speaker admits to feeling the 'irrational need / to forgive myself' for being like those 'Others' who, 'over the centuries had left' the 'loved valley' (the Irfon: RB). 'I had not thought', the poem's speaker observes with significant emotional frankness, 'to be one of them'. In such frankness, then, this piece suggests the same sort of confessional mood that was apparent in the closing poem of 'Riding the Flood', perhaps confirming an (albeit still occasional) increase in the personal openness of Bidgood's poetry by this point in her career. Indeed, by the end of 'Back', the Irfon Valley itself is effectively approached in terms of the poet-speaker's emotional state, as the poem observes that:

> June sun
> seemed uncensorious. Today
> all the valley's imagined words
> were warm. I sat by the stream
> and listened.

However much the poem may present its speaker as feeling guilty about leaving, the valley itself attributes no blame. As such, the closing lines here suggest an ongoing friendship between the place and its former resident, in what might cautiously be interpreted as a poetic coming-to-terms with Bidgood's changed circumstances. Certainly, some poems in *Time Being* respond to her personal history. 'Shape' (*TB*, p. 48), for example, is an engagement with fragmentary childhood memories and a consideration of what to do with them in age, whilst the opening lines of 'Reading a Landscape' (*TB*, p. 44) suggest the challenges of settling into Beulah ('I'm reading a landscape, / searching for the word "home" / in this new context'). However, other pieces that might appear to be autobiographical are not. 'Morning' is an especially pertinent case in point (*TB*, p. 26). According to Bidgood herself, this poem has 'been (quite wrongly) interpreted as being about my husband leaving me', leading her to comment, rather drily, that a 'bit of autobiography seems to be craved for sometimes!' (RB). Rather than being about her own life story, then, this poem is resolutely intertextual, in the sense that it is what Bidgood has called a 'variation' on another poem. Specifically, Bidgood is responding to Glyn Jones's 1930s piece 'Esyllt ferch Brychan', which she describes as 'a favourite poem of mine' (RB).[1] Far from being work that points outwards to a life, in other words, 'Morning' is caught in a textual web as a poem that points backwards to another poem. Indeed, given that Jones has described 'Esyllt ferch Brychan' as 'a sort of dramatic lyric after the manner of Robert Browning', the textual web here stretches still further.[2] Glyn Jones's piece, then, considers the reactions of the eponymous woman whose lover has just gone away 'for a long time' (as Jones has explained),[3] and whom she now watches walking away 'down our hill' in the sunshine. What is perhaps most striking about Jones's poem is Esyllt's description of 'last moment's parting' as feeling merely 'unreal' and her consequent suggestion that it was less painful than those moments in the past when her lover had to leave for just a short while. For Bidgood, these are reactions which suggest that Esyllt is fundamentally 'in denial' in the immediate aftermath of separation (RB). Bidgood's own poem, echoing Jones's, is also about the departure of a woman's lover. It thus begins by observing how, as her lover leaves the house in the morning, the woman does not 'go with him / down the stairs' but is nonetheless compelled to follow his dwindling form through 'the small grudging window / [that] was too available, too near'. 'Morning', however, does not retain the defining contrast in Jones's 'Esyllt ferch Brychan' between this long-term, present sundering of the lovers and their earlier, shorter separations. Rather, Bidgood's piece focuses all of its emotional force on the current moment which is, as a consequence, rather more fully explored than in Jones's original, in which the emotional drama is primarily located in the couple's previous, very temporary partings and in Esyllt's contrasting of such past events with the present. Initially, then, for Bidgood's protagonist, the experience of separation is one of 'shapeless pain'. However, this quickly shifts to a more mediated sense of the necessity that 'to live this, / without struggle, was all she could do / to save their yesterday'. Whilst such an acceptance of the lovers' changed circumstances might seem relatively calm, the poem fundamentally undercuts this by subsequently referring to the woman's 'shocked mind' and to her final, bleak 'wondering what it was / that might in the end be saved'. With all of these shifts taking place in the last of the poem's three stanzas, the poem's close is a moment of richly concentrated emotional portraiture. It is also a significant departure from the seemingly numbed experience of Jones's Esyllt, for whom the instant of long-term separation is 'never sad' and is, indeed, 'less felt' than her observation of a snail's nearby silver 'calligraphy' which is presented as a far more 'intense' generator of feeling. Moreover, just as Bidgood changes the emotional tenor of the original poem by substituting for a sense of unreality in the present the raw and confusedly shifting feelings of her final stanza, so she also fundamentally alters its visual character. Thus, whilst the present moment of Jones's piece is set in sunshine, with 'snapping bracken' and 'gold broom's / Outcropping quartz', Bidgood's is a matter of rain, 'wet trees' and 'muddy track'. Indeed, Bidgood even removes the colour from the departing lover's clothes: in 'Esyllt ferch Brychan' he wears 'new soft orange hunting-boots' as he goes, but in 'Morning' he lifts 'his old grey coat from the nail'. Bidgood's poem, in short, seems visually far bleaker than Jones's – and her protagonist far closer to a state of immediate emotional crisis. As such, 'Morning' is not only a 'variation' on 'Esyllt ferch Brychan'; it is arguably also a reply to it, even a riposte, in the sense that it figures, on the part of its female protagonist, a response to her current circumstances which is much less numb and rather more riven with conflicting shifts of present feeling than that of the earlier poem. Moreover, in its emergence out of text rather than life, 'Morning' also stands as something of a warning about the potential dangers of pursuing too biographical a reading of Bidgood's work. Within this context, 'Assembling the Pieces' (*TB*, p. 18) is also worth noting, given the way in which it initially seems to recall memory poems such as 'Shape' and the *Symbols of Plenty* sequence 'Riding the Flood'. Here, then, Bidgood seems to begin with precisely the sort of physically focused impressions which so significantly characterize those memory pieces:

> There's a shadowy porch; outside it
> a sunlit herringbone
> of brick tiles, uneven as if
> insecurely covering something.[4]

However, the poem takes a distinctly dream-like turn in its third stanza, which introduces a 'pin-headed stick-man' who 'gleams in pale sharp blue'. Following this, the fourth and fifth stanzas respectively consider seemingly alternative scenarios in which the stick-man either goes 'inwards' ('into the porch') where 'A black hall swallows him' or 'outwards', just escaping over the tiles before they 'break / this way and that, pushed by the upward thrust / of a tempest of black leaves'. As such, it should be no surprise that Bidgood points away from any root of personal recollection here, instead indicating that this poem is what she calls 'a kind of daydream' or 'visualization' (RB). One may wish to concur with the poet herself that this poem contains hints of resurrection ('though I didn't plan that', she concedes: RB) and that it thus broadly relates to the various mythical strands of her work that I discussed in chapter 3 above. However, what is perhaps more important is the sense that, as what is effectively a dream sequence, 'Assembling the Pieces' suggests a willingness on Bidgood's part quietly to pursue new directions even in her mid-eighties. Indeed, the heightened rhetorical patterning of both 'Slide-lecture, "Universe"' and 'Shape' shows a similar capacity to depart from dominant patterns – in this case, from the typically conversational nature of her poetic. Thus, 'Slide-lecture, "Universe"' (*TB*, p. 53) begins with five short stanzas, all of which start with the phrase 'We have seen', whilst 'Shape' (*TB*, p. 48) likewise uses repeated words and phrases at each stanza's conclusion. Thus, in this latter poem, the first stanza closes by considering memories from childhood as 'Fragments. A sense / of something lost. / Echoes. Longing', whilst the second likewise observes 'Fragments. A sense / of springing up through grey / to waking light. / Anticipation. Longing.' Finally, the third stanza closes its observations on memory in age by noting 'Fragments. A sense / of shape, not yet clear. / Longing. A fitful hope.' In an interesting echo of the poem's sense itself, what Bidgood achieves here in her use of single-word and very short sentences is an unusually fragmentary poetic, as well as one that is rooted in a striking structural parallelism. (Indeed, one might wish to suggest that, in such material, Bidgood is successfully articulating the formal variousness that she had explored, albeit rather less effectively, at the very beginning of her poetic career.)

However, it is perhaps in her increasingly obvious attention to the non-human as a point of focus in and of itself rather than primarily as a context for human life that *Time Being* most obviously displays Bidgood's still-continuing development. I have already observed 'the extent to which Bidgood's sensibility tends towards the built rather than the natural', but as my previous chapter suggests, her later poetry certainly raises some significant issues about the environment itself.[5] However, *Time Being*'s 'Ice' arguably goes further than previous work in terms of environmental engagement in the sense that it moves towards an explicitly 'green' concern about issues of climate change. Thus, recalling a previous winter in which the Irfon Valley (RB) 'seemed helpless / in an agony of white' and in which the 'hurt air savagely / seeking a victim, burn[t] / my lungs with cold', Bidgood's mid-Wales takes on global significance in 'this winter's / threatening warmth' which leaves the poet-speaker wishing for the return of 'gelid extremes' and 'an unchanging pole' (*TB*, p. 41). The warmth of the winter as 'threatening' is of primary significance, of course, as is the speaker's dissatisfaction with the word 'unseasonable' to describe it. As such, unlike 'Camarch in Sun' (see chapter 5 above), the point of 'Ice' certainly is to express that sense of planetary crisis which Greg Garrard identifies as being central to the contemporary environmentalist movement.[6] A different perspective, but one that is equally oriented towards the non-human world, is to be found in the Camarch poem 'Lives' (*TB*, pp. 19–20),[7] in which Bidgood's central concern is to evoke the richness of the environment in which she walks. Thus, shifting her focus emphatically away from those marks of human culture which normally so dominate her work, the poem's second stanza significantly observes that 'The valley is full of life, / hardly any of it human', whilst the third is a long and nearly ecstatic piece of nature writing:

> All through the valley, in its mould,
> its waters, grasses, old fallen leaves;
> under its bark, stones, rushes,
> carried on its winds, motes in its sunrays,
> are the secret living things,
> the valley's nodes and ganglions,
> blood-vessels, flesh and bone –
> trillions of wings, carapaces,
> hairs, feathers, scales,
> flakes and films of skin,
> horde on horde of scuttling legs,
> tiny puffs of breath, and with them
> juice of leaf and stem, powder of pollen,
> channelled fountaining of sap.

Apart from the splendid example this gives of Bidgood's persisting use of the long, winding sentence, it also suggests what the environmental critic Lawrence Buell calls 'the ability to read landscapes from the mountaintop, so to speak' – by which he means the capacity to produce a 'distilled and panoramic image, dependent on knowledge of how the various biotic and geological constituents interlink'.[8] Of course, Bidgood's poem does not present such a reading of the Camarch Valley in any technical or scientific way. However, in its evocation of the valley as a combination of water, stone, wind, sunshine, plant-matter (both rotting and alive) and a range of animal life – as well as being a place through which humanity also passes, as the rest of the poem makes clear – 'Lives' offers up a dynamic vision of a place's ecology. It is, moreover, precisely the vibrant life of that ecology which takes the poem's attention as it draws to a close. Thus, having left the valley itself, Bidgood considers its potential for regeneration:

> Minute beings disrupted
> by our clearing of wood from the path,
> our thrusting back of brambles;
> everything crushed by our trampling;
> will soon be replaced by the irresistible
> fecundity of the place.

Here, then, Bidgood's mid-Wales is a place of astonishing non-human richness, the landscape being more than just a context for humanity; rather, it is a space of significant drama in its own right. Indeed, in 'Film, "Gwesyn"' (*TB*, p. 61), Bidgood seemingly puts aside almost entirely her typically dominant human focus, as she observes that 'I felt / it mattered little to be there / or far away, young or old, even / alive or dead, as long as that / uncompromising beauty stayed.' The value of remote mid-Wales at this point is the land itself, with even the poet's own life seeming to be a matter of little concern by comparison.

*   *   *

Responding as they do to the Irfon, Camarch and Gwesyn valleys, such poems suggest with absolute clarity the ongoing significance to Bidgood's oeuvre of that mid-Wales space which is the generative heart of her entire poetic. I have previously argued that Bidgood's poetic work is, in its mid-Wales orientation, a writerly process of what is called (in certain environmentalist circles) reinhabitation.[9] As Lawrence Buell explains, reinhabitation is a commitment to *being in* and *being moulded by* a particular location (often one that has suffered degradation in some way) in a 'long-term reciprocal engagement with a place's human and nonhuman environments'. This is not a solitary act; rather, it is undertaken in a manner that 'involve[s] participation in community both with fellow inhabitants in the present and with past generations, through absorption of history and legend'.[10] Buell's description of this process seems to me to be a remarkably close fit for Bidgood's mid-Wales work which, as I put it in my earlier analysis, is precisely 'an artwork of being-in-place, amongst the conifers and the ruins; it is a vision of what grows and dies and what may grow back again in "the last vast emptiness at the heart of Wales"'.[11] Indeed, the sort of sensitivity to the richness of mid-Wales's non-human life suggested by 'Lives' adds still further to Bidgood's status in this respect, in the sense that it demonstrates with new force her engagement with the non-human aspect of the place to which she has, exactly, committed herself. In her interview with Jason Walford Davies in 1999, Bidgood unequivocally declared that she was 'not a nature poet' ('HW', 50). However, recent poems such as 'Ice', 'Lives' and 'Film, "Gwesyn"' suggest a clear capacity for work in which the non-human is given a significant primacy of attention. Indeed, 'Winter Coming' (*TB*, p. 23) is ultimately nothing less than a celebration of seasonal change in the minutiae of leaf and hedgerow life:

> Soon each small withering of leaf,
> each miniscule hedgerow difference,
> will be like a little boy

running towards us along
the empty road, calling
'It's coming! It's coming!', and we'll hear
at last, far off, drums
and, slowly growing, pulse of the dance.

However, of arguably greater importance than all of this is the sense that, as I intimated in my discussion of 'Chapel' (*N&S*, p. 242) in chapter 5, it is the *totality* of what Bidgood offers up, in terms of her mid-Wales poetic engagements, which is of primary significance. The point of her work, in this sense, is never the individual mid-Wales poem; rather, it is the intertwined richness between poem and poem, over years of poetic thought. To quote Bidgood's own words about what she calls her 'home patch', 'One sees different facets [of it] and the whole thing is always shifting' (RB). This is, then, the variation between her focus on the built space ('Llanddewi Hall, Radnorshire': *GT*, pp. 13–14) and on the non-human ('Lives': *TB*, pp. 19–20); it is her shifts between the land as underpinned by darkness ('Slate-quarry, Penceulan': *K*, p. 49) and as the locus of heaven-like brightness ('Chwefru': *FM*, p. 55); it is her manifestation of mid-Wales as both blessing ('Mid-Wales': *GT*, p. 12) and curse ('Rhyd y Meirch': *SP*, pp. 38–40); it is her awareness of a social scale, across the present and the past, which draws into its scope, and just to choose three areas, poverty and wealth ('Banquet': *K*, pp. 10–11; 'Cae Newydd': *K*, pp. 19–20), the long-established and the incomer ('Drinking Stone': *PM*, p. 21; 'Invaders': *PM*, p. 22), the medieval and the modern ('Carreg yr Adar (Rock of the Birds)': *SP*, pp. 16–19; 'Party Night': *FM*, p. 59). This interpretive range is, I believe, the primary significance of Ruth Bidgood's poetic achievement – which, in terms of her mid-Wales work, has now effectively achieved the scale of epic. In the sheer breadth of engagement which it has come to offer, in other words, Bidgood's poetry of mid-Wales is emphatically to do with what Georg Lukács suggests is the defining concern of epic with 'the extensive totality of life'.[12] Indeed, Bidgood's regional and multi-generational mid-Wales concerns find a pertinent heritage in the traditions of the classical epic itself, in the form of what Peter Toohey calls the *historical epic* which, in one of its manifestations, was 'characterized by a large time frame (events usually take place over several generations) and by a concentration on the fortunes of a single city or region rather than on an individual hero'.[13] Of course, no such parallel should be pushed too far. Bidgood's work is clearly not annalistic in the manner of this particular branch of the classical epic. But such contexts do generally suggest that, in her temporal scope, in her focus on the long-term outworkings of a place and in her capacity to engage with 'social reality on a broad scale' her extended mid-Wales work has now manifestly established itself within epic territory.[14] Moreover, the fact that Bidgood's mid-Wales is clearly a matter of numerous, variously directed incidents rather than a central driving story interestingly echoes Franco Moretti's assessment of the 'modern epic' as a form that precisely demands attention in terms of digression rather than plot.[15] From such perspectives, then, Bidgood's individual poems of her *bro* are, in isolation, shorn of their primary significance. Rather, their true weight is to be felt only in their extended combination and interaction, as her consequent creation of what is, precisely, a mid-Wales epic constitutes one of the most important and substantial achievements of anglophone Welsh poetry since its revival in the 1960s.

Appendix A
Publication in Magazines during the 1960s

This appendix lists Ruth Bidgood's poetry publications in magazines during the 1960s. (Listing is by magazines in alphabetical order, then by poems in publication order.)

The Anglo-Welsh Review
'Passer-by', 39 (summer 1968), 135.
'Chimneys', 39 (summer 1968), 135.
'Old Film', 41 (summer 1969), 184.
'Old Pump-house, Llanwrtyd Wells', 41 (summer 1969), 185.
'The Given Time', 41 (summer 1969), 186.

Country Life
'Shepherd's Cottage', 3669 (29 June 1967), 1657.
'Llanddewi Hall, Radnorshire', 3670 (6 July 1967), 42.
'Spiders', 3723 (11 July 1968), 69.
'Distance', 3744 (5 December 1968), 1451.
'Mid-Wales', 3749 (9 January 1969), 53.
'Log Fire', 3749 (9 January 1969), 59.
'Nant-y-Cerdin', 3762 (10 April 1969), 869.

The Countryman
'Mole-trap', 71/2 (winter 1968/9), 303.
'Map Reading', 72/1 (spring 1969), 82.
'The Salamander', 72/2 (summer 1969), 331.
'Broiler Fowl', 73/2 (winter 1969/70), 370.

Country Quest
'Tree-felling', 8/1 (June 1967), 49.
'Little of Distinction', 8/4 (September 1967), 35.
'Cammarch Valley, Breconshire', 8/7 (December 1967), 41.
'Winter Evening', 8/9 (February 1968), 34.
'The Bee-keeper', 8/11 (April 1968), 24.
'Turner's Painting of Hafod', 9/2 (July 1968), 29.
'Roads', 9/3 (August 1968), 20.
'Carreg-y-Fran', 9/4 (September 1968), 36.
'Walls', 9/7 (December 1968), 41.
'Manor House', 9/8 (January 1969), 25.
'In the Suburbs', 9/11 (April 1969), 35.
'Cefn Cendu', 10/1 (June 1969), 20.
'Courtesy', 10/3 (August 1969), 35.

London Welshman
'Children Playing', 22/7 (July/August 1967), 19.
'The Malcontent', 22/9 (October 1967), 13.
'Trespass', 22/10 (November 1967), 8.
'Storm', 23/5 (May 1968), 3.
'Shoes', 23/6 (June 1968), 18.
'Gladestry, Radnorshire', 23/7 (July/August 1968), 19.
'The Chapel', 24/7 (July/August 1969), 17.
'Cardiganshire Story', 24/10 (November 1969), 8.

Manifold
'Towns', 27 (autumn/winter 1968), 17 [as D. E. Bidgood].
'A Barn', 28 (summer 1969), 12–13.

Poetry Wales
'Warning', 4/2 (winter 1968), unpaginated.
'At Fanog', 5/2 (winter 1969), 14–15.

Appendix B
Two Unpublished Early Poems

These two previously unpublished pieces are taken from the files of Bidgood's uncollected and unpublished poetry held in the National Library of Wales: see Ruth Bidgood, *Ruth Bidgood Poems, 1966–2011*, NLW MS 23946iD, National Library of Wales, fol. 38, typescript with manuscript note, and fol. 42, typescript with manuscript alterations.

Specific composition dates are handwritten at the foot of the typescript of 'The Zombie-makers' (reproduced here in square brackets following the poem itself). No such dates are given on the typescript of 'Brianne 1970', but this piece is collected between poems that have handwritten dates of early 1970 to early 1971.

The Zombie-makers

Seventh hell is for the zombie-makers
who cut the heart out while it faintly beats,
and clamp whole valleys to a heart-and-lung machine
of reservoir and forestry – work now, die later –
then switch off. As the blood congeals,
here come corpse cosmeticians, bland embalmers,
to prettify the violated body
with labelled forest trail and picnic area,
and fake a ghoulish animation
that is not life, and mocks at death.

If you must kill a land,
let it die, then.

Llewelyn's head, a death-in-life on Cheapside once,
rotted at last to the dignity
of dust, like the sundered body
under the altar in remote Cwmhir.

[3.12.69 – -.5.70]

Brianne 1970

I stumble on a stone. Over it goes,
down the scar-line of the riven mountain,
Down, down to the platform of monstrous fragments
where the monstrous dam will rise.
Sunday evening now – only one stone-crusher
grinds with a small relentless noise. Soon, arc-lights
will glare down from these lunar cliffs
on the great stage dwarfed by its theatre's height –
a Calvary with no crosses, that awaits
the enactment of a valley's passion.
But by this agony what soul is saved?
and in this cleft rock who can hide?

Appendix C
Unpublished Letter to *Poetry Wales*

(Ruth Bidgood, unpublished letter to *Poetry Wales*, 7 April 1989, Ruth Bidgood's private papers, typescript with manuscript notes).

7 April 1989

Dear Mike[1]

I've followed Ken Smith's series with interest. I enjoyed meeting him; we had a most amicable chat, despite what might have seemed an unpropitious start, when I had to tell him I don't much like being called a 'woman poet': I'm pleased that he found my work interesting enough to study in some detail and write about at length in company with that of three notable poets.

May I have a bit of space to develop what Ken has written about my radio poem 'Hymn to Sant Ffraid[']? This poem (though it is due to come out from a small press)[2] hasn't yet been published as a whole, so readers can't refer to it to see whether or not they agree with his interpretation. Hence my remarks.

The 'Hymn' is a praise-poem to the Celtic saint (called Brigid in Ireland and Ffraid in Wales) who partially absorbed a pagan fertility-goddess, rather than to the goddess (as stated by Ken Smith).

He is quite right about the strong influence of David Jones on the manner, at least, of this poem, written ten years ago (1979) when I was soaked in his poetry – though 'Protectress of the peat-stack' was one of Ffraid's traditional titles, not an imitation of Jones. It's hardly surprising that when I followed Jones too closely it was obvious that he was much better – after all, he is one of the 20th century's major poets!

As for the matter of the poem: it's not irrelevant that it was a commissioned ode. I was constrained in part by two technical requirements. It was to be a celebratory poem, and it was to take about 30 minutes of radio time. No choice of subject is entirely a matter of chance; the reasons unknown to reason are working away. Still, my choice of Sant Ffraid was as near chance as these things ever are. I had just been reading Brigid/Ffraid legends, having been interested in a friend's remarks about the process of Christianisation. When I was suddenly asked to produce an ode lasting ten times or more as long as my usual poems, I happened to have to hand a possible subject. If I had been reading about a male saint, I might have written an ode to *him*.

I can't pretend that I had a consuming desire to praise either the goddess or the saint, but I hoped to do a workmanlike job; and of course I got far more deeply involved that [*sic*] I had expected. The heart will speak, given half a chance.

I think Ken Smith's pigeonholing of 'Sant Ffraid' as a product of the 'Feminine stage' as distinct from Feminist or Female is a bit too slick. There was a lot of power in that Celtic saint, despite the rusting of the sacrificial knives (not a development to be lamented, perhaps)? I found myself increasingly surprised by the strength and diversity of images and rôles bound up into a figure I have called a 'concocted saint.' I don't think it's so much that the poem (as Ken rather reproachfully writes) doesn't question male domination, as that domination of one sex by the other is not what the poem is about.

I'm interested in Ken's white/red/black pattern, but I don't think it's as simple as he does. The goddess (not the saint) had as one of her titles, 'White Swan'; I have also associated her with 'red-gold fire,' blood, and 'darkness within fire.' The saint who took over so many of her rôles had a similar mixture of colour-associations – not only white, but the black/white of her bird (the orange-red-billed oystercatcher), the gold of the sun and the rayed dandelion (her flower), and gold and red-gold of fire.

It is the 'saint of poets', not the pagan goddess, of whom the poem says 'You are fire, as a poem is . . . Power sprang in you like flame.'

Ken Smith says that Part II is 'dedicated to the Mother goddess.' No – it's headed 'The Legend,' and is concerned with what most interested and moved me, the creation of an inclusive body of legend, the 'concoction' (starting from a historical figure, an Irish abbess) of the saint people needed to fill the gap after the interdicted 'old worship.' A whiter-than-white 'wraith' wouldn't have satisfied them. The saint had somehow to combine life-giving fire, 'lavish' love, with a share of Mary's gentleness; her domain was an extraordinarily wide one. There was nothing of the surface-pretty 'feminine' about this powerful figure.

I don't think one can say that Part III 'deals with Ffraid the destroyer.' There's just one glimpse of a vengefulness more easily associated with the pagan goddess – in the example Ken quotes of the desecrated chapel. (I find it unhelpful to alternate and equate the words 'saint' and 'goddess' as he does; this blurs the distinction between the linked but separate figures). This final section is called 'The Saint Invoked.' After stanzas about Ffraid's shrines on the coast and inland and her rôle as successor to the fertility goddess in the farming year, the poem ends with a litany for Sant Ffraid, in which those prayed for are associated with her symbols – animal, flower, light and fire.

The maiden/bride/hag trinity may seem to 'reflect control by men over the lives of women'; nevertheless the concept surely comes from very ancient Mother-worshipping times. The Hag was certainly not just 'an ugly old woman whom no man would want.' She was (as far as one can explain such an enigmatic figure): a personification of age and death as part of the nature of things, feared and accepted – no death, no new life.

I do see that the battle of the snakes (in the 'Hymn') echoes the fight of the white and red dragons, though I wasn't *consciously* writing about the 'silencing of the Welsh language' any more that [sic] I was promulgating 'sexist stereotypes.' When the poem refers to Sant Ffraid translating worshippers' prayers into God's language, I was trying to find an image for her rôle (demanded of her by the people) of intermediary between unlettered worshippers and their many-dimensioned God. And when the saint is asked to smile on those 'whose words dart and flicker/like the tongue of the snake' I was not thinking of Welsh-speakers, as Ken suggests, but of the witty and devious, who need praying for as much as do the brash (like blundering bullocks) or the slow (like heavy submissive cows). If all this adds up to 'criticisms of colonisation,' then so be it. As I've said in the 'Hymn,' a poem is mysterious. One of the mysteries is the way it can hold so many meanings that its writer never intended.

Yours,
Ruth Bidgood

Notes

I

1   Personal communication. All quotations from and observations by Ruth Bidgood that are not otherwise attributed are drawn from the poet's many letters and e-mails to the author of this volume and are subsequently marked 'RB' in the main text.

2   William Herbert Jones took up his post in St Mary's, Seven Sisters in 1912. The church had been built only the year before to replace the initial corrugated iron building which is now the church hall. I am grateful to Stephen Barnes, current vicar of St Mary's, Seven Sisters, for information about the church's history. See also the section about St Mary's church in the leaflet *Dulais Valley Heritage Trail / Taith Dreftadaeth Cwm Dulais* (Seven Sisters: Dulais Valley Partnership, 2010), *http://www.dulaisvalley.org.uk/heritagetrail/docs/Dulais Valley Heritage Trail leaflet.pdf* (accessed 9 February 2011).

3   In the 1911 census, Hilda Garrett is listed as an 'Elementary School Teacher', born in Shepton Beauchamp, Somerset, and living at 13 Richmond Terrace, Abernant, Aberdare. William Herbert Jones is listed as a 'Clergyman (Established Church)', living in a boarding house at 15 Glanant Street, Aberdare. Herbert and Hilda married in 1913.

4   See Clare Jones, *Aberconwy House & Conwy Suspension Bridge/Tŷ Aberconwy a Phont Grog Conwy* (London: National Trust, 2005), p. 12, which notes that 'William and Jane Jones ran Aberconwy House as a Temperance Hotel from 1850 to 1910'. The 1881 census shows Jane Ann Jones (widow) living at 1 High Street, Conwy, citing as her occupation 'Temperance Hotel Keeper'. William H. Jones, son, aged seven, is resident in the same household. In the 1891 census, 1 High Street is also specifically recorded as 'Aberconwy Temp. Hotel'.

5   For the incident with the scythe, see Sabine Baring-Gould, *Eve: A Novel* (1888; London: Chatto & Windus, 1891), chapters 21 and 22 (pp. 138–51).

6   For a history of this ancient parish, see Raymond Preece, *A History and Guide to St Mary's Church, Parish of Aberavon, 1199–1999* (N.p.: n.p., 1999). Preece notes William Herbert Jones in the list of incumbents

(p. 7) and also in reference to a 'screen' within St Mary's church that is dedicated to his memory (p. 28).

7   I am grateful to Sally Roberts Jones for information about Port Talbot Secondary School.

8   Ruth Bidgood, 'A poet in her place – an interview with Ruth Bidgood', with Sally Roberts Jones and Alexandra Trowbridge-Matthews, *Roundyhouse*, 7 (2001), 21.

9   For Burton's somewhat dismissive reaction to Bidgood's school-days poetry, see ibid.

10 David Edgar Bidgood died shortly afterwards, in 1978.

11 Ruth Bidgood, 'Interview', with Angela Morton, *New Welsh Review*, 10 (1990), 38.

12 *Country Quest* had first been published in the summer of 1960.

13 In terms of her initial appearances in these magazines, Bidgood's first poems to be published were: 'Tree-felling', in *Country Quest* (June 1967); 'Shepherd's Cottage', in *Country Life* (29 June 1967), and 'Children Playing', in *London Welshman* (July/August 1967). In the following year, she made initial appearances in: *The Anglo-Welsh Review* ('Passer-by' and 'Chimneys', summer 1968); *Manifold* ('Towns', autumn/winter 1968, as D. E. Bidgood, thus using her husband's initials); *The Countryman* ('Mole-trap', winter 1968/9), and *Poetry Wales* ('Warning', winter 1968).

14 Most prominent amongst Bidgood's publication outlets during these first months (up to the end of 1969) were *Country Quest* (thirteen poems), *London Welshman* (eight poems) and *Country Life* (seven poems). For a list of Bidgood's 1960s poetry publications, see Appendix A. I am grateful to both Miriam Valencia of The Poetry Library and Paula Fahey of the *Country Life* Picture Library for assistance in compiling this material.

15 Ruth Bidgood, 'Tree-felling', *Country Quest*, 8/1 (June 1967), 49.

16 For the period of particularly intense coniferization of Welsh land, see W. Linnard, *Welsh Woods and Forests: A History* (Llandysul: Gomer, 2000), p. 211; for the replacement of broadleaved woodland, see p. 209 (emphasis added). Linnard notes that, whilst the Forestry Commission's 1980 census of woodland indicated that there was actually no decrease in 'the total area of broadleaves in Wales' over the previous thirty years, areas of oak had declined 'by some 7,000 hectares' (p. 211).

17 I am grateful to Ruth Bidgood's son Martin for identifying the precise location referred to in 'Tree-felling' as NGR SN 882 540 – i.e. the north-facing slope of Bryn Mawr. Throughout this volume, six-figure and eight-figure National Grid Reference (NGR) identifiers are used to locate small features, such as a particular hillside or an

individual building, on contemporary Ordnance Survey mapping. Four-figure NGR identifiers are used for larger landscape features.

[18] Ordnance Survey maps from 1905 until the 1960s indicate the presence of this area of mixed woodland in Coed Trallwm: see, for example, *Brecknockshire*, Sheet VII.14, 1:2,500 (2nd edn; Southampton: Ordnance Survey, 1905), parcel 219b.

[19] Kirsti Bohata, *Postcolonialism Revisited* (Cardiff: University of Wales Press, 2004), p. 86.

[20] Ruth Bidgood, 'Llanddewi Hall, Radnorshire', *Country Life*, 3670 (6 July 1967), 42.

[21] H. Brooksby, 'Llanddewi Hall', *Transactions of the Radnorshire Society*, 50 (1980), 68. Llanddewi Hall is at NGR SO 1085 6871.

[22] Full references are provided in the 'Local history: articles and essays' section of the Select Bibliography in this volume. However, all of these articles are now also available online via the National Library of Wales's Welsh Journals Online project (*http://welshjournals.llgc.org.uk/*).

[23] Ruth Bidgood, 'Families of Llanddewi Hall, Radnorshire. Part I: the Phillips and the Probert families', *Transactions of the Radnorshire Society*, 44 (1974), 8.

[24] Mircea Eliade, *The Sacred and the Profane: The Nature of Religion*, trans. by Willard R. Trask (San Diego: Harcourt Brace Jovanovich, 1959), p. 20.

[25] Ruth Bidgood, 'In the Suburbs', *Country Quest*, 9/11 (April 1969), 35.

[26] Terry Gifford, 'Towards a post-pastoral view of British poetry', in John Parham (ed.), *The Environmental Tradition in English Literature* (Aldershot: Ashgate, 2002), p. 52.

[27] Ruth Bidgood, 'Trespass', *London Welshman*, 22/10 (November 1967), 8.

[28] The typescript of the poem held at the National Library of Wales indicates, in a handwritten note, that this piece was composed between 18 April 1966 and 21 August 1966 (see Ruth Bidgood, *Ruth Bidgood Poems, 1966–2011*, NLW MS 23946iD, National Library of Wales, fol. 3, typescript with manuscript notes). As such, it was indeed amongst Bidgood's very earliest material.

[29] I have suggested elsewhere that 'Literary analysis typically does a disservice to poetry by reducing it merely to the life of its author': Matthew Jarvis, 'On love', *New Welsh Review*, 91 (2011), 22.

[30] Ruth Bidgood, 'Shoes', *London Welshman*, 23/6 (June 1968), 18.

[31] See also Deryn Rees-Jones, 'Facing the present: the emergence of female selves in the poetry of Ruth Bidgood', *Poetry Wales*, 26/3 (1991), 9–12.

[32] Ruth Bidgood, unpublished letter to *Poetry Wales*, 7 April 1989, Ruth Bidgood's private papers, typescript with manuscript notes; see Appendix C above, p. 135 See also Kenneth R. Smith, 'Praise of the

past: the myth of eternal return in women writers', *Poetry Wales*, 24/4 (1989), 51–3.

33 Ruth Bidgood, 'Warning', *Poetry Wales*, 4/2 (winter 1968), unpaginated.

34 Bidgood, 'A poet in her place', 21.

35 See Matthew Jarvis, 'Voices of renewal: anglophone Welsh poetry in the 1960s', *Poetry Wales*, 44/2 (2008), 22–3.

36 Tony Conran, *Frontiers in Anglo-Welsh Poetry* (Cardiff: University of Wales Press, 1997), p. 177.

37 Meic Stephens, 'The Second Flowering', *Poetry Wales*, 3/3 (1967), 4.

38 John Tripp, 'Poetry at Cardiff', *London Welshman*, 21/11 (1966), 12.

39 Stephens, 'Second Flowering', 6.

40 Ibid., 7.

41 For a discussion of the ways in which the poetry of the Second Flowering engaged with issues to do with Wales, see Jarvis, 'Voices of renewal', 25–6 and n. 28. See also Matthew Jarvis, 'Repositioning Wales: poetry after the Second Flowering', in Daniel G. Williams (ed.), *Slanderous Tongues: Essays on Welsh Poetry in English 1970–2005* (Bridgend: Seren, 2010), pp. 24–8.

2

1 Jeremy Hooker, '*The Given Time* by Ruth Bidgood', *Anglo-Welsh Review*, 49 (1973), 220.

2 Ibid., 221 and 222.

3 David Shayer, 'Ruth Bidgood: *The Given Time*; Florence Bull: *St. David's Day*', *Poetry Wales*, 8/2 (1972), 84.

4 Ibid.

5 John Tripp, 'Round the poets', *Planet*, 16 (1973), 69.

6 Hooker ('*Given Time*', 221–2) notes, for example, the 'deadening' effect of clichés in the collection: 'The quality of word choice in "Nightmare", however, is too common in *The Given Time*. In this poem the speaker escapes "the horror in the *stunted* trees", scrambles uphill "*against the wind's malice*" and "the *treachery* of slithering stones", to where "Great rocks *loomed* suddenly"' (emphases in original).

7 Peter Elfed Lewis, '*Ten Anglo-Welsh Poets* edited by Sam Adams', *Anglo-Welsh Review*, 53 (1974), 165.

8 For Bidgood's Welsh Arts Council prize, see Welsh Arts Council/ Cyngor Celfyddydau Cymru, *Annual Report for the Year Ending 31 March 1976/Adroddiad Blynyddol am y Flwyddyn Hyd at 31 Mawrth 1976* (N.p.: n.p., n.d.), unpaginated. The central white pages contain pictures of all those who received the year's 'Prizes to writers'

(Bidgood is photograph number eleven), whilst the final green page lists the authors, the winning publication of each individual (if applicable) and the amounts in question. The prizes – not to be confused with 'Awards', which were writing bursaries and travel grants – were primarily 'for books published during the previous calendar year which, in the Literature Committee's opinion, were of exceptional literary merit', although two further prizes were awarded for 'distinguished contributions to the literatures of Wales over many years'. Bidgood's prize of £250, specifically for *Not Without Homage*, was one of the former. The English-language recipients for 1976 are, from a later perspective, an especially distinguished list: alongside Bidgood, the others to be honoured were Bernice Rubens, Kenneth O. Morgan, R. S. Thomas and Gwyn Thomas.

9   The mid-Wales emphasis in these three collections is overwhelmingly on Breconshire, with poems that emerge from or somehow engage with Breconshire making up around half of each volume.

10 Only sixty-four poems are listed in the contents page of the volume; the one that is missed out is 'Roads', the sixth poem in the collection (*GT*, p. 16).

11 Shayer, '*Given Time*', 84.

12 W. Linnard, *Welsh Woods and Forests: A History* (Llandysul: Gomer, 2000), p. 209.

13 For Cluniau-fawr, see *Brecknockshire*, Sheet VII.10, 1:2,500 (Southampton: Ordnance Survey, 1888), parcel 10; NGR SN 8872 5571. The conifers have recently been cut down, so the house is now visible on the hillside again (RB).

14 Tony Curtis, '*Not Without Homage* by Ruth Bidgood; *Poetry Dimension Annual 3* edited by Dannie Abse', *Anglo-Welsh Review*, 56 (1976), 175.

15 Bidgood writes of 'Roads' that 'I sometimes feel it's the only poem of mine anyone seems to know! It has several times been requested for weddings, a marriage blessing, and funerals' (RB).

16 Yi-Fu Tuan, *Space and Place: The Perspective of Experience* (Minneapolis, Minn.: University of Minnesota Press, 1977), p. 86.

17 Ibid., p. 87.

18 For Hennant ('Hen-nant' on Ordnance Survey maps), see *Brecknockshire*, Sheet IX.4, 1:2,500 (Southampton: Ordnance Survey, 1889), parcel 133; NGR SN 8473 5288.

19 Jeremy Hooker, *The Presence of the Past: Essays on Modern British and American Poetry* (Bridgend: Poetry Wales Press, 1987), p. 170.

20 J. Lloyd, 'Angladd yn yr ucheldiroedd', *Cymru*, 255 (1912), 173–5. Bidgood was helped in her translation of this piece by Dai Jones of Abergwesyn Post Office, an important figure in terms of her local history knowledge of Abergwesyn: for her acknowledgement of his

'constant help over many years', see *PB*, p. 7. For generous help with Lloyd's essay I am grateful to Dr Lionel Madden.

21   For Blaen-Glasffrwd, see NGR SN 7665 6328.

22   Tripp, 'Round the poets', 69.

23   Greg Garrard, *Ecocriticism* (Abingdon: Routledge, 2004), p. 38.

24   Charles Darwin, *Autobiographies*, ed. Michael Neve and Sharon Messenger (London: Penguin, 2002), p. 72.

25   David Pepper, *Modern Environmentalism: An Introduction* (London: Routledge, 1996), p. 183.

26   For Soar y Mynydd, see NGR SN 7847 5328. J. Lloyd ('Angladd', 173) describes it as 'y capel ar lan y Camddwr' (the chapel on the banks of the Camddwr).

27   For Bidgood's description of the event in 1876 on which the poem is based, see *PB*, p. 52. J. Lloyd's original essay identifies the deceased woman as 'Shân, gwraig John Jones, Pysgotwr' (Shân, wife of John Jones, of Pysgotwr), and describes the announcement of her funeral as being made 'Ar fore'r Sabbath cyntaf yn y flwyddyn 1876, yng nghapel Bethesda, Llanddewi Brefi' (On the morning of the first Sabbath of the year 1876, in Bethesda Chapel, Llanddewi Brefi): see Lloyd, 'Angladd', 173. For the starting and ending points of the journey itself, see (respectively) NGR SN 7344 5182 and SN 8510 5262.

28   My tentative attempts to reconstruct this journey suggest that it is more likely to have been around eight-and-a-half miles in length. For Lloyd's remarks, see 'Angladd', 174.

29   Given that Pysgotwr is on the northern bank of Afon Pysgotwr Fawr, it seems unlikely that the funeral party would have crossed this river, contrary to the poem's suggestion. However, Lloyd's essay indicates that the coffin's route crossed both Doethie Fawr and Doethie Fach (ibid.), so the poem's notion of passing over 'four rivers' still stands (the other two being the Camddwr and the Tywi). Of the route's 'four mountains', the most challenging ascent – particularly bearing in mind that a coffin was being carried – was from the banks of the Tywi up past Nant yr Ych, where the path rises from a little over 900 to 1,560 feet in about two-thirds of a mile.

30   W. Rhys Nicholas, *The Folk Poets*, Writers of Wales ([Cardiff]: University of Wales Press, 1978), p. 6. For distinctions between *canu bro* and the work of the *bardd gwlad*, I am grateful to Wynn Thomas.

31   Jeremy Hooker, 'Ceridwen's daughters: Welsh women poets and the uses of tradition', *Welsh Writing in English: A Yearbook of Critical Essays*, 1 (1995), 133–4.

32   'Boy in a Train' draws on an incident 'on a suburban line between Coulsdon and London' (RB).

33   Nicholas, *Folk Poets*, p. 6.

34 Terry Gifford, *Pastoral* (London: Routledge, 1999), p. 2.

35 For 'Daren hill' ('Darren' on current Ordnance Survey maps), see NGR SN 908 568. Bidgood notes, however, that 'The geography of this poem is a bit of a mixture', drawing together Breconshire and 'North Carmarthenshire, which was a great resort at the time [for] hippies and drop-outs, of whom my daughter was one' (RB).

36 For Bidgood's discussion of droving and the Abergwesyn area, see *PB*, pp. 189–93.

37 Nicholas, *Folk Poets*, p. 6.

38 For Blaennant ('Blaen-y-Nant' on Ordnance Survey maps), see *Brecknockshire*, Sheet VII.13, 1:2,500 (2nd edn; Southampton: Ordnance Survey, 1905), parcel 69; NGR SN 8643 5463. For Bidgood's own remarks on this house, and on 'Rhys Jones, once a drover, who became a roadmender', see *PB*, p. 189.

39 Pamela J. Stewart and Andrew Strathern (eds), *Landscape, Memory and History: Anthropological Perspectives* (London: Pluto, 2003), p. 229.

40 Nicholas, *Folk Poets*, p. 6.

41 A. M. Allchin, 'The mystery that complements precision: reading Ruth Bidgood's poetry', *Logos: The Welsh Theological Review/Cylchgrawn Diwinyddol Cymru*, 4/5/6 ([1993]), 9.

42 Matthew Jarvis, *Welsh Environments in Contemporary Poetry* (Cardiff: University of Wales Press, 2008), p. 66.

43 Ibid., pp. 65–6. For the notion of 'Watershed Aesthetics', see Lawrence Buell, *Writing for an Endangered World: Literature, Culture, and Environment in the U.S. and Beyond* (Cambridge, Mass.: Belknap, 2001), p. 246.

44 A. M. Allchin, 'The return of the angels', *New Fire*, V/37 (1978), 205.

45 Linnard, *Welsh Woods and Forests*, p. 211.

46 Ruth Bidgood, *Ruth Bidgood Poems, 1966–2011*, NLW MS 23946iD, National Library of Wales, fol. 38, typescript with manuscript notes. The poem is reproduced in this volume in Appendix B, along with what can be seen as its companion piece, the similarly unpublished 'Brianne 1970' (fol. 42, typescript with manuscript alterations). Neither poem was unpublished for want of trying on Bidgood's part, although she now describes them as 'vitriolic' (RB).

47 Kirsti Bohata, *Postcolonialism Revisited* (Cardiff: University of Wales Press, 2004), p. 85.

48 Ibid., p. 84. For Bohata's useful discussion of specific appropriative actions by such bodies (and thus ultimately by 'the London government'), see pp. 81–3.

49 For pastoral as 'complacent', see Gifford, *Pastoral*, p. 2.

3

[1] As the poem includes prose sections, the line count is problematic. I refer here to the poem as set out in *SoP*, pp. 3–20.

[2] For the 1981 extract from the 'Hymn', see Ruth Bidgood, 'Hymn to Sant Ffraed', *Anglo-Welsh Review*, 69 (1981), 5–11. Apart from its use of the spelling 'Ffraed' and the basic fact that it is not a full version of the poem (over 180 lines of the complete text are missing from the 1981 extract), the two main differences between this publication and that of 2006 are: (a) the lack of specified 'voices' in the earlier extract; (b) the change in the 2006 publication to numbered rather than titled sections. There are also differences in lineation and stanza breaks, as well as some small variations in the wording of the text itself. Unless specified otherwise, my discussion here will refer to the complete text as published in *Symbols of Plenty* (*SoP*, pp. 3–20).

[3] Gwasg Boase was run by *Western Mail* journalist Charles Boase. The publication of Bidgood's 'Hymn' with this press reached proof stage, and was letterpress work, produced 'using metal type I had cast in my workshop' (personal communication from Charles Boase). See also Appendix C above, p. 135, which indicates that there was still hope for the project in early 1989.

[4] For Kenneth R. Smith's discussion of the 'Hymn', see his 'Praise of the past: the myth of eternal return in women writers', *Poetry Wales*, 24/4 (1989), 51–3.

[5] Ibid., 51.

[6] These details are given on the cover sheet of Ruth Bidgood, *Poems for Radio: Hymn to Sant Ffraed*, BBC Radio Wales script [1979], Ruth Bidgood's private papers, typescript with manuscript notes.

[7] Identification of sources for the 'Hymn' has been made in the course of numerous written exchanges between Ruth Bidgood and the author of this volume.

[8] See Smith, 'Praise of the past', 51, and the observation in Bidgood's letter that Smith was 'quite right about the strong influence of David Jones on the manner, at least, of this poem, written . . . when I was soaked in his poetry' (Appendix C above, p. 135).

[9] David Jones, *The Anathémata* (1952; London: Faber, 1972), p. 9.

[10] Anne Ross, 'Ritual and the druids', in Miranda J. Green (ed.), *The Celtic World* (London: Routledge, 1995), p. 436. Dorothy Bray emphasizes that this process should be seen in terms of syncretism rather than 'direct borrowing': Dorothy Bray, 'Brigit (goddess)' in John T. Koch (ed.), *Celtic Culture: A Historical Encyclopedia*, vol. I (Santa Barbara, Calif.: ABC-CLIO, 2006), p. 288. Indeed, Elissa R.

Henken points out that the saint is herself not just one saint; rather, 'St Brigid as she is honoured in Wales is a conglomeration of a number of Brigids, especially St Brigid of Kildare . . ., a St Brigid who lived in North Wales, and the Swedish St Brigid': Elissa R. Henken, *Traditions of the Welsh Saints* (Cambridge: Brewer, 1987), p. 161.

[11] Bidgood, 'Hymn to Sant Ffraed', 5.

[12] Proinsias Mac Cana, *Celtic Mythology* (new rev. edn; Feltham: Newnes, 1983), p. 34.

[13] Bray, 'Brigit (goddess)', p. 287.

[14] Mac Cana, *Celtic Mythology*, p. 34.

[15] Fiona Macleod, *Where the Forest Murmurs: Nature Essays* (London: Country Life, 1906), p. 77.

[16] Donald A. Mackenzie, *Scottish Folk-lore and Folk Life: Studies in Race, Culture and Tradition* (London: Blackie & Son, 1935), p. 188.

[17] G. R. D. McLean, *Poems of the Western Highlanders* (London: SPCK, 1961), p. 307; for the sources of this poem, see p. 469, notes to item 369. For the precise notion of the two-stage touch of Bride opposing the ice, see 'The coming of Angus and Bride', in Donald A. Mackenzie, *Wonder Tales from Scottish Myth & Legend* (London: Blackie & Son, [1917]), specifically pp. 41 and 48.

[18] For a text of this *cywydd*, see Eurys I. Rowlands (ed.), *Poems of the Cywyddwyr: A Selection of Cywyddau c.1375–1525* ([Dublin]: Dublin Institute for Advanced Studies, 1976), pp. 63–5.

[19] Anita Tregarneth, *Founders of the Faith in Wales* (1947; Bangor: Welsh National Centre for Religious Education, 1996), p. 43. See also Sabine Baring-Gould and John Fisher, *The Lives of the British Saints: The Saints of Wales and Cornwall and Such Irish Saints as have Dedications in Britain*, vol. I (London: Honourable Society of Cymmrodorion, 1907), p. 288 and Lewis Morris, *Celtic Remains* (London: J. Parker for the Cambrian Archæological Society, 1878), p. 386.

[20] For miraculous replenishments, see Whitley Stokes (ed. and trans.), *Lives of Saints from the Book of Lismore* (Oxford: Clarendon Press, 1890), pp. 185–7; for the origins of the *Book of Lismore*, see p. v and also Robert Welch (ed.), *The Oxford Companion to Irish Literature* (Oxford: Clarendon Press, 1996), p. 55. Bidgood's quotation from Stokes constitutes the last fourteen lines of Part I of the 'Hymn' (*SoP*, p. 7), her use of quotation marks identifying this material as a direct citation – although it should be noted that Bidgood does make some changes to her source. For Stokes's original, see *Book of Lismore*, p. 198.

[21] Stokes, *Book of Lismore*, p. 187.

22 Baring-Gould and Fisher, *Lives of the British Saints*, p. 271.
23 Ross, 'Ritual and the druids', p. 436; John O'Donovan (trans.), *Cormac's Glossary*, ed. by Whitley Stokes (Calcutta: Irish Archæological and Celtic Society, 1868), p. 23.
24 Robert Graves, *The White Goddess: A Historical Grammar of Poetic Myth* (London: Faber, 1948), p. 343.
25 For Graves's use of these titles, see ibid., pp. 94 and 346.
26 Pamela Berger, *The Goddess Obscured: Transformation of the Grain Protectress from Goddess to Saint* (London: Robert Hale, 1988), p. 72.
27 For Saint Brigid as 'foster-mother of Christ', see Mackenzie, *Scottish Folk-lore*, p. 190.
28 Another volume that Bidgood consulted in writing the poem was T. C. Lethbridge, *Gogmagog: The Buried Gods* (London: Routledge and Kegan Paul, 1957), which pertinently declares Brigid to be 'Chiefly a goddess of fire' (p. 165).
29 See, for example, Bidgood's remarks in her unpublished letter to *Poetry Wales* about 'Hymn' as a 'praise-poem' (Appendix C above, p. 135).
30 Smith, 'Praise of the past', 52. Bidgood; 'Hymn to Sant Ffraed', 6.
31 See Appendix C above, p. 137.
32 Tregarneth, *Founders of the Faith*, p. 43. The tale of the famine miraculously relieved by Ffraid is perhaps more typically associated with Afon Conwy: see Baring-Gould and Fisher, *Lives of the British Saints*, p. 288, and William Payne, 'A legend of St. Ffraid', *Notes and Queries* (10 December 1892), 465.
33 Herbert Thurston and Donald Attwater (eds), *Butler's Lives of the Saints*, vol. I (2nd edn; London: Burns & Oates, 1956), p. 226.
34 See, respectively, Stokes, *Book of Lismore*, pp. 188 and 184.
35 Bidgood, 'Hymn to Sant Ffraed', 8.
36 For the fishing-related rituals of Part III, stanzas one and two (*SoP*, p. 13), see Seán Ó Súilleabháin, *Irish Folk Custom and Belief* (Dublin: Three Candles, 1967), pp. 26–7; for the Bride's Eve traditions of Part III, stanzas eight and nine (*SoP*, pp. 15–16), see Mackenzie, *Scottish Folk-lore*, pp. 191–3.
37 For Llansantffraed, see NGR SO 122 235. Henry Vaughan's second collection of poetry, dated 1647 but not published until 1651, was called *Olor Iscanus* ('The Swan of Usk'): see Margaret Drabble (ed.), *The Oxford Companion to English Literature* (rev. edn; Oxford: Oxford University Press, 1995), p. 1033. For Vaughan's burial, see John Davies et al. (eds), *The Welsh Academy Encyclopaedia of Wales* (Cardiff: University of Wales Press, 2008), p. 908.
38 Smith, 'Praise of the past', 51.

[39] The association between Brigid and the peat-heap is articulated in McLean, *Poems of the Western Highlanders*, p. 119 ('Bride of the veils, of the peat-heap stock'), which itself draws on Alexander Carmichael, *Carmina Gadelica: Hymns and Incantations*, vol. III (Edinburgh: Oliver and Boyd, 1940), p. 157 ('Brigit of the mantles, / Brigit of the peat-heap').

[40] On the complexity of 'myth' as a concept, see Laurence Coupe, *Myth* (London: Routledge, 1997), pp. 5–6; my quotation from theologian Don Cupitt is drawn from Coupe's discussion.

[41] One of Saint Brigid's particular associations is with 'milch cows and the dairy': see Henken, *Traditions of the Welsh Saints*, p. 163.

[42] For the *Mirabilia Britanniae* ('the title of a tract which is appended to texts of the eleventh-century Cambridge recension of the *Historia Brittonum*, which attributes the work to Nennius'), see Meic Stephens (ed.), *The New Companion to the Literature of Wales* (Cardiff: University of Wales Press, 1998), p. 498.

[43] See Charlotte Guest (trans.), *The Mabinogion* (London: Dent, 1906), pp. 331–2. For the location of what contemporary Ordnance Survey maps call 'Carn Gafallt', two-and-three-quarter miles south-west of Rhayader, see NGR SN 944 647. For a discussion of the name Carn Cafall and the observation that *carn* can, in fact, 'in no way . . . denote a dog's softer paw', see Rachel Bromwich and D. Simon Evans (eds), *Culhwch and Olwen: An Edition and Study of the Oldest Arthurian Tale* (Cardiff: University of Wales Press, 1992), pp. lxvi–lxvii.

[44] Quoted in Coupe, *Myth*, p. 6.

[45] See Giraldus Cambrensis, *The Itinerary through Wales and the Description of Wales* (London: Dent, 1908), p. 32.

[46] For a reference to this myth, see Christopher J. Evans, *Breconshire* (Cambridge: Cambridge University Press, 1912), p. 24.

[47] Giraldus Cambrensis, *Itinerary through Wales*, p. 33, editorial matter (by Richard Colt Hoare).

[48] Quoted in Coupe, *Myth*, p. 6.

[49] Ibid., p. 8 (emphases in original).

[50] Lucy Toulmin Smith (ed.), *The Itinerary in Wales of John Leland in or about the Years 1536–1539* (London: George Bell, 1906), p. 119.

[51] *PB*, p. 253; for a photograph of the hoofprints, see *PB*, plate 60. For Alltyrhebog (Allt yr Hebog), see NGR SN 8506 5302.

[52] Mircea Eliade, *The Sacred and the Profane: The Nature of Religion*, trans. by Willard R. Trask (San Diego: Harcourt Brace Jovanovich, 1959), pp. 20 and 27 (emphasis in original).

[53] Matthew Jarvis, *Welsh Environments in Contemporary Poetry* (Cardiff: University of Wales Press, 2008), p. 68.

54 For Dowsing's destructions at Clare, see Trevor Cooper (ed.), *The Journal of William Dowsing: Iconoclasm in East Anglia during the English Civil War* (London: Ecclesiological Society; Woodbridge: Boydell, 2001), p. 214; for those at Little St Mary's, see p. 192; for those at Peterhouse, see pp. 155–6. For the particular wording used by Bidgood of God the Father 'holding a Glass in his Hand', see the version of the destructions at Little St Mary's as reproduced in David Cressy and Lori Anne Ferrell (eds), *Religion & Society in Early Modern England: A Sourcebook* (2nd edn; Abingdon: Routledge, 2005), p. 216.

55 Eliade, *The Sacred and the Profane*, p. 26.

56 *PB*, p. 54; Bidgood's quotation here is from G. Hartwell Jones, *Celtic Britain and the Pilgrim Movement* (London: Honourable Society of Cymmrodorion, 1912), p. 38. Carreg Clochdy is at NGR SN 8117 5026, at an elevation of around 1,200 feet.

57 Jones, *Celtic Britain*, pp. 38–9.

58 Eliade, *The Sacred and the Profane*, p. 20.

59 Ibid., p. 27.

60 Ibid.

61 The incident to which Bidgood refers here is from the entry for 14 October 1870: see David Lockwood (ed.), *Kilvert, the Victorian: A New Selection from Kilvert's Diaries* (Bridgend: Seren, 1992), p. 81.

4

1 The volumes published in the 1970s, plus 'Hymn to Sant Ffraid', constitute around 170 pages of new work; the total is almost exactly the same for the four books published in the 1980s and 1990s. Bidgood's uncollected and unpublished poetry held in the National Library of Wales suggests a similar situation, preserving around eighty pages of such poems from the period up to 1979 and seventy pages from 1980 to 1999 (see Ruth Bidgood, *Ruth Bidgood Poems, 1966–2011*, NLW MS 23946i–iiD, National Library of Wales, both files, typescripts).

2 Amy Wack has worked for Seren since 1989, having taken on the post of poetry editor in 1992: see 'Amy Wack', *Seren*, http://www.serenbooks.com/author/amy-wack (accessed 16 January 2012), and 'About Seren', *Seren*, http://www.serenbooks.com/about (accessed 16 January 2012). The first of Bidgood's collections on which Wack worked was 1992's *Selected Poems* (personal communication from Amy Wack).

3 Bidgood's collections in these years brought together only a little over one hundred pages of new work.

4   See 'Past winners and judges', *Literature Wales/Llenyddiaeth Cymru*, *http://www.literaturewales.org/past-winners-and-judges/* (accessed 16 January 2012).

5   Bidgood had been one of a number of writers proposed as fellows of The Welsh Academy at The Welsh Academy Members' Committee in January 1999. These fellowships were approved in the meeting that followed in September 1999. (I am grateful to Bronwen Price of Literature Wales for this information.)

6   David Annwn, '*Lighting Candles, New and Selected Poems* by Ruth Bidgood', *Anglo-Welsh Review*, 74 (1983), 101.

7   Katie Jones [Gramich], 'Cabaret and kin', *Planet*, 65 (1987), 102.

8   Hilary Llewellyn Williams, '*With the Offal Eaters*, Douglas Houston; *Beware Falling Tortoises*, Sheenagh Pugh; *Kindred*, Ruth Bidgood', *Book News from Wales/Llais Llyfrau* (summer 1987), 13.

9   Douglas Houston, '*Taken for Pearls*, Tony Curtis; *Selected Poems*, Ruth Bidgood', *Books in Wales/Llais Llyfrau* (winter 1993), 15.

10 Merryn Williams, 'Ruth Bidgood: *Selected Poems*', *Poetry Wales*, 28/2 (1992), 62 and 63.

11 A. M. Allchin, 'Poet of the haunted present', *Planet*, 98 (1993), 102.

12 Don Dale-Jones, 'Beyond the blinkered metropolis', *New Welsh Review*, 37 (1997), 56.

13 Eddie Wainwright, 'Parts and wholes', *Envoi*, 117 (1997), 156.

14 Paul Groves, 'The haunted brink', *Poetry Review*, 87/4 (1997/8), 67.

15 Gareth Owen, '*Selected Poems*: Ruth Bidgood', *BWA: Bulletin of the Welsh Academy*, 29 (1993), 10.

16 Caroline Sylge, 'Home and all the rest of it', *PN Review*, 115 (1997), 72.

17 Williams, 'Ruth Bidgood: *Selected Poems*', 62.

18 Dai Griffiths, '*Selected Poems*: Ruth Bidgood', *BWA: Bulletin of the Welsh Academy*, 31 (1993), unpaginated.

19 For Digiff, see 'Digyff' on the nineteenth-century Ordnance Survey map *Brecknockshire*, Sheet IX.4, 1:2,500 (Southampton: Ordnance Survey, 1889), parcel 129. Although no longer named on contemporary Ordnance Survey maps, the location of Digiff is NGR SN 8455 5318.

20 Keith Silver, 'Voices in the trees', *PN Review*, 94 (1993), 61.

21 Griffiths, '*Selected Poems*', unpaginated.

22 For telephone boxes, see 'Small Town Afternoon' and 'Telephones' (*GT*, pp. 27 and 66); for trains, see 'Boy in a Train' (*NWH*, p. 5), 'Afternoon in Pantyffynnon' and 'The Smile' (*PM*, pp. 48–9 and 50); for lorries, see 'Broiler Fowl' (*GT*, p. 59) and 'Native' (*PM*, p. 33).

23 Robert C. Morgan, 'Gary Hill: beyond the image', in Robert C. Morgan (ed.), *Gary Hill* (Baltimore: John Hopkins University Press, 2000), p. 7.

[24] Allchin, 'Poet of the haunted present', 101.

[25] Griffiths ('*Selected Poems*', unpaginated) notes that, in *Kindred*, 'the poems begin, perhaps overdue, to lengthen', with the 'main development' of *Selected Poems* being the 'confirmation of length'. Allchin ('Poet of the haunted present', 102) simply remarks that, 'the inclusion of longer poems' in *Selected Poems* is 'particularly new'.

[26] Allchin, 'Poet of the haunted present', 102 and 101.

[27] Ibid., 102.

[28] 'All Souls'' had originally been published in the winter 1973/4 edition of *Poetry Wales*: see Ruth Bidgood, 'All Souls'', *Poetry Wales*, 9/3 (1973/4), 36.

[29] The poem notes that the Dutchman's 'girl', Marion, had painted 'again and again from across the river / the house Bryndolau': Bryndolau is to be found on the north-west side of Afon Gwesyn at NGR SN 8607 5313.

[30] Yi-Fu Tuan, *Space and Place: The Perspective of Experience* (Minneapolis, Minn.: University of Minnesota Press, 1977), p. 43.

[31] For the high land (which rises to over 1,500 feet) of Llethr Dôl-iâr, Rhiw Garreg-lwyd and Cefn Waun-lwyd, see the area covered by NGR square SN 86 52.

[32] Tuan, *Space and Place*, p. 43.

[33] For the 'derelict lead-mine' in the hills nearly two miles south-west of Abergwesyn to which the eponymous path of the poem leads, see *PB*, pp. 209–14.

[34] Tuan, *Space and Place*, p. 43.

[35] Jane Aaron, 'Valleys' women writing', in Alyce von Rothkirch and Daniel Williams (eds), *Beyond the Difference: Welsh Literature in Comparative Contexts* (Cardiff: University of Wales Press, 2004), pp. 91–2.

[36] Ruth Bidgood, 'Interview', with Angela Morton, *New Welsh Review*, 10 (1990), 42.

[37] See Abhishiktananda, *Guru and Disciple*, trans. by Heather Sandeman (London: SPCK, 1974), p. 165.

[38] Tuan, *Space and Place*, p. 43; Abhishiktananda, *Guru and Disciple*, p. 165.

[39] Bidgood notes that the eponymous spout appeared 'in a very wet field below Glangwesyn farm in Abergwesyn' (RB). Glangwesyn is at NGR SN 8635 5366.

[40] The upper Camarch Valley lies some three to four miles east of the upper Irfon Valley, in which Abergwesyn is situated.

[41] Alwyn Rees and Brinley Rees, *Celtic Heritage: Ancient Tradition in Ireland and Wales* (London: Thames and Hudson, 1961), p. 83.

[42] Ibid., pp. 84 and 83.

[43] Coedtrefan is at NGR SN 9196 5261.

⁴⁴ Quoted in Alice Entwistle, *In These Stones: Women Writing Poetry In and Out of Wales* (Bridgend: Seren, forthcoming). For a useful and related approach to this poem through the notion of the uncanny, see Entwistle's chapter 2, '"Not without strangeness": Ruth Bidgood's unhomely mid-Wales'.

⁴⁵ Allchin, 'Poet of the haunted present', 102.

⁴⁶ For the farm of Rhyd-y-meirch (which is 'long gone', according to the poem's opening stanza), see *Brecknockshire*, Sheet VI.SW, 1:10,560 (2nd edn; Southampton: Ordnance Survey, 1905); the ford is a short distance downriver to the south-west of the house. On contemporary Ordnance Survey maps, the location of the ford is NGR SN 7745 5598.

⁴⁷ D. C. Rees, *Tregaron: Historical and Antiquarian* (Llandysul: J. D. Lewis, 1936), p. 71.

⁴⁸ It should be noted, however, that overturning Rees's error regarding the outcome of the battle of Camddwr means that the princes whose 'cause was just vengeance' at the poem's end, but who were actually defeated, must stand as figures of noble tragedy. For the battle of Camddwr, which took place in 1075, see K. L. Maund, *Ireland, Wales, and England in the Eleventh Century* (Woodbridge: Boydell, 1991), pp. 29–30. Maund concedes that this battle is 'one of the most confused events of eleventh-century Wales' (p. 29).

⁴⁹ For the notion of being washed in the blood of Christ – and thus redeemed — see Revelation 1: 5 and 7: 14.

⁵⁰ Allchin, 'Poet of the haunted present', 101.

⁵¹ Tuan, *Space and Place*, p. 43.

5

¹ See my observations at the start of chapter 4 above.

² As of February 2012, this volume has reached final proofs stage (RB).

³ The amount of new work in the volumes from this period, including the upcoming *Above the Forests*, would seem to suggest a similar degree of sustained productivity to that which characterized Bidgood's initial energy of the late 1960s and 1970s.

⁴ Glyn Mathias, 'The Roland Mathias Prize', *Brycheiniog*, 37 (2005), 20.

⁵ 'Veteran poet Ruth Bidgood wins Roland Mathias Prize', *BBC News*, 9 April 2011, *http://www.bbc.co.uk/news/uk-wales-13023960* (accessed 16 January 2012).

⁶ The other volumes on the Roland Mathias Prize 2011 shortlist were: Oliver Reynolds, *Hodge* (Oxford: Areté, 2010); Huw Lawrence, *Always the Love of Someone* (Talybont: Alcemi, 2010); M. Wynn Thomas, *In the Shadow of the Pulpit: Literature and Nonconformist Wales* (Cardiff:

University of Wales Press, 2010). See 'Four Welsh writers shortlisted for top literary prize', *BBC Press Office*, 4 March 2011, *http://www. bbc.co.uk/pressoffice/pressreleases/stories/2011/03_march/04/wales.shtml* (accessed 16 January 2012).

7   For an acknowledgement by Fiona Sampson (then editor of *Poetry Review*) of the Martian element within what she called, in 2006, 'the British house style', see 'The practice of poetry: Fiona Sampson interviewed by Matthew Jarvis', *English*, 214 (2007), 84. For the relatively brief Martian 'moment' itself in the late 1970s/early 1980s, see Anthony Thwaite, *Poetry Today: A Critical Guide to British Poetry 1960–1995* (London: Longman, 1996), pp. 141–2 and the chapter 'Grammars of civilization? The "Martian" poetry of Craig Raine and Christopher Reid', in Neil Corcoran, *English Poetry Since 1940* (London: Longman, 1993), pp. 235–43. For the later significance of what I have called 'surrea*lish*' verse in Wales-identified poets, see Matthew Jarvis, 'Divergent paths: poetic divisions in the 1990s', *Poetry Wales*, 45/1 (2009), 29–30 and 33.

8   Merryn Williams, 'Ruth Bidgood, *The Fluent Moment*', *Poetry Wales*, 32/3 (1997), 68.

9   Lawrence Buell, *The Future of Environmental Criticism: Environmental Crisis and Literary Imagination* (Oxford: Blackwell, 2005), p. 134. I am grateful to Matthew Walker for drawing Buell's discussion of anthropomorphism to my attention.

10   Val Plumwood, *Environmental Culture: The Ecological Crisis of Reason* (London: Routledge, 2002), p. 4.

11   Ibid., pp. 4 and 167.

12   This is the same hill, in other words, to which the poem 'Blizzard' also refers (see chapter 4 above), much of which has been subject to coniferous plantation (see the area around NGR SN 86 52).

13   Kate Soper, *What is Nature? Culture, Politics and the Non-human* (Oxford: Blackwell, 1995), p. 99. Soper goes on to observe that the construction of the non-human world as feminine 'has also been said by anthropologists to be cross-cultural and well-nigh universal'.

14   Plumwood, *Environmental Culture*, p. 97.

15   Greg Garrard, *Ecocriticism* (Abingdon: Routledge, 2004), p. 85.

16   Plumwood, *Environmental Culture*, p. 112.

17   'Into the Wind' is the closing sequence of *Singing to Wolves*.

18   For Blaennant and the nineteenth-century reports of death omens associated with the house, see *PB*, p. 258. For the location of Blaennant, see chapter 2 above, n. 38.

19   Bidgood observes that she essentially fictionalized the events which lay behind this poem: in reality, 'the illness was diphtheria, not consumption, and the daughter was not in fact the last to die' (RB).

[20] Bidgood identifies the chapel as Gelynos Congregational Chapel, just north-west of Llanwrtyd Wells, of which only the burial ground now remains (RB). For this chapel, see *Brecknockshire*, Sheet X.13, 1:2,500 (2nd edn; Southampton: Ordnance Survey, 1905), parcel 930; NGR SN 8711 4713.

[21] Matthew Jarvis, *Welsh Environments in Contemporary Poetry* (Cardiff: University of Wales Press, 2008), p. 69.

[22] Both of these sequences were originally published, in part or in earlier versions, in *Scintilla*; see Ruth Bidgood, 'Cwm Pennant', *Scintilla*, 1 (1997), 79–82, and Ruth Bidgood, 'Riding the Flood', *Scintilla*, 6 (2002), 86–9.

[23] For example, the closing poem of the volume, 'Bringing Home the Bride' (*HV*, pp. 59–63) was written in 2002: see the typescript held in the National Library of Wales, which bears the handwritten date of 'March '02' on its second page (Ruth Bidgood, *Ruth Bidgood Poems, 1966–2011*, NLW MS 23946iiD, National Library of Wales, fols 169–70, typescript with manuscript notes).

[24] See O. E. Craster, *Llanthony Priory, Monmouthshire* (London: HMSO, 1963), pp. 4 and 5.

[25] Giraldus Cambrensis had observed that the monks could 'behold the tops of the mountains, as it were, touching the heavens, and herds of wild deer feeding on their summits': see Thomas Forester and Richard Colt Hoare (trans.), *The Historical Works of Giraldus Cambrensis*, rev. and ed. by Thomas Wright (London: George Bell, 1905), p. 356.

[26] Garrard, *Ecocriticism*, p. 61.

[27] Jarvis, *Welsh Environments*, p. 60.

[28] 'Cwmyoy' is the version of the name on contemporary Ordnance Survey maps. 'Cwm-iou' is the rendition in the landmark volume Elwyn Davies (ed.), *A Gazetteer of Welsh Place-names* (3rd edn; Cardiff: University of Wales Press, 1975), p. 35.

[29] Bidgood further observes that 'The weather was marvellous, company congenial and places powerfully magnetic!' (RB).

[30] For the place names of Clodock/Merthyr Clydawg, see A. T. Bannister, *The History of Ewias Harold, Its Castle, Priory, and Church* (Hereford: Jakeman & Carver, 1902), p. 5.

[31] Ian Gregson, *The New Poetry in Wales* (Cardiff: University of Wales Press, 2007), p. 13.

[32] For Ewias, see John Davies, *A History of Wales* (rev. edn; London: Penguin, 2007), pp. 226 and 227, and John Davies et al. (eds), *The Welsh Academy Encyclopaedia of Wales* (Cardiff: University of Wales Press, 2008), p. 274. I am grateful to Nina Wedell of the Ewyas Lacy Study Group for detailed information about territorial development

between the commote of Ewias, the Marcher lordship of Ewyas Lacy, and the post-1536 Herefordshire hundred of Ewyas Lacy. For the website of the Ewyas Lacy Study Group, see *http://www.ewyaslacy.org.uk* (accessed 16 January 2012).

33 Davies et al., *Encyclopaedia of Wales*, p. 94.

34 The date is questionable, as acknowledged in David Hugh Farmer, *The Oxford Dictionary of Saints* (5th edn; Oxford: Oxford University Press, 2004), p. 112. For further information about the saint, see also Sabine Baring-Gould and John Fisher, *The Lives of the British Saints: The Saints of Wales and Cornwall and Such Irish Saints as have Dedications in Britain*, vol. II (London: Honourable Society of Cymmrodorion, 1908), pp. 153–4 and John Edward Lloyd, 'Clydog', *Welsh Biography Online*, *http://wbo.llgc.org.uk/en/s-CLYD-APC-0500.html* (accessed 16 January 2012).

35 Davies, *History of Wales*, p. 226.

36 For a photograph of the mural in question, and an interesting discussion, see Anne Marshall, 'Warning to Sabbath breakers: Michaelchurch Escley, Hereford & Worcester', *Medieval Wall Painting in the English Parish Church: A Developing Catalogue, http://www.painted church.org/micaesc.htm* (accessed 16 January 2012).

37 Joan Evans, *English Art 1307–1461* (Oxford: Clarendon Press, 1949), p. 226. This rejection of the artistic category of 'Christ of the Trades' continues emphatically into the present: see Roger Rosewell, *Medieval Wall Paintings in English & Welsh Churches* (Woodbridge: Boydell, 2008), pp. 87–9. I am grateful to Anne Marshall's observations (see n. 36 above) for pointing me towards Evans's analysis, and to Martin Crampin of the Centre for Advanced Welsh and Celtic Studies, Aberystwyth, for directing me towards Rosewell's.

38 Garrard, *Ecocriticism*, p. 60. Garrard's extremely helpful discussion of the word 'wilderness' explains that it 'derives from the Anglo-Saxon "wilddeoren", where "deoren" or beasts existed beyond the boundaries of cultivation. So useful is the word "wild" to designate the realms of the "deoren" that neither its spelling nor its simple meaning have changed in a millennium and a half.'

39 Claire Boyle, *Consuming Autobiographies: Reading and Writing the Self in Post-war France* (London: Legenda, 2007), p. 12.

40 See n. 22 above.

41 The 'windbitten valley' of this poem is the Culent (RB).

42 For the Shropshire Archives (in Shrewsbury), see Shropshire Council, *Archives, http://www.shropshire.gov.uk/archives.nsf* (accessed 16 January 2012). For the Hanmer collection (and a very useful introduction to the material it contains), see 'A collection of deeds and papers relating to the Hanmer family of Pentrepant', *National Archives,*

http://www.nationalarchives.gov.uk/a2a/records.aspx?cat=166-894
(accessed 16 January 2012).

43 See the 'Administrative history' of 'A collection of deeds and papers relating to the Hanmer family of Pentrepant'.

44 The poem itself is not of recent origin, however: the earliest version of the piece held in the National Library of Wales (Bidgood, *Ruth Bidgood Poems*, NLW MS 23946iD, fols 70–1, typescript with manuscript alterations and note) bears the handwritten date of 23 February 1977.

45 Ruth Bidgood, 'Families of Llanddewi Hall. Part III (second instalment)', *Transactions of the Radnorshire Society*, 47 (1977), 63.

46 Soper, *What is Nature?*, p. 101.

47 For Cobbing's 'Alphabet of Fishes', see Gillian Allnutt et al. (eds), *The New British Poetry 1968–88* (London: Paladin, 1988), p. 149.

48 For John Powell, see Robert Thomas Jenkins, 'John Powell (d.1743)', *Welsh Biography Online*, *http://wbo.llgc.org.uk/en/s-POWE-JOH-1700.html* (accessed 16 January 2012). For a brief introduction to the major figure of Howell Harris ('One of the founders of Welsh Calvinistic Methodism'), see Davies et al., *Encyclopaedia of Wales*, p. 354.

6

1 For Jones's poem, see Meic Stephens (ed.), *The Collected Poems of Glyn Jones* (Cardiff: University of Wales Press, 1996), pp. 3–4.

2 Ibid., p. 138.

3 Ibid.

4 In *Time Being* itself, the text of the first line of this poem erroneously reads 'There's a shadowy perch'.

5 Matthew Jarvis, *Welsh Environments in Contemporary Poetry* (Cardiff: University of Wales Press, 2008), p. 60. See chapter 5 above.

6 Greg Garrard, *Ecocriticism* (Abingdon: Routledge, 2004), p. 85.

7 The identification of this piece as a Camarch poem is Bidgood's (RB).

8 Lawrence Buell, *Writing for an Endangered World: Literature, Culture, and Environment in the U.S. and Beyond* (Cambridge, Mass.: Belknap, 2001), p. 17.

9 See Jarvis, *Welsh Environments*, pp. 71–2.

10 Buell, *Writing for an Endangered World*, p. 84. Buell explains that reinhabitation is a 'term used since the 1970s by place-committed writers of bioregionalist persuasion'.

11 Jarvis, *Welsh Environments*, p. 72. In this analysis, my quotation is from Brian Morris, *Harri Webb*, Writers of Wales (Cardiff: University of Wales Press, 1993), p. 62.

[12] Georg Lukács, *The Historical Novel*, trans. by Hannah Mitchell and Stanley Mitchell (London: Merlin, 1962), p. 133.

[13] Peter Toohey, *Reading Epic: An Introduction to the Ancient Narratives* (London: Routledge, 1992), p. 4.

[14] The phrase 'social reality on a broad scale' is taken from M. H. Abrams's discussion of Lukács's notion of the bourgeois epic: see M. H. Abrams, *A Glossary of Literary Terms* (5th edn; London: Holt, Rinehart and Winston, 1988), p. 53.

[15] As Moretti puts it, describing the developments of his thinking about the modern epic, 'Digression became interesting, and the plot secondary': see Franco Moretti, *Modern Epic: The World-system from Goethe to García Márquez*, trans. by Quintin Hoare (London: Verso, 1996), p. 237.

Appendices

[1] Bidgood handwritten note: 'Jenkins (editor)' – i.e. Mike Jenkins, then editor of *Poetry Wales*.

[2] Bidgood handwritten note: 'in Monmouth – it folded'. See chapter 3 above, n. 3.

Select Bibliography

Material by Ruth Bidgood

Poetry collections

The Given Time (Swansea: Christopher Davies, 1972).
Not Without Homage (Swansea: Christopher Davies, 1975).
The Print of Miracle (Llandysul: Gomer, 1978).
Lighting Candles: New and Selected Poems (Bridgend: Poetry Wales Press, 1982).
Kindred (Bridgend: Poetry Wales Press, 1986).
Selected Poems (Bridgend: Seren, 1992).
The Fluent Moment (Bridgend: Seren, 1996).
Singing to Wolves (Bridgend: Seren, 2000).
New & Selected Poems (Bridgend: Seren, 2004).
Symbols of Plenty: Selected Longer Poems (Norwich: Canterbury Press, 2006).
Hearing Voices (Blaenau Ffestiniog: Cinnamon, 2008).
Time Being (Bridgend: Seren, 2009).

Poetry pamphlet

'Sheep in the Hedge', in Ruth Bidgood, Alison Bielski, Gillian Clarke, Leslie Norris, John Tripp and Harri Webb, *Creatures*, Illustrated Poetry Broadsheets: Writing from Wales (Treforest: National Language Unit of Wales, 1990), loose leaf.

Poetry: archival material

Poems for Radio: Hymn to Sant Ffraed, BBC Radio Wales script [1979], Ruth Bidgood's private papers, typescript with manuscript notes.
Ruth Bidgood Poems, 1966–2011, NLW MS 23946i–iiD, National Library of Wales, two files of material, typescripts and manuscripts.

Local history: volumes (books/pamphlets)

Penry Lloyd of Dinas, 1831–1913 (N.p.: n.p., [1976]).

Eglwys Oen Duw Church & Parish: A Guide (N.p.: n.p., 1993).

Abergwesyn: Bwlch y Ddau Faen, illus. Bernice Carlill (Newtown: Gwasg Gregynog, 1997).

Parishes of the Buzzard (Port Talbot: Gold Leaf, 2000).

The Churches of Abergwesyn (Beulah, Llanwrtyd Wells: Minffordd Private Press, 2006).

Local history: leaflet

Two Church Trails Around Builth Wells/Dwy Daith i Eglwysi Cylch Llanfair ym Muallt, trans. by Gwyneth Rowlands ([Llanelwedd]: Menter Powys [1998]).

Local history: articles and essays

'"English is spoke"', *Country Quest*, 7/12 (1967), 15–16.

'Thrashing the hen', *Country Quest*, 8/1 (1967), 44–5.

'Don't be rude to a parson', *Country Quest*, 8/5 (1967), 18.

'For whom the death bell tolls', *Country Quest*, 8/9 (1968), 7–8.

'Going to the fair', *Country Quest*, 8/12 (1968), 19–20.

'Ribbons for the king of summer holly for the king of winter', *Country Quest*, 9/5 (1968), 30, 43.

'Pageant of the parish', *Country Quest*, 9/8 (1969), 36–7.

'Dancing in the flames', *Country Quest*, 9/11 (1969), 9–10.

'At the end of all things', *Country Quest*, 10/4 (1969), 7–9.

'Carols at cock-crow', *Country Quest*, 10/7 (1969), 45, 47.

'Lost churches', *Country Quest*, 10/11 (1970), 33, 35, 37.

'A stone to cure you of a mad dog's bite', *Country Quest*, 10/12 (1970), 37, 39.

'Wastes of Eppynt', *Country Quest*, 11/2 (1970), 20–1, 23.

'No defence for a martyr', *Country Quest*, 11/4 (1970), 10–11.

'Giants of Claerwen Valley', *Country Quest*, 11/6 (1970), 1–4.

'A stone for five saints', *Country Quest*, 11/8 (1971), 35, 37.

'At war with the devil', *Country Quest*, 11/11 (1971), 20–1.

'When Peg of Ffrydie was battered to death', *Country Quest*, 11/12 (1971), 6–8.

'Kilsby – a man loved for his generosity and hated for his wit', *Country Quest*, 12/1 (1971), 5–7.

'Brave but eccentric Lady Hester', *Country Quest*, 12/2 (1971), 14–16.

'Congregation in the kitchen', *Country Quest*, 12/3 (1971), 14–17.

'The story of the cymorth', *Country Quest*, 12/9 (1972), 32–3.

'Villagers lived to a ripe old age', *Country Quest*, 12/11 (1972), 31–3.

'In the land of the lost saint', *Country Quest*, 12/12 (1972), 9–11.

'Cold waters creep over Fanog's ruined walls', *Country Quest*, 13/6 (1972), 19–21.

'Ancient dames and lusty lasses', *Country Quest*, 13/7 (1972), 6–8.

'So many have passed through its open doors', *Country Quest*, 14/10 (1974), 19–20.

'Homeward with the hay', *Country Quest*, 14/11 (1974), 39, 41, 43.

'Overbeek curse', *Country Quest*, 15/1 (1974), 30, 32.

'Troublesome goats', *Country Quest*, 15/4 (1974), 10–12.

'Families of Llanddewi Hall, Radnorshire. Part I: the Phillips and the Probert families', *Transactions of the Radnorshire Society*, 44 (1974), 7–25.

'Dark signs that death is on its way', *Country Quest*, 15/9 (1975), 12–13.

'Those other Harrises', *Country Quest*, 15/12 (1975), 41, 43.

'Fetes that turned into fights', *Country Quest*, 16/6 (1975), 35–6.

'Families of Llanddewi Hall – part II', *Transactions of the Radnorshire Society*, 45 (1975), 22–35.

'An old craft lives on', *Country Quest*, 17/5 (1976), 11.

'Families of Llanddewi Hall. Part III (first instalment): the Hanmers of Pentrepant and Llanddewi Hall', *Transactions of the Radnorshire Society*, 46 (1976), 37–50.

'Families of Llanddewi Hall. Part III (second instalment)', *Transactions of the Radnorshire Society*, 47 (1977), 62–74.

'New life at the old farmstead', *Country Quest*, 18/8 (1978), 10–11.

'Murder at Nant-y-Stalwyn', *Country Quest*, 19/2 (1978), 33.

'Families of Llanddewi Hall, Radnorshire. Part IV (first instalment): the 18th-century owners, and the Burton estate', *Transactions of the Radnorshire Society*, 48 (1978), 48–66.

'Families of Llanddewi Hall, Radnorshire. Part IV (second instalment): tenants of Llanddewi Hall from the 1770s to the 1840s', *Transactions of the Radnorshire Society*, 49 (1979), 47–59.

'Families of Llanddewi Hall, Radnorshire – part V. Conclusion: from the 1840s to the present day', *Transactions of the Radnorshire Society*, 50 (1980), 56–67.

'Before the waters came', *Country Quest*, 22/1 (1981), 9–11.

'Household and personal possessions in Radnorshire wills of the 16th, 17th and 18th centuries', *Transactions of the Radnorshire Society*, 51 (1981), 16–28.

'Churches and gentry in the Abergwesyn area', *Brycheiniog*, 21 (1984/5), 34–51.

'Last will and testament', *Country Quest*, 26/3 (1985), 17.

'To Brecon with a thousand sheep . . .', *Country Quest*, 27/3 (1986), 7–8.

'Early families of Rhydoldog, Llansanffraid Cwmteuddwr. Part one', *Transactions of the Radnorshire Society*, 56 (1986), 35–51.

'The Price family of Dôlmenyn', *Brycheiniog*, 22 (1986/7), 63–70.

'Early families of Rhydoldog, Llansanffraid Cwmteuddwr. Part two', *Transactions of the Radnorshire Society*, 57 (1987), 34–48.

'Thomas Price of Gwarafog and Strand House and his family', *Brycheiniog*, 23 (1988/9), 49–63.

'Lawrence families of the Builth and Llanelwedd area in the 18th and 19th centuries [I and II]', *Transactions of the Radnorshire Society*, 59 (1989), 90–115.

'Pool Hall, Crucadarn and its owners and occupiers from the late 17th to early 19th centuries', *Brycheiniog*, 24 (1990/2), 67–83.

'A farm rooted in history', *Country Quest*, 31/10 (1991), 8–9.

'Breconshire hero of the French wars', *Country Quest*, 32/7 (1991), 22–3.

'Lawrence families of the Builth and Llanelwedd area in the 18th and 19th centuries (continued). III: the Lawrences of Llanelwedd Hall (first instalment)', *Transactions of the Radnorshire Society*, 61 (1991), 37–53.

'Lawrence families of the Builth and Llanelwedd area in the 18th and 19th centuries (conclusion). III: the Lawrences of Llanelwedd Hall (second instalment)', *Transactions of the Radnorshire Society*, 62 (1992) 40–50.

'"Pool Hall": correction', *Brycheiniog*, 26 (1992/3), 133.

'The Williams family, nonconformist squires of Trawscoed and Talachddu', *Brycheiniog*, 26 (1992/3), 119–33.

'Nantgwyllt: part 1', *Transactions of the Radnorshire Society*, 65 (1995), 33–46.

'"A gentleman of the name of Jones" (part 1)', *Brycheiniog*, 28 (1995/6), 81–101.

'Nantgwyllt: part 2', *Transactions of the Radnorshire Society*, 66 (1996), 16–30.

'"A gentleman of the name of Jones" (part 2)', *Brycheiniog*, 29 (1996/7), 87–104.

'The Prices of Tŷ'nycoed, Llanlleonfel', *Brycheiniog*, 33 (2001), 105–15.

'Neuadd Fawr, Cilycwm: the early years', *Carmarthenshire Antiquary*, 38 (2002), 5–13.

'After Mr Jones', *Brycheiniog*, 36 (2004), 51–68.

'The Prices of Abergwenlais, Bwlch Triban(n)au and Erryd, Cilycwm: a north Carmarthenshire kinship network', *Carmarthenshire Antiquary*, 43 (2007), 51–64.

Miscellaneous writings

'Some sorts of Welshness', written for the Welsh Union of Writers, undated, Ruth Bidgood's private papers, typescript with manuscript alterations.

'Statement', written for the Welsh Academy, April 1984, Ruth Bidgood's private papers, typescript.

Unpublished letter to *Poetry Wales*, 7 April 1989, Ruth Bidgood's private papers, typescript with manuscript notes.

'Heartland', *Poetry Wales*, 26/3 (1991), 7–9.

'Ruth Bidgood', in Sandra Anstey and Rhiannon Vaughan Griffiths (eds), *Poetry from Wales II: Resource Pack* (Cardiff: BBC Wales Education, 1995), pp. 21–9 (pp. 21, 23, 25, 27).

Untitled contribution, in Sheenagh Pugh, Neal Mason, Ruth Bidgood, H. G. A. Hughes, Nicholas Murray and Linden Peach, '"Exhausted tradition" bites back', *New Welsh Review*, 28 (1995), 23–8 (25).

'Writer's diary', *Books in Wales/Llais Llyfrau*, 96/2 (1996), 4.

Untitled contribution, in 'Books 99', *Planet*, 138 (1999/2000), 47–50 (47–8).

Untitled note to two poems, *Interpreter's House*, 13 (2000), 13.

'Author's notes: Ruth Bidgood', *WalesOnline.co.uk*, *Western Mail*, 30 April 2011, *http://www.walesonline.co.uk/showbiz-and-lifestyle/books/news/2011/04/30/author-s-notes-ruth-bidgood-91466-28600059/* (accessed 16 January 2012).

Interviews

'Interview', with Angela Morton, *New Welsh Review*, 10 (1990), 38–42.

'History is now and Wales: Ruth Bidgood interviewed by Jason Walford Davies', *Planet*, 137 (1999), 47–54.

'A poet in her place – an interview with Ruth Bidgood', with Sally Roberts Jones and Alexandra Trowbridge-Matthews, *Roundyhouse*, 7 (2001), 21–5.

Videos

'Ruth Bidgood at Ledbury Poetry Festival', filmed by Neil Astley, *vimeo.com*, July 2010, *http://vimeo.com/25378104* (accessed 17 January 2012).

'Poetry by Ruth Bidgood from Seren Books', *YouTube.com*, 9 December 2010, *http://www.youtube.com/watch?v=PjJSG_nrUu0* (accessed 17 January 2012).

Material about Ruth Bidgood

Substantial critical discussions

Allchin, A. M., 'The mystery that complements precision: reading Ruth Bidgood's poetry', *Logos: The Welsh Theological Review/Cylchgrawn Diwinyddol Cymru*, 4/5/6 ([1993]), 7–15.

——, 'Ruth Bidgood: an afterword', in Ruth Bidgood, *Symbols of Plenty: Selected Longer Poems* (Norwich: Canterbury Press, 2006), pp. 65–81.

Entwistle, Alice, '"Little to say of home": Ruth Bidgood's un/homely mid-Wales', *Gothic Locations*, Cardiff University (2008), unpublished conference paper.

——, '"Not without strangeness": Ruth Bidgood's unhomely mid-Wales', in Alice Entwistle, *In These Stones: Women Writing Poetry In and Out of Wales* (Bridgend: Seren, forthcoming).

Jarvis, Matthew, 'Ruth Bidgood: reinhabiting mid Wales', in Matthew Jarvis, *Welsh Environments in Contemporary Poetry* (Cardiff: University of Wales Press, 2008), pp. 54–72, 158–62.

Maro, Judith, 'Rooted, intrinsic, aboriginal', *New Welsh Review*, 37 (1997), 55–6.

Rees-Jones, Deryn, 'Facing the present: the emergence of female selves in the poetry of Ruth Bidgood', *Poetry Wales*, 26/3 (1991), 9–12.

Smith, Kenneth R., 'Women writers in Wales: Anglo-Welsh themes and characteristics as transformed by a female poetic' (unpublished MA thesis, University College of Wales, Aberystwyth, 1985).

——, 'Poetry of place: the haunted interiors', *Poetry Wales*, 24/2 (1988), 59–65.

——, 'Praise of the past: the myth of eternal return in women writers', *Poetry Wales*, 24/4 (1989), 50–8.

Thurston, Bonnie, '"A scatter of little sights and happenings": the poetic vision of Ruth Bidgood', *The Way*, 45/1 (2006), 93–104.

Williams, Merryn, 'The poetry of Ruth Bidgood', *Poetry Wales*, 28/3 (1993), 36–41.

——, 'The poetry of Ruth Bidgood', in James A. Davies and Glyn Pursglove (eds), *Writing Region and Nation: Proceedings of the Fourth International Conference on the Literature of Region and Nation*, a special number of *The Swansea Review* (Swansea: Department of English, University of Wales Swansea, 1994), 561–72.

Other discussions or citations

Aaron, Jane, 'Finding a voice in two tongues: gender and colonization', in Jane Aaron, Teresa Rees, Sandra Betts and Moira Vincentelli (eds), *Our Sisters' Land: The Changing Identities of Women in Wales* (Cardiff: University of Wales Press, 1994), pp. 183–98 (p. 196).

——, 'Towards devolution: new Welsh writing', in Laura Marcus and Peter Nicholls (eds), *The Cambridge History of Twentieth-century English Literature* (Cambridge: Cambridge University Press, 2004), pp. 685–99 (pp. 690, 691–2).

——, 'Valleys' women writing', in Alyce von Rothkirch and Daniel Williams (eds), *Beyond the Difference: Welsh Literature in Comparative Contexts* (Cardiff: University of Wales Press, 2004), pp. 84–96 (pp. 90–3, 96).

——, 'Welsh women writers (1700–2000)', in John T. Koch (ed.), *Celtic Culture: A Historical Encyclopedia*, vol. V (Santa Barbara, Calif.: ABC-CLIO, 2006), pp. 1785–9 (pp. 1788, 1789).

—— and M. Wynn Thomas, '"Pulling you through changes": Welsh writing in English before, between and after two referenda', in M. Wynn Thomas (ed.), *Welsh Writing in English*, A Guide to Welsh Literature, vol. VII (Cardiff: University of Wales Press, 2003), pp. 278–309 (pp. 288–9).

Allchin, A. M., *Pennant Melangell: Place of Pilgrimage* (Pennant Melangell: Gwasg Santes Melangell, 1994), pp. 34–8, 43.

Annwn, David, 'Her pulse their pace: women poets and Basil Bunting', in James McGonigal and Richard Price (eds), *The Star You Steer By: Basil Bunting and British Modernism* (Amsterdam: Rodopi, 2000), pp. 123–48 (p. 125).

Anon., 'Bidgood, Ruth', in Jenny Stringer (ed.), *The Oxford Companion to Twentieth-century Literature in English* (Oxford: Oxford University Press, 1996), p. 65.

——, 'Bidgood, Ruth', in Meic Stephens (ed.), *The New Companion to the Literature of Wales* (Cardiff: University of Wales Press, 1998), pp. 49–50.

——, 'Veteran poet Ruth Bidgood wins Roland Mathias Prize', *BBC News*, 9 April 2011, *http://www.bbc.co.uk/news/uk-wales-13023960* (accessed 16 January 2012).

——, 'Poetry vet scoops prestigious prize', *Western Mail*, 11 April 2011, 4.

Anstey, Sandra and Rhiannon Vaughan Griffiths (eds), *Poetry from Wales II: Resource Pack* (Cardiff: BBC Wales Education, 1995), pp. 2, 21–9.

Barker, Jonathan, *Poetry in Britain and Ireland since 1970: A Select Bibliography* (London: British Council, 1995), p. 17.

Brightmore, Gillian, '"Stonking" in the valleys', *Books in Wales/Llais Llyfrau*, 96/2 (1996), 5–6 (6).

Cluysenaar, Anne, 'Introduction', in Anne Cluysenaar and Norman Schwenk (eds), *The Hare that Hides Within: Poems about St. Melangell* (Cardigan: Parthian, 2004), pp. ix–xii (p. x).

Conradi, Peter J., *At the Bright Hem of God: Radnorshire Pastoral* (Bridgend: Seren, 2009), pp. 13, 173–7, 193, 233.

Davies, Oliver and Fiona Bowie, 'Introduction [modern poetry]', in Oliver Davies and Fiona Bowie (eds), *Celtic Christian Spirituality: Medieval and Modern* (London: SPCK, 1995), pp. 165–77 (pp. 168, 169).

——, 'Ruth Bidgood (b. 1922)', Introductory Note, in Oliver Davies and Fiona Bowie (eds), *Celtic Christian Spirituality: Medieval and Modern* (London: SPCK, 1995), p. 194.

de Waal, Esther, *Living on the Border: Connecting Inner and Outer Worlds* (Norwich: Canterbury Press, 2001), pp. 40, 55.

——, *Lost in Wonder: Rediscovering the Spiritual Art of Attentiveness* (Norwich: Canterbury Press, 2003), pp. 58, 94, 138, 167, 181.

——, *Seeking Life: The Baptismal Invitation of the Rule of St Benedict* (Norwich: Canterbury Press, 2009), pp. 19–20, 140.

Earle, Mary C. and Sylvia Maddox, *Holy Companions: Spiritual Practices from the Celtic Saints* (Harrisburg, Pa.: Morehouse, 2004), pp. 48–9.

Entwistle, Alice, 'Now you see her?', *New Welsh Review*, 74 (2006), 32–8 (33).

Eyres, Harry, 'The daily poem', *Daily Express*, 21 June 2000, 32.

——, 'The final stanza', *Guardian*, 5 February 2001, *http://www.guardian.co.uk/media/2001/feb/05/mondaymediasection.dailyexpress* (accessed 17 January 2012).

Glick, Nada Beth and Sarah L. Prakken (eds), *The Bowker Annual of Library and Book Trade Information* (22nd edn; New York: Bowker, 1977), p. 465.

Gramich, Katie, 'Editorial: poetry for supper (breakfast, dinner and tea)', *Books in Wales/Llais Llyfrau*, 96/2 (1996), 3.

——, 'Mountains and mirrors', *Planet*, 128 (1998), 70–5 (75).

——, 'Welsh greats of the century no. 1: poets', *New Welsh Review*, 40 (1998), 9–12 (11).

——, *Twentieth-century Women's Writing in Wales: Land, Gender, Belonging* (Cardiff: University of Wales Press, 2007), pp. 159, 225, 231.

Holt, Constance Wall, *Welsh Women: An Annotated Bibliography of Women in Wales and Women of Welsh Descent in America* (Metuchen, NJ: Scarecrow, 1993), pp. 53, 85, 474, 486, 501, 510, 514–17, 771.

Hooker, Jeremy, *The Presence of the Past: Essays on Modern British and American Poetry* (Bridgend: Poetry Wales Press, 1987), pp. 168, 169–71.

——, 'Seeing place', in C. C. Barfoot (ed.), *In Black and Gold: Contiguous Traditions in Post-war British and Irish Poetry* (Amsterdam: Rodopi, 1994), pp. 27–44 (p. 35).

——, 'Ceridwen's daughters: Welsh women poets and the uses of tradition', *Welsh Writing in English: A Yearbook of Critical Essays*, 1 (1995), 128–44 (133, 134, 136–7, 142, 144).

——, *Imagining Wales: A View of Modern Welsh Writing in English* (Cardiff: University of Wales Press, 2001), pp. 25, 203.

——, 'Poets, language and land: reflections on English-language Welsh poetry since the Second World War', *Welsh Writing in English: A Yearbook of Critical Essays*, 8 (2003), 141–56 (150).

Houston, Douglas, 'Welsh poetry', in Neil Roberts (ed.), *A Companion to Twentieth-century Poetry* (Oxford: Blackwell, 2003), pp. 329–42 (p. 331).

James, Siân, 'Feminist poets', *Planet*, 138 (1999/2000), 91–2.

Jarvis, Matthew, *Welsh Environments in Contemporary Poetry* (Cardiff: University of Wales Press, 2008), pp. 6, 16, 22, 31, 32, 82, 90, 94, 141, 142, 187–8.

——, 'A poetry of diversification: new voices of the 1970s', *Poetry Wales*, 44/3 (2008/9), 43–8 (44–5, 47).

——, 'Welsh environments: a dialogue', with John Kinsella, *Poetry Wales*, 45/2 (2009), 39–44 (39, 40, 42, 43).

——, 'Repositioning Wales: poetry after the Second Flowering', in Daniel G. Williams (ed.), *Slanderous Tongues: Essays on Welsh Poetry in English 1970–2005* (Bridgend: Seren, 2010), pp. 21–59 (pp. 33–7).

Jenkins, Randal, 'The new Anglo-Welsh poets', *Poetry Wales*, 8/2 (1972), 5–16 (8–9).

Jones, Andrew, *Every Pilgrim's Guide to Celtic Britain and Ireland* (Norwich: Canterbury Press, 2002), p. 27.

Jones, Glyn and John Rowlands, *Profiles: A Visitors' Guide to Writing in Twentieth Century Wales* (Llandysul: Gomer, 1980), p. 360.

Jones, Sally Roberts, *Women Writers in Wales in the English Language: A Preliminary List, with Notes and Select Bibliographies* (N.p.: n.p., n.d.), unpaginated.

——, untitled contribution, in Sheenagh Pugh, Gloria Evans Davies, Christine Evans, Sally Roberts Jones and Val Warner, 'Symposium: is there a women's poetry?', *Poetry Wales*, 23/1 ([1987]), 51–2 (52).

Le Nevez, Catherine, Mike Parker and Paul Whitfield, *The Rough Guide to Wales* (6th edn; London: Rough Guides, 2009), p. 508.

Lewis, Peter Elfed, '*Ten Anglo-Welsh Poets* edited by Sam Adams', *Anglo-Welsh Review*, 53 (1974), 159–65 (165).

Lloyd, David T., 'Interview with Gillian Clarke', in David T. Lloyd (ed.), *The Urgency of Identity: Contemporary English-language Poetry from Wales* (Evanston, Ill.: TriQuarterly Books/Northwestern University Press, 1994), pp. 25–31 (p. 29); repr. in David T. Lloyd (ed.), *Writing on the Edge: Interviews with Writers and Editors of Wales* (Amsterdam: Rodopi, 1997), pp. 141–7.

——, 'Interview with Jeremy Hooker', in David T. Lloyd (ed.), *The Urgency of Identity: Contemporary English-language Poetry from Wales* (Evanston, Ill.: TriQuarterly Books/Northwestern University Press, 1994), pp. 68–77 (p. 72); repr. as 'Interview with Jeremy Hooker (I)', in David T. Lloyd (ed.), *Writing on the Edge: Interviews with Writers and Editors of Wales* (Amsterdam: Rodopi, 1997), pp. 41–50.

Mathias, Glyn, 'The Roland Mathias Prize', *Brycheiniog*, 37 (2005), 19–22 (20).

Mathias, Roland, 'Literature in English', in Meic Stephens (ed.), *The Arts in Wales 1950–75* (Cardiff: Welsh Arts Council, 1979), pp. 207–38 (p. 237).

——, 'Poets of Breconshire', *Brycheiniog*, 19 (1980/1), pp. 27–49 (pp. 47–8).

——, *Anglo-Welsh Literature: An Illustrated History* (Bridgend: Poetry Wales Press, 1987), pp. 115, 116.

Peach, Linden, 'The environment in twentieth-century Welsh writing in English', in Patrick D. Murphy (ed.), *Literature of Nature: An International Sourcebook* (Chicago: Fitzroy Dearborn, 1998), pp. 191–9 (pp. 196, 197).

Reynolds, S. Rhian, 'English-language poetry from Wales', in Ray Keenoy, S. Rhian Reynolds and Sioned Puw Rolands, *The Babel Guide to Welsh Fiction* (Oxford: Boulevard, 2009), pp. 149–55 (p. 154).

Rhydderch, Francesca, '(Re)mapping "Anglo-Welsh" poetry: a century of verse', *Poetry Wales*, 33/2 (1997), 12–17 (12, 14).

Saunders, Benjamin David, 'Bidgood, Ruth', in Mark Willhardt and Alan Michael Parker (eds), *Who's Who in Twentieth-century World Poetry* (London: Routledge, 2000), p. 35.

Shortt, Rupert, *Rowan's Rule: The Biography of the Archbishop* (London: Hodder & Stoughton, 2008), pp. 225, 449.

[Simpson, Mercer], 'Anglo-Welsh literature', in Marion Wynne-Davies (ed.), *English Literature A–Z* (N.p.: Bloomsbury, 1994), unpaginated.

Smith, Ken [Kenneth R.], 'Women, criticism and the Anglo-Welsh', *Poetry Wales*, 20/3 (1985), 60–6 (64).

——, 'The portrait poem: reproduction of mothering', *Poetry Wales*, 24/1 (1988), 48–54 (50, 51).

——, 'A vision of the future?', *Poetry Wales*, 24/3 (1989), 46–52 (48).

Stephens, Meic, *Literature in Twentieth-century Wales: A Select Bibliography* (London: British Council, 1995), p. 43.

——, 'Ruth Bidgood', in Meic Stephens (ed.), *Poetry 1900–2000: One Hundred Poets from Wales*, Library of Wales, vol. X (Cardigan: Parthian, 2007), p. 275.

Stevens, Catrin, '"The funeral made the attraction": the social and economic functions of funerals in nineteenth-century Wales', in Katie Gramich and Andrew Hiscock (eds), *Dangerous Diversity: The*

Changing Faces of Wales; Essays in Honour of Tudor Bevan (Cardiff: University of Wales Press, 1998), pp. 83–104 (p. 95).

Thomas, M. Wynn, 'Prints of Wales: contemporary Welsh poetry in English', in Hans-Werner Ludwig and Lothar Fietz (eds), *Poetry in the British Isles: Non-metropolitan Perspectives* (Cardiff: University of Wales Press, 1995), pp. 97–114 (p. 104).

——, 'Staying to mind things: Gillian Clarke's early poetry', in Menna Elfyn (ed.), *Trying the Line: A Volume of Tribute to Gillian Clarke* (Llandysul: Gomer, 1997), pp. 44–68 (p. 46).

——, 'R. S. Thomas and modern Welsh poetry', in Neil Corcoran (ed.), *The Cambridge Companion to Twentieth-century English Poetry* (Cambridge: Cambridge University Press, 2007), pp. 159–72 (p. 171).

Tunnicliffe, Stephen, *Poetry Experience: Teaching and Writing Poetry in Secondary Schools* (London: Methuen, 1984), pp. 45–6, 210, 262, 263, 283.

Ward, John Powell, 'Editorial', in Cary Archard (ed.), *Poetry Wales 25 Years* (Bridgend: Seren, 1990), pp. 129–33 (p. 131); partial repr. of 'Editorial', *Poetry Wales*, 13/1 (1977), 3–11.

Welsh Arts Council/Cyngor Celfyddydau Cymru, *Annual Report for the Year Ending 31 March 1976/Adroddiad Blynyddol am y Flwyddyn Hyd at 31 Mawrth 1976* (N.p.: n.p., n.d.), unpaginated.

Williams, Euriona Lucretia, 'Lost in the shadows: Welsh women poets writing in English, c.1840–1970' (unpublished Ph.D. thesis, University of Wales, Bangor, 2005), 292, 304–5, 400.

Reviews and review articles

The Given Time

Hooker, Jeremy, '*The Given Time* by Ruth Bidgood', *Anglo-Welsh Review*, 49 (1973), 220–2.

Shayer, David, 'Ruth Bidgood: *The Given Time*; Florence Bull: *St. David's Day*', *Poetry Wales*, 8/2 (1972), 82–6 (84–6).

Tripp, John, 'Round the poets', *Planet*, 16 (1973), 61–72 (69).

Not Without Homage

Curtis, Tony, '*Not Without Homage* by Ruth Bidgood; *Poetry Dimension Annual 3* edited by Dannie Abse', *Anglo-Welsh Review*, 56 (1976), 175–8 (175–6).

Shayer, David, 'Ruth Bidgood: *Not Without Homage*', *Poetry Wales*, 11/2 (1975), 154–7.

The Print of Miracle

Allchin, A. M., 'The return of the angels', *New Fire*, V/37 (1978), 202–8.

Hooker, Jeremy, 'Inside knowledge', *PN Review*, 9 (1979), 57–8.

Morgan, Gerald, '*The Sundial* by Gillian Clarke; *The Print of Miracle* by Ruth Bidgood', *Anglo-Welsh Review*, 63 (1978), 136–8 (137–8).

Werson, Gerard, 'Michael Schmidt: *A Change of Affairs*; Gillian Clarke: *The Sundial*; Ruth Bidgood: *The Print of Miracle*', *Poetry Wales*, 14/3 (1978/9), 82–5 (82, 84–5).

Lighting Candles: New and Selected Poems

Annwn, David, '*Lighting Candles, New and Selected Poems* by Ruth Bidgood', *Anglo-Welsh Review*, 74 (1983), 96–101.

Bird, Michael, 'Litter & detail', *PN Review*, 35 (1983), 79–80 (80).

Hill, Greg, '*Letter from a Far Country*, Gillian Clarke; *Lighting Candles*, Ruth Bidgood', *Book News/Llais Llyfrau* (spring 1983), 12–13.

Lloyd, Jo, 'Ruth Bidgood: *Lighting Candles, New and Selected Poems*', *Poetry Wales*, 18/4 (1983), 85–7.

Morgan, Alison M., '*Lighting Candles* by Ruth Bidgood', *Rural Wales: The Journal of CPRW*, 47 (1983), 25.

Kindred

Davies, Diane, 'Ruth Bidgood: *Kindred*', *Poetry Wales*, 22/3 (1987), 106–9.

Dixon, Peter, 'Ruth Bidgood, *Kindred*; David Lockwood, *Winter Wheat*', *Brycheiniog*, 22 (1986/7), 121–4 (121–3).

Jones [Gramich], Katie, 'Cabaret and kin', *Planet*, 65 (1987), 101–3 (102–3).

Llewellyn Williams, Hilary, 'With the *Offal Eaters*, Douglas Houston; *Beware Falling Tortoises*, Sheenagh Pugh; *Kindred*, Ruth Bidgood', *Book News from Wales/Llais Llyfrau* (summer 1987), 12–13 (13).

Morton, Angela, '*Kindred*, by Ruth Bidgood', *Window on Wales*, 1/3 (?1988), 98–9.

Simpson, Mercer, '*Kindred*, by Ruth Bidgood', *Anglo-Welsh Review*, 85 (1987), 116–19.

Williams, Merryn, 'Welsh voices', *Prospice*, 22 (1987), 153–5 (153–4).

Selected Poems

Allchin, A. M., 'Poet of the haunted present', *Planet*, 98 (1993), 101–2.

——, 'Poet rising', *Church Times*, 19 February 1993, 13.

Anon., 'Selected Poems', *The Brecon & Radnor Express and Powys County Times*, 17 December 1992, 9.

Dale-Jones, Don, '*Selected Poems*, Ruth Bidgood', *New Welsh Review*, 21 (1993), 112–13.

Griffiths, Dai, '*Selected Poems*: Ruth Bidgood', *BWA: Bulletin of the Welsh Academy*, 31 (1993), unpaginated.

Houston, Douglas, 'Taken for Pearls, Tony Curtis; Selected Poems, Ruth Bidgood', Books in Wales/Llais Llyfrau (winter 1993), 14–15 (15).

Mason, John, 'Ruth Bidgood, Selected Poems', Transactions of the Radnorshire Society, 63 (1993), 81–3.

Monaghan, Patricia, 'Selected Poems', Booklist, 15 October 1993, http://www.booklistonline.com/Selected-Poems-Ruth-Bidgood/pid=125684 (accessed 28 July 2011).

Owen, Gareth, 'Selected Poems: Ruth Bidgood', BWA: Bulletin of the Welsh Academy, 29 (1993), 10.

Silver, Keith, 'Voices in the trees', PN Review, 94 (1993), 60–2 (61).

Williams, Merryn, 'Ruth Bidgood: Selected Poems', Poetry Wales, 28/2 (1992), 62–3.

The Fluent Moment

Allchin, A. M., 'Poet of the real place', Church Times, 15 November 1996, 16.

Blundell, Colin, 'Ruth Bidgood: The Fluent Moment', New Hope International Review, 19/4 (1997), 19.

Dale-Jones, Don, 'Beyond the blinkered metropolis', New Welsh Review, 37 (1997), 56–7.

Groves, Paul, 'The haunted brink', Poetry Review, 87/4 (1997/8), 65–8 (67).

Morton, Angela, 'The Fluent Moment, Ruth Bidgood; Genesis, John Powell Ward', Books in Wales/Llais Llyfrau, 96/4 (1996), 14–15.

Oxley, William, 'Personal feeling and philosophical consideration', Acumen, 28 (1997), 108–10 (109).

Sylge, Caroline, 'Home and all the rest of it', PN Review, 115 (1997), 70–2 (72).

Wainwright, Eddie, 'Parts and wholes', Envoi, 117 (1997), 155–60 (155–6).

Williams, Merryn, 'Ruth Bidgood, The Fluent Moment', Poetry Wales, 32/3 (1997), 67–8.

Singing to Wolves

Allchin, A. M., 'In pursuit of the real', Planet, 145 (2001), 108–9.

Anon., 'Poet sings to wolves', Brecon & Radnor Express and Powys County Times, 1 June 2000, 9.

Beagan, Glenda, 'Ruth Bidgood, Singing to Wolves', Poetry Wales, 36/3 (2001), 69–70.

Fulwood, Neil, 'Singing to Wolves. Poems by Ruth Bidgood', Poetry Monthly, 52 (2000), 4–5.

Gruffydd, Peter, 'Ordinary Time, Joseph P. Clancy; A Gwynedd Symphony, Tony Conran; Singing to Wolves, Ruth Bidgood; Simmer Dim, William Greenway', New Welsh Review, 50 (2000), 82–3 (83).

Stephens, Meic, Untitled, Western Mail Magazine (section 4), 6 January 2001, 14.

New & Selected Poems

Allchin, A. M. [Donald], 'New and Selected Poems: Ruth Bidgood', Fairacres Chronicle, 38/1 (2005), 50–2.

——, 'Ruth Bidgood: New and Selected Poems', David Jones Journal, 6/1 & 2 (2007), 260–1.

Cluysenaar, Anne, 'How different is real from ordinary', Planet, 173 (2005), 97–9.

Jarvis, Matthew, 'New & Selected Poems, Ruth Bidgood', New Welsh Review, 67 (2005), 113–14.

Keogan, Kate, 'New and Selected Poems, Ruth Bidgood', Poetry Wales, 40/4 (2005), 68–9.

Roberts, Dewi, 'New and Selected Poems, Ruth Bidgood', gwales.com, http://www.gwales.com/bibliographic/?isbn=9781854113771 (accessed 17 January 2012).

Stephens, Meic, 'Books', Cambria, 7/3 (2005), 69.

Symbols of Plenty: Selected Longer Poems

Gill, Caroline, 'Symbols of Plenty, Ruth Bidgood', Roundyhouse, 21 ([?2007]), 35.

Hill, Greg, 'Of saints, angels and wolves', Planet, 183 (2007), 105–6.

Jarvis, Matthew, 'Symbols of Plenty, Ruth Bidgood; A Moment in the Field, Margaret Lloyd; Missed Chances, Sam Adams; Early Departures, Late Arrivals, Mercer Simpson', New Welsh Review, 77 (2007), 69–71 (69–70).

Hearing Voices

Finch, Peter, 'The insider', Western Mail, 27 December 2008, http://docs.newsbank.com/openurl?ctx_ver=z39.88-2004&rft_id=info:sid/iw.newsbank.com:WLSNB:CWMC&rft_val_format=info:ofi/fmt:kev:mtx:ctx&rft_dat=1255C908E0CC9F28&svc_dat=InfoWeb:aggdocs&req_dat=F40D1930047444E2B32A215A4E7AC431 (accessed 17 January 2012).

Owen, Fiona, 'Ruth Bidgood, Time Being and Hearing Voices; John Powell Ward, Variations on Four Places and The Last Green Year', Poetry Wales, 45/2 (2009), 61–4 (62).

Stephens, Meic, 'Nothing invented or added', Planet, 194 (2009), 129–30.

Time Being

Crowther, Claire, 'Ruth Bidgood, Time Being', Times Literary Supplement, 21 and 28 August 2009, 25.

Finch, Peter, 'The insider', WalesOnline.co.uk, Western Mail, 25 April 2009, http://www.walesonline.co.uk/showbiz-and-lifestyle/books-in-wales/2009/04/25/the-insider-peter-finch-91466-23458533/ (accessed 17 January 2012).

King, Henry, 'Habitations and names', *PN Review*, 194 (2010), 74–6 (75).

Milne, W. S., 'Omnium gatherum of Welsh books', *Agenda*, 44/2–3 (2009), 133–49 (133, 141, 142).

Owen, Fiona, 'Ruth Bidgood, *Time Being* and *Hearing Voices*; John Powell Ward, *Variations on Four Places* and *The Last Green Year*', *Poetry Wales*, 45/2 (2009), 61–4 (61–2).

Poole, Richard, 'Urban and rural', *Planet*, 199 (2010), 143–4.

Index

Aaron, Jane 83
Aberafan 2, 113, fig. 2
Aberconwy House (Conwy) 2, 139
Aberdare 2, 139
Abergwesyn 1, 2, 5, 7, 9, 21, 24, 27, 29,
  32, 33, 34, 36, 40–1, 44, 56, 61, 62,
  71, 80, 87, 99, 102–3, 105, 111, 119,
  121, 143, 145, 152, fig. 6, fig. 7;
  see also arrival in Abergwesyn
  (under Bidgood, Ruth); Jones, Dai
  (of Abergwesyn Post Office);
  Llanddewi Abergwesyn; Powell,
  John (of Abergwesyn); Tŷhaearn
  (under Bidgood, Ruth)
Abhishiktananda (Henri Le Saux)
  85
Abrams, M. H. 158
Adams, Sam 23
afforestation 7–8, 24–6, 42–3, 97, 140,
  154
Afon Camddwr see Camddwr
Afon Claerddu 61
Afon Conwy see Conwy
Afon Doethie Fach 144
Afon Doethie Fawr 144
Afon Gwesyn see Gwesyn
Afon Honddu 103
Afon Irfon see Irfon
Afon Llynfi 59–60
Afon Pysgotwr Fawr 144
Afon Tywi 64, 144
agriculture see farms and
  farming/agriculture
Alexandria 3
Allchin, A. M. ('Donald') 42, 52–3, 69,
  78–9, 86, 90, 93, 152
Alltyrhebog/Allt yr Hebog (Irfon
  Valley) 62, 149
angels 63–4, 65–7, 77
Anglesey see Ynys Môn

Anglo-Welsh Review, The 6, 15, 22, 45,
  69, 131, 140, 146
Annwn, David 69
anthropomorphism 98–100
anti-Arcadianism 31–2
anti-pastoral 28
antiquarianism 27, 55
Aran Islands 35
Arthur, King 57–8, 61
Attwater, Donald 54
autobiography 103, 111–16, 121–2, 124

Baez, Joan 76
bardd gwlad 34, 36, 38, 40, 41, 144
Bardsey Island see Ynys Enlli
Baring-Gould, Sabine 2, 50
BBC Radio Wales 45
Berger, Pamela 51
Beulah 121, 122
Bidgood, David Edgar 4, 5, 122, 140,
  fig. 5
Bidgood, Ruth
  arrival in Abergwesyn ix, 1, 5
  birth 2, 113
  childhood and youth 2–3, 4–5, 77,
    112–14, 122, fig. 1, fig. 2
  children 4, 145, fig. 4
  divorce 5
  feminism 13, 136
  grandchildren 88
  grandmother (maternal) 112
  grandparents (paternal) 2, 139
  husband see Bidgood, David
    Edgar
  local historian ix, 1, 4, 5, 8–9, 25,
    30, 116–17, 143–4; see also
    Parishes of the Buzzard (under
    Bidgood, Ruth: works)
  marriage 4
  move to Beulah 121

parents 2, 4, 139–40, fig. 1
poetic style 12, 15–19, 22, 23, 46,
    47, 69, 96–7, 100, 125, 127
prizes, nominations and honours
    24, 68–9, 96, 142–3, 151, fig. 8
school-days poetry 1, 140
schooling 2–3
Tŷhaearn 5, 81, 99, fig. 6, fig. 7
university 3
variations in volume of poetic
    output 68, 95–6
wartime service 3–4, 115, fig. 3
Welsh language 2
women's poetry 13, 135
works: *Above the Forests* 95, 153;
    Fluent Moment, The 28, 61, 63,
    68, 69–70, 76–7, 86, 93–4, 95,
    129; *Given Time, The* 1, 15–21,
    22–34, 35, 39, 42, 44, 55, 56, 57,
    64–5, 70, 75, 76, 80, 102, 111,
    114, 129, 142, 143, 151; *Hearing
    Voices* 95, 103–4, 116–20, 155;
    'Hymn to Sant Ffraid' 13,
    45–56, 57, 62, 66–7, 68, 78–9,
    87–8, 103, 109, 135–8, 146, 147,
    148, 150; *Kindred* 68, 69, 70–5,
    76, 77, 78, 83–4, 95, 129, 152;
    *Lighting Candles: New and
    Selected Poems* 68, 69, 74–5,
    79–83, 85, 89, 90, 93, 95; *New
    & Selected Poems* 95, 96, 97,
    101–2, 103, 111, 113, 129; *Not
    Without Homage* 23–4, 34–5,
    36–8, 39–40, 57–8, 78, 116, 143,
    151; *Parishes of the Buzzard* 25,
    40, 62, 64, 143–4, 145, 149, 152,
    154; *Print of Miracle, The* 24,
    34, 35, 36, 39, 40–3, 58–61,
    61–2, 63–4, 79, 80, 82, 90, 129,
    151; *Selected Poems* 65, 68, 69,
    70, 73, 76, 78–9, 84, 85–93, 102,
    109, 129, 150, 152; *Singing to
    Wolves* 65, 74, 95, 96, 97–101,
    102, 103, 104–11, 112–3, 126,
    154; *Symbols of Plenty: Selected
    Longer Poems* 45, 46–56, 57,
    65–7, 68, 77, 95, 103, 111,
    113–16, 124, 146, 147, 148;
    Time Being 95–6, 103, 120,
    121–9, 157

Black Mountains 104
Blaendulais *see* Seven
    Sisters/Blaendulais
Blaen-Glasffrwd (Cardiganshire) 30,
    144
Blaennant/Blaen-y-Nant (Gwesyn
    Valley) 40, 41, 101, 145, 154
Boase, Charles 146
Bohata, Kirsti 8, 43–4, 145
Book of Lismore 50, 54, 147
Boyle, Claire 111
Bray, Dorothy 146
Breconshire 1, 5, 11, 24, 25, 28, 58, 72,
    104, 132, 143, 145, 149
Bride 46, 48–9, 51, 55, 147, 148, 149
Brigid (goddess) 46, 47–9, 51–3, 54, 56,
    67, 135–7, 146, 148
Brychan 107–8
Bryn Mawr (Cnyffiad Valley) 7, 140
Bryndolau (Gwesyn Valley) 152
Buell, Lawrence 42, 98, 127, 128, 157
Bugeilyn (Montgomeryshire) 101, 102
Builth/Buellt 57
Builth Wells 1
Burton, Philip 2–3, 4, 140
Burton, Richard (Richard Jenkins) 2–3

Cafall 57–8, 149
Camarch
    houses *see* Cluniau-fawr
        (Camarch Valley); Coedtrefan
        (Camarch Valley)
    valley 25, 26, 37, 87–90, 99–101,
        102, 121, 126–7, 128, 152, 157,
        fig. 11, fig. 14
Cambrian Mountains 101, 104
Cambridge 63
Camddwr
    battle 91, 92, 153
    places *see* Rhyd-y-meirch
        (Camddwr Valley); Soar y
        Mynydd (Camddwr Valley)
    river 32, 90–1, 144
    valley 91–2
canu bro 34, 36, 144
Cardiff 113
Cardiganshire 24, 30–2, 33, 34, 70,
    132
Carmarthenshire 24, 145
Carmichael, Alexander 48, 149

Carmina Gadelica (Alexander Carmichael) 48–9, 149
Carn Cafall/Carn Gafallt (near Rhayader) 57–8, 149
Carreg Clochdy (Tywi Valley) 64, 75, 150
Celtic Christianity 52
Chambers's Encyclopædia 4
Christ 52, 63, 80, 148, 153
    Christ of the Trades 107, 108–9, 156
Christianization 47, 51–3, 136, 137
Christopher Davies, Swansea 15, 20, 22
Cinnamon Press 95
Clarke, Gillian 107
climate change 126
Clodock 107–8, 155
Cluniau-fawr (Camarch Valley) 25, 143, fig. 11
Clynnog Fawr 109, 110
Cnyffiad
    landscape features *see* Coed Trallwm (Cnyffiad Valley); Bryn Mawr (Cnyffiad Valley)
    valley 7, fig. 9
Cobbing, Bob 119
Coed Trallwm (Cnyffiad Valley) 7–8, 141, fig. 9
Coedtrefan (Camarch Valley) 88, 89, 152
community 5, 19, 32–3, 34, 36, 37–41, 57, 70, 94, 102, 128
confessionalism 77, 116, 121–2
conifers/coniferization/coniferous plantation 7–8, 24–6, 41, 42–3, 97–8, 128, 140, 143, 154
Conwy
    river 148
    town 2, 139
    see also Aberconwy House (Conwy)
Cornwall 3
Coulsdon 4, 10, 144
Country Life 6, 8, 131, 140
Country Quest 6, 132, 140
Countryman, The 6, 131, 140
Coupe, Laurence 61, 149
Culent Valley 156
Cupitt, Don 57, 58, 60, 149

Curtis, Tony 26
Cwm Pennant (Montgomeryshire) 103, 155
Cwmyoy/Cwm-iou 106, 155

Dale-Jones, Don 69
Daren/Darren (Breconshire) 37, 38, 145
Darran, John 46
Darwin, Charles 31
David, Tudor 6, 14
Davies, Idris 15
Davies, John 108
death omens 87–8, 101–2, 154
dechreunos 89–90
depopulation 40–1, 43–4, 88
Devon 3
Digiff (Irfon Valley) 71–2, 151, fig. 12
Donne, John 3
Doors, The 27, 76
Dowsing, William 63–4, 150
droving 40, 145
Dylan, Bob 76

ekphrastic poetry 76–7, 108–9
Elan Valley 5
Eliade, Mircea 10, 63, 64–5
Entwistle, Alice 153
environmental crisis 100, 126
environmental disaster 76
environmentalism/green movement 42, 98–100, 125–6, 128
epic 32, 129–30, 158
Escley Brook 103
Eve (Sabine Baring-Gould) 2, 139
Ewias (commote) 107, 109, 155–6
Eyton, Frances 118

farms and farming/agriculture 22, 26, 27, 30, 33, 36–8, 71, 72, 88, 91, 93, 137, 152, 153
feminism *see* feminism (*under* Bidgood, Ruth)
Fisher, John 50
Forestry Commission 8, 25, 44, 140
found poetry 78, 103–4, 116–20

Garlick, Raymond 15, 20
Garrard, Greg 31, 100, 104, 110, 126, 156

Garrett, Hilda *see* Jones, Hilda (Hilda Garrett)
Gelynos Congregational Chapel (near Llanwrtyd Wells) 102, 155
geological time 100–1
Gifford, Terry 11, 37, 145
Giraldus Cambrensis 58–60, 104, 155
Glangwesyn (Gwesyn Valley) 40, 152
Gramich, Katie (Katie Jones) 69
Graves, Robert 51
Gregson, Ian 107
Griffiths, Dai 70–1, 74, 75, 76, 78, 152
Groves, Paul 70
Gruffudd ap Rhys ap Tewdwr 58–60
Guest, Charlotte 57
Gusdorf, Georges 111
Gwasg Boase 45, 135, 146
Gwesyn
    high land *see* Rhiw Garreg-lwyd (Gwesyn Valley)
    houses *see* Blaennant/Blaen-y-Nant (Gwesyn Valley); Bryndolau (Gwesyn Valley); Glangwesyn (Gwesyn Valley)
    river 81, 99, 152
    valley 40–1, 81, 127, 128

Hanmer collection (Shropshire Archives) 116, 117, 156–7
Harris, Howell 119, 157
Hendrix, Jimi 27, 76
Henken, Elissa R. 146–7, 149
Hennant/Hen-nant (Irfon Valley) 29, 76, 114, 143
Herefordshire 35, 104, 156
Hill, Gary 76–7
Hooker, Jeremy 22, 23, 29, 34, 142
houses 2, 5, 8–10, 12, 24–6, 27, 29, 30, 32, 33, 37, 39, 40–1, 42, 43, 63, 71, 72, 79–80, 86, 88, 89–90, 92, 101, 106, 113–14, 122, 131, 132, fig. 6, fig. 7, fig. 10, fig. 11, fig. 12; *see also entries for specific houses e.g.* Digiff (Irfon Valley)
Houston, Douglas 69

incomers to mid-Wales 37–9, 41, 129
Iorwerth Fynglwyd 49–50
Ireland 35, 47
    folk customs 55, 56, 148

mythology 47, 48, 50–1, 52, 56, 87, 135, 137
Irfon
    houses *see* Alltyrhebog/Allt yr Hebog (Irfon Valley); Digiff (Irfon Valley); Hennant/Hen-nant (Irfon Valley)
    river 62
    valley 29, 62, 71–2, 121, 126, 128, 152, fig. 12
Isle of Wight festival 76

Jenkins, Mike 135, 158
John, Margaret 46
Jones, Dai (of Abergwesyn Post Office) 143–4
Jones, David 47, 135–6, 146
Jones, G. Hartwell 64
Jones, Glyn 122–4
Jones, Hilda (Hilda Garrett) 2, 139, fig. 1
Jones, Katie *see* Gramich, Katie (Katie Jones)
Jones, William Herbert 2, 139, 139–40, fig. 1

Kilvert, Francis 65, 150

Largs 115
Le Saux, Henri *see* Abhishiktananda (Henri Le Saux)
Leland, John 61
Lethbridge, T. C. 148
Lewis, Peter Elfed 23
light/dark dialogue 79–90, 93–4
Linnard, William 7–8, 24, 140
Llanafan Fawr 87
Llanddewi Abergwesyn 32, 64
Llanddewi Brefi 32, 144
Llanddewi Hall (Radnorshire) *see* Radnorshire
Llandrindod 4
Llansantffraed (Breconshire) 55, 148
Llanthony Priory (Vale of Ewyas) 104–5, 110
Llewellyn Williams, Hilary 69
Llŷn Peninsula see Pen Llŷn
Llyn Safaddan/Llyn Syfaddan 58–60
Lochard, Elizabeth 117–18, 119

London 4, 6, 8, 14, 144, 145
London Welshman 6, 12, 15, 19, 132, 140
Lukács, Georg 129, 158

Mabinogion, The 57
Machynlleth 101
Mackenzie, Donald A. 48, 55
Macleod, Fiona (William Sharp) 48
Manifold 6, 132, 140
Martian poetry 96, 154
Mary, Mother of Christ 52
Mathias, Glyn 96
Mathias, Roland 15
    Roland Mathias Prize 96, 153–4,
        fig. 8
Mayan civilization 76, 84
McLean, G. R. D. 49, 147, 149
memory/memories 2, 22, 24, 26, 40,
    41–3, 44, 57–8, 73, 80, 87, 111,
    113–16, 122, 124, 125
Michaelchurch Escley 107, 108–9, 156
mines and mining/quarries 2, 71, 81,
    82–4, 86, 129, 152
Ministry of Defence 44
Mirabilia Britanniae 57, 149
Mitchell, Joni 27, 76
Monmouthshire 104, 106
Moretti, Franco 130, 158
Morgan, Kenneth O. 143
Morgan, Robert C. 77
myth/mythology 47–8, 49, 51–2, 53,
    55, 56, 57–62, 76, 124–5, 149
mythical space 28

Nant yr Ych (Tywi Valley) 144
nature poetry 125–9
Nicholas, W. Rhys 34, 36, 40, 41
non-human/feminine equation 99,
    154
nostalgia 9

Oliver, R. C. B. 116–17
ordinary lives 70–5
Ó Súilleabháin, Seán 55
Owen, Gareth 70

pastoral 11, 31, 37, 44, 145
patriarchy 13–14
Pen Llŷn 109–11
Pepper, David 31

Planet 23, 69, 78
Plumwood, Val 98–100
Poetry Book Society 96
Poetry Wales 6, 13, 14–15, 19, 21, 22,
    45, 47, 69, 132, 135, 140, 152, 158
poverty/the poor 50, 71, 72, 129
Powell, John (of Abergwesyn) 119,
    157
praise poetry 52, 53, 56, 135, 136, 148
pre-Christian Wales 38
Pugh, Sheenagh 69
Pysgotwr (Cardiganshire) 32, 144

Radnorshire 1, 4–5, 11, 24, 28, 132
    Llanddewi Hall 8–10, 11, 19, 21,
        26, 63, 75, 129, 131, 141, fig. 10
    Radnorshire Society 117
    Transactions of the Radnorshire
        Society 8
Rees, Alwyn 87, 88
Rees, Brinley 87, 88
Rees, D. C. 90–1, 153
Rees, Olwen 46
Rees-Jones, Deryn 13
reinhabitation 128, 157
restoration 26, 29, 39, 56, 74–5, 94
Rhayader 57, 149, fig. 4
Rhiw Garreg-lwyd (Gwesyn Valley)
    81, 152, fig. 13
Rhyd-y-meirch (Camddwr Valley) 78,
    86, 90–1, 92, 109, 129, 153
Ricoeur, Paul 61
River Monnow 103
Roland Mathias Prize *see* Mathias,
    Roland
Roman empire 76, 93–4
Ross, Anne 47, 51
Rubens, Bernice 143
ruins 5, 7, 21, 24, 26, 28–9, 35, 41, 42,
    43, 71, 80, 88, 92, 105, 128, fig. 11,
    fig. 12

sacred space 10, 21, 33, 62–3, 64–5
Saint Brigid/Sant Ffraid 47, 48, 49–50,
    51, 52–6, 57, 66–7, 135–8, 147, 148,
    149
    'Hymn to Sant Ffraid' *see* 'Hymn
        to Sant Ffraid' (*under*
        Bidgood, Ruth: Works)
Saint Clydog 107–8, 156

St Hugh's College, Oxford 3
Sampson, Fiona 154
Sant Ffraid *see* Saint Brigid/Sant
    Ffraid
Scintilla 113, 155
Scotland 3, 115
    folk customs 55, 56, 148
    mythology 48–9, 51, 56, 147
Second Flowering 14–15, 17, 19–21,
    23, 97, 142
'Second Flowering, The' (Meic
    Stephens) 19–21
Seren 68, 150
Seven Sisters/Blaendulais 2, 83,
    113–14, 139, fig. 1
sexism 137
Sharp, William *see* Macleod, Fiona
    (William Sharp)
Shayer, David 22–3, 24
Shelley, Percy Bysshe 2
Silver, Keith 73
Smith, Kenneth R. 13, 45–6, 47, 53, 56,
    135–8, 146
Soar y Mynydd (Camddwr Valley) 32,
    144
Somerset 139
Soper, Kate 99, 118, 154
Stephens, Meic 14–15, 19–21
Stewart, Pamela J. 41
Stokes, Whitley 50, 147
stone/stones 18, 21, 26, 27, 28–9, 38,
    40, 42–3, 52, 57–8, 61, 64, 71, 79,
    80, 114, 126, 127, 129, 134, 142
    gravestones 106
    see also ruins
Strata Florida 30
Strathern, Andrew 41
suburbia 4, 10–11, 34, 132, 144
Suffolk 63
Surrey 4, 5
Sylge, Caroline 70

Tenby 112
Thomas, Dylan 15
Thomas, Edward 5–6, 28
Thomas, Gwyn 143

Thomas, R. S. 143
Thurston, Herbert 54
Toohey, Peter 130
Transactions of the Radnorshire Society
    see Radnorshire
Tregarneth, Anita 50, 53
Tripp, John 15–17, 19, 20, 23, 24, 31,
    33, 44
Troynt/Twrch Trwyth 57, 58
Tuan, Yi-Fu 28, 80–1, 83, 84, 85, 94

UK landscape policy 7, 8, 24–5, 43–4,
    145

Vaughan, Henry 55, 148

Wack, Amy 68, 150
Wainwright, Eddie 70
Wales Book of the Year 68–9
Walford Davies, Jason 1, 3, 26–7,
    128
Water Board 44
watershed aesthetics (Lawrence
    Buell) 42
weather 17, 30, 32, 81–2, 93, 110, 123,
    155
Webb, Harri 20
Welsh Academy 69, 151
    *BWA: Bulletin of the Welsh
        Academy* 70
Welsh Arts Council 24, 45, 142–3
Welsh language 2, 30, 34, 38, 107, 108,
    137–8
West Country 2
Western Mail 146
wilderness 29, 104–6, 110–11, 156
Williams, Merryn 69, 70, 96–7
Women's Royal Naval Service
    (WRNS) 3–4, 115, fig. 3
World War II 3–4, 7, 25
Wyatt, Thomas 3

Ynys Enlli 109, 110
Ynys Môn 53

zoomorphism 99